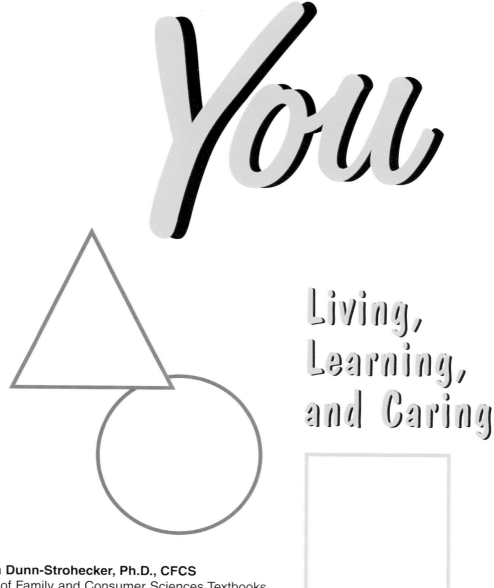

You

Living, Learning, and Caring

Martha Dunn-Strohecker, Ph.D., CFCS
Author of Family and Consumer Sciences Textbooks
and Management Consultant
Boston, Massachusetts

Deborah Tunstall Tippett, Ph.D., CFCS
Professor and Head
Department of Human Environmental Sciences
Meredith College
Raleigh, North Carolina

Publisher
The Goodheart-Willcox Company, Inc.
Tinley Park, Illinois

Library of Congress Catalog Card Number
International Standard Book Number 1-56637-472-3

2 3 4 5 6 7 8 9   99   03 02 01 00 99

Library of Congress Cataloging-in-Publication Data

Dunn-Strohecker, Martha.
    You: living, learning, and caring/Martha Dunn-Strohecker, Deborah Tunstall Tippett.
        p.   cm.
    Includes index.
    ISBN 1-56637-472-3
    1. Home economics.   I. Tippett, Deborah Tunstall.   II.Title.
TX167.D86   1998
640--dc21   98-20608
                                               CIP

Cover photos:
Background photo: Thomas Croke/Tony Stone Images©
Left to right: ©The Stock Market/T&D McCarthy, 1997
        Hunter Freeman/Tony Stone Images©
        Steve A. Wilson

Introduction

You: Living, Learning, and Caring is a book about you. It's about understanding yourself. It's about being a responsible member of your family and community. It's about managing your resources. It's about the foods you eat, the clothes you wear, and the job you may choose in the future.

You are a special person. You are growing, developing, and learning responsibility. You are also learning about life. This book will teach you skills that can make a difference in your life and the lives of others.

This book also will help you enjoy your life because you will feel more confident about making decisions. Your life is affected by the decisions you make each day. You will learn to make decisions concerning yourself, others, and your environment. You will also learn how your decisions affect others and the world in which you live.

Life is an adventure! This book will help you enjoy, understand, and value life's adventure.

About the Authors

Martha Dunn-Strohecker's professional background includes secondary and higher education teaching, public management practice, and community service in nonprofit and religious organizations. Martha's extensive career combines family and consumer sciences, community nutrition, and public service focused on helping individuals and families use their resources more effectively and efficiently.

Martha presently serves as a consultant in management and diversity training. Among her numerous honors, she received Ohio State University's highest award, the Centennial Award, and also Ohio State's Outstanding Leadership Recognition for services to families. Further, she has been listed in *Who's Who of American Women*, and received volunteer service awards from Goodwill Industries and the American Red Cross.

Deborah Tunstall Tippett's background includes 12 years as a family and consumer sciences junior high teacher with 3 concurrent years as a family and consumer sciences teacher educator at the University of North Carolina at Greensboro. Deborah is currently a family and consumer sciences teacher educator at Meredith College in Raleigh, North Carolina, where she is Head of the Department of Human Environmental Sciences. She has published research and presented workshops and courses on middle school family and consumer sciences.

Dr. Tippett served as a national officer in the Family and Consumer Sciences Education Association. She has won such awards as honorary membership of North Carolina's FHA/HERO and the Presidential Award for Outstanding Service at Meredith College. She has also received such local and regional awards as Teacher of the Year and Outstanding Young Careerist. She is listed in *Who's Who in Education*.

Table of Contents

Unit 1 You and Others

Unit 2 You — A Manager

Unit 3 You and Food

Unit 4 You and Your Clothes

Unit 5 The World of Work

Topic 13 Preparing for Work

Unit 1
You and Others

Learning more about yourself can make it easier to leave childhood behind and look forward to adulthood.

Lesson 1-1
Looking at Yourself

Objectives

After studying this lesson, you will be able to
- *define physical traits, heredity, personality, environment, self-concept, and self-esteem.*
- *explain how physical traits identify a person.*
- *describe how personality traits describe a person.*
- *tell how you can change your physical traits and personality.*

New Words

physical traits: *distinguishing characteristics of each human body.*
heredity: *the result of receiving traits from parents or ancestors.*
personality: *the group of traits that makes each person a unique individual.*
environment: *the conditions, objects, places, and people that are all around a person.*
self-concept: *the way a person sees himself or herself.*
self-esteem: *the way a person feels about his or her self-concept.*

New Ideas

- *The physical traits and personality of each person are unique.*
- *The physical traits and personality of each person are influenced by heredity and environment.*
- *Learning how to become the person you want to be is important in growth and development.*

Have you ever looked in a mirror and asked, "Who am I?" It can be fun and exciting to do that sometimes. When you look in the mirror you may think about the person you want to become. You are an individual, a special and unique person. No other human being in the whole world is just like you. You can become whoever you want to be. See 1-1.

During the next few years, your body will grow and develop. Your feelings will grow and develop, too. You will experience new feelings about yourself and others.

1-1 Taking a close look at yourself can help you identify all your special qualities.

Physical Traits

Your **physical traits** are the distinguishing characteristics of your body. These characteristics are ones people can see, such as your height and your body build. The color of your hair, eyes, and skin are also physical traits.

Some of your physical traits are *inherited.* You received them from your parents. Your parents inherited their physical traits from their parents. The result of receiving these traits from your ancestors is called **heredity.**

In some families, brothers and sisters look alike. In other families, the children may not look like each other or their parents. Sometimes children begin to look more like their parents as they grow older. The reason people look like other family members is heredity. See 1-2.

Certain factors can affect the physical traits that you inherit. One is the lifestyle you adopt. For instance, if your lifestyle is active and busy, you can maintain your desired weight. This affects the appearance of your inherited body build. Another factor is how you change your features. Changing the color of your hair is an example.

1-2 Children inherit many physical traits from their parents, such as their hair and skin color.

Your diet can affect your physical traits. The food you eat can influence your weight and your height. It also affects the appearance of your hair and the condition of your skin.

✔ Check What You Have Learned

1. What are some physical traits that you can inherit from your parents?
2. Why may you resemble other members of your family?
3. What are some factors that can affect the physical traits you inherit?

Personality

The way you act and feel makes you unique. These traits create your **personality**. They start developing early in life. Throughout your life, they continue to grow and develop.

Think about your personality for a moment. You have to think about everything you are. The way you look, act, think, and behave are all part of your personality. Your personality should reflect what you are, not what others think you should be.

How you get along with people and what your family and friends think of you reflects your personality. Words such as friendly, nice, thoughtful, pleasant, and funny may be used to describe your personality. Perhaps you use other words to describe yourself and the personalities of other people.

You may have wondered why a person has a certain personality. Two factors affect personality. You learned that heredity determines physical traits. These physical traits affect your personality.

Environment is the other factor that affects your personality.

Your **environment** is your surroundings and the people in your life. Your environment includes your home, your neighborhood, and your school. It also includes family members, neighbors, classmates, and teachers. See 1-3. You are affected by all the people and places in your environment. However, your family and friends probably have the greatest effect on you. They are closer to you than anyone else. They are part of your environment every day.

1-3 Your friends at school are part of your environment.

✔ Check What You Have Learned

1. What causes each person to have a unique personality?
2. How are you affected by the people and places in your environment?

Self-Concept

Your **self-concept** is the way you see yourself. This includes the way you think about yourself. For example, the feelings you have about your appearance are part of your self-concept.

The feelings others have about you are reflected in your self-concept. The trust your parents have in you influences your self-concept. You feel confident and good about yourself when others trust you. The respect of your friends shapes your self-concept.

Self-Esteem. Think for a moment about your self-concept. Do you think about yourself in positive ways? Do you feel good about your appearance? Do you feel proud about your accomplishments? These feelings are part of your self-esteem. How you feel about your self-concept is called **self-esteem.**

People with good self-esteem feel positive about themselves and enjoy life. They see themselves as able to do things. They feel confident. They accept and respect themselves and others.

Your self-esteem should reflect confidence in, and satisfaction with, yourself. You will feel worthwhile as a result. You will do better in school, and you will feel like trying new activities.

You can boost the self-esteem of your family members and friends. You can do this by making them feel appreciated, worthwhile, and loved.

✔ Check What You Have Learned

1. How can the feelings others have about you affect your self-concept?
2. How can you boost the self-esteem of others?

How You Can Change

Do you like the person you are? Are you happy with your appearance and your personality? People who feel good about themselves enjoy life. Other people like them and enjoy being with them.

Suppose you are not happy with the way you look. You may wish you could change. There are ways you can do this. You can exercise to help tone your muscles and feel more energetic. You can change your appearance by updating your wardrobe, wearing contact lenses, or changing your hairstyle.

You can also make changes if you do not feel good about your personality. Making changes may not be easy, but they are possible. You have control over who you are.

Ask yourself the questions in chart 1-4. You may think of others. Some of your answers may please you, and some may not. However, your answers should be honest. These answers will give you a true picture of your own personality. Then you are ready to plan for changes.

Some changes you can work on alone. For others, you may need the help and advice of other people. Ask your parents, teachers, or other adults what they think about your ideas. Their comments

Who Am I?

★ Am I happy with my appearance, my weight, my hairstyle, my complexion, and my posture? Why or why not? How can I make changes?

★ Do I do things I like to do, or do I do things only because my friends do them? How do I feel about this?

★ Do I behave in ways that are comfortable for me? Do I copy someone else's ways? How do I feel about this?

★ Do I talk a lot, or am I quiet much of the time? Do I talk a lot about myself, or do I try to learn about other people? How does this make me feel?

★ Do I enjoy being with other people? Do others enjoy being with me? How does this make me feel?

★ Am I comfortable spending time alone, or do I always have to be with other people? How do I feel about this?

1-4 Spend a few private moments thinking about who you are and how you feel.

may help you as you try to understand yourself. Try to be patient as you work on improving your personality and your appearance. Remember that changes do not happen at once. They take time.

 Check What You Have Learned

1. What are some physical traits that are possible to change? Explain your answer.
2. What are some ways you can change personality traits?

The Main Ideas

The physical traits and personality of each person are unique. Some physical traits are inherited. Personality develops and changes as a person grows and matures. A person can change his or her appearance and personality. Self-concept is the way a person sees himself or herself. Self-esteem is how a person feels about his or her self-concept.

Apply What You Have Learned

1. Write down all the words you can think of to describe personalities. Which words do you feel describe you? Which words would you like to have others use to describe you? Why?
2. Look at pictures of yourself as a baby. Compare these with pictures taken of you recently. In what ways have you changed? Compare these pictures with pictures of other members of your family. In what ways do you look like the rest of your family? How are you different? Try to find some pictures of your parents and other relatives when they were about your age. Do you look like any of them? Make a mini family album with these pictures. Write captions for the pictures to explain what you learned about inherited physical traits.
3. Talk to one or two family members, such as your mother, father, aunt, uncle, or grandparent. Ask them how their personalities as children are different from their personalities today. How and why did their personalities change? Take notes about what they tell you. Then write a short story about how their personalities have changed.
4. Think about a special friend. How can you help your friend see himself or herself in a more positive way? List five actions you could take to improve your friend's self-esteem.

Lesson 1-2
Changing and Growing

Objectives

After studying this lesson, you will be able to
→ *define* growth, development, accept, developmental tasks, independence, adolescence, *and* responsibility.
→ *give examples of ways people continually grow and develop.*
→ *explain how adolescence prepares you to become an adult.*

New Words

growth: *an increase in size, strength, or ability that occurs over time.*
development: *gradual changes that take place as the result of growth.*
accept: *view as normal or proper.*
developmental tasks: *skills or behavior patterns people should accomplish at certain stages of their life.*
independence: *the freedom to decide, act, and care for yourself.*
adolescence: *the stage of growth between childhood and adulthood.*
responsibility: *something a person is expected or trusted to do.*

New Ideas

→ *The process of growth and development continues throughout life.*
→ *Adolescence is a period of time between childhood and adulthood.*
→ *Adolescence is a stage of life that prepares you for greater responsibilities and more independence as an adult.*

Life is a continuous process of growth and development. From birth to death, people grow and change in many ways. You know that you have changed in many ways since childhood. You will keep on changing and growing during adolescence and adulthood.

Your Growth and Development

Experts in human development study the growth and development of people. **Growth** is an increase in size, strength, or ability that occurs over time. **Development** is the gradual changes that take place as the result of growth. These experts usually agree upon four major types of growth and development. They are physical, social, emotional, and intellectual.

Physical growth and development involve body changes. Some examples are growing taller and changing in body shape as you grow from childhood to adulthood. Although actual growth stops in the late teens or early twenties, physical changes continue through adulthood until death.

Social growth and development is concerned with the ways people behave and act. A sign of social growth in young children is learning to share. In older children, obeying rules without being reminded is an example of social growth. What other examples can you think of? See 1-5.

Emotional growth and development involves feelings. People learn to recognize, respect, and **accept** their feelings. In other words, they realize their feelings are normal. People find ways to express feelings that do not hurt themselves or others. For instance, expressing anger through talking, instead of through having a temper tantrum, is a sign of emotional growth. Trying to understand ideas from a different point of view is another sign of emotional growth.

Intellectual growth and development refers to learning. It includes developing the ability to think. When children learn to read and tell time they are growing intellectually. Young people begin to question ideas they learned earlier in life. They debate points of view and search for facts. They try performing tasks different ways. Adults keep growing intellectually through classes, reading, and contact with other people.

1-5 Part of social growth is making friends and learning to get along with others.

✓ **Check What You Have Learned**

1. Explain the statement: "Life is a continuous process of growth and development."
2. What are the four major types of growth and development?
3. Which of these four types of growth and development can you influence? Give examples.

Stages of Growth and Development

A normal life span has three main stages of growth and development. These are childhood, adolescence, and adulthood. Some experts divide these stages into smaller stages. For instance, they may divide adolescence into early and late adolescence.

People change during each life stage. They grow and develop physically, emotionally, intellectually, and socially. These types of growth and development are closely related. More than one type of growth can occur at a time. See 1-6. As your body grows, so do your abilities. You are able to show emotions, learn new ideas, and get along with others better.

Experts in human development have identified developmental tasks for each stage of life. **Developmental tasks** are skills or behavior patterns people should achieve at certain stages of their lives. You can think of developmental tasks as

1-6 As a baby grows physically, he or she is also growing emotionally, socially, and intellectually.

goals of growth. Some examples are learning to stand, walk, talk, and care about others. Another example is making career choices.

People need to achieve the developmental tasks in each stage of development. If they do not, they may have problems reaching the goals of the next stage. For instance, learning to share is a developmental task of childhood. Forming mature relationships is a developmental task of the teen years. If a young child does not learn to share, he or she may find it hard to form close friendships as a teen.

✔ Check What You Have Learned

1. What are the three different stages of growth and development?
2. Why is it important to achieve the developmental tasks during each stage of development?

Childhood

Childhood is the stage of growth from birth to about 11 or 12 years old. A great deal of growth and development happens during this stage. Babies learn to sit up, crawl, walk, and talk. Later, children learn to play with other children and share their toys. They begin developing ideas about what is right and what is wrong. They also start learning about their emotions and how to deal with them. These are just some of the goals of growth during early childhood. Learning how to read and write, and learning to accept responsibilities at home and at school are also goals. See 1-7.

Beginning to develop independence is another goal of childhood. **Independence** is the freedom to decide, act, and care for yourself. For instance, babies depend on others to meet all their needs. Others must feed them, dress them, and try to soothe them when they are upset. As children grow, they learn how to perform many tasks for themselves. This is how they learn to become more independent and prepare for adolescence and adulthood.

1-7 Learning to read independently is an important goal of childhood.

✔ Check What You Have Learned

1. What are some important goals of development in childhood?
2. How do children begin to show their independence? Give examples.

Adolescence

Adolescence is the stage of growth between childhood and adulthood. People in this stage of growth are called *adolescents*. Adolescence begins when a child's body starts to develop into an adult size and shape.

During adolescence, many changes occur. You are probably in this stage of life now. Adolescents are more aware of themselves. They are trying to understand themselves better. They begin to think more about the direction of their lives and ask important questions. They have important hopes and dreams for the future. Intense feelings about families and friends often develop.

Many young people develop strong interests during adolescence. They may begin to work on causes for other people. They may become active in clubs, sports, or religious groups. These interests may change, or they may last for a long time.

As an adolescent, you may not act as you feel. You may act bold, but feel scared inside. You may say you don't need love, but inside you want love. You may claim to be grown up, but seek out adults who praise you. You may not act upset when you make a mistake, but feel embarrassed inside.

All of these feelings are normal. You are a changing, growing person. Each year will bring new growth and development for you. See 1-8. Adolescence is the time when you are moving from childhood to adulthood. You must allow yourself time to move through this period of your life.

Growth and development in adolescence do not happen all at once. They happen at different times for different people. Some children begin adolescence at age 9 or 10. Others don't start their growth into adulthood until they are 15 or 16 years old. Adolescence usually starts around 11 or 12 years of age.

During adolescence, you take on many new responsibilities. A **responsibility** is something you are expected or trusted to do. You may have responsibilities at home. Your family may expect you to keep your room clean. They may expect you to do other chores, too. You have responsibilities at school. Teachers expect you to get to class on time and do your homework. You have responsibilities to your friends. They expect you to be thoughtful, patient, and honest.

One of the important goals of adolescence is fulfilling your responsibilities. You need to show others they can count on you. This will let them know you are ready to begin taking on even more responsibilities as an adult.

1-8 You will see changes in your appearance, as well as in your attitudes, as you grow and develop during adolescence.

Another important goal of adolescence is to become more independent from adults. To do this, you must reach smaller goals first. You need to learn how to get along with others and prepare for a career. You must find your identity and become responsible for yourself and your actions.

Meeting the goals of becoming an adolescent takes work. You need to think about the type of person you want to become. You need to set goals and plan steps to achieve these goals. This effort helps prepare you for adulthood.

Developmental Needs of Young Adolescents

The ages between 11 and 14 are sometimes called early adolescence. If you are in this age group, you may be having many new feelings. You may feel family members, teachers, and friends are suddenly expecting a lot from you.

You may wonder whether your friends have some of the same feelings and thoughts. You may feel that everyone expects more of you than they expect of others. You may think everyone is watching to see how you perform. You have many needs during this time of your life. Your parents and teachers are trying to meet those needs.

What are the needs of young adolescents? The basic needs are listed here. You should be aware of these needs so that you can understand yourself and your peers better. As a young adolescent you have the following needs:

- You need to understand yourself. You want to learn about yourself, your interests, and your capabilities.

- You need to have many different experiences. Your interests and concerns may vary from day to day. You want to explore the world around you. You want to use your knowledge at home, at school, and in the neighborhood.

- You need to have meaningful relationships in family, school, and the community.

- You need to have positive relationships with peers. You want to have time for casual conversations with your peers. You want to be able to spend time with small groups of your friends.

- You need to be successful. You want to gain skills. You want to receive praise and rewards for doing tasks well.

- You need to achieve your desirable weight and height. Your body grows and develops rapidly during early adolescence. Your nutritional needs increase to help your muscles and bones develop.

- You need to have opportunities for physical activity. You have lots of energy. Your body needs to move and get exercise. You want to enjoy physical activities and learn new skills.

Adulthood

Adulthood is the stage of growth following adolescence. This stage begins as people gain greater independence. They do not depend on parents or other adults all the time. They support themselves by holding a job. Adults take care of problems without becoming upset easily. They are able to develop good relationships with many people. They enjoy being with family members and friends. They know what they want from life. They know how to express their emotions properly. They value communication.

During adulthood, physical growth levels off, but other types of growth and development continue. Many people marry and have children. This adds responsibilities and calls for more learning to take place. See 1-9. If the goals of adolescence have not been reached, adults may have problems dealing with marriage and a family. They may not be willing or able to make the changes needed.

Life is confusing for adults sometimes. Although adults are more mature than teens, they may sometimes feel as they did during adolescence. They may question who they are. They may feel confused about what they want from life. Some adults find growing old hard to understand and accept. They may try to act younger than their age. This type of behavior can sometimes cause problems. However, aging is a normal part of life.

People in their 20s are in early adulthood. The major goal of early adulthood centers on finding a place in society. Every person wants to become the best person he or she can be. This goal may be achieved through choosing a certain job or lifestyle.

People in their 30s and 40s try to fit the goals of early adulthood into the present. As young adults, these people may have chosen careers and started families. Now, they may focus on advancing in their careers and raising their children. Striving to reach these goals gives their lives purpose and meaning.

People in their 50s and 60s continue working toward their goals. They also begin to think about retirement. Preparing for the later years in life is an important task. Adults need to feel useful and stay active. See 1-10. They need to develop interests they can still have after they retire.

People today live longer than ever before. Many people in their 70s, 80s, and 90s enjoy good health and active lifestyles. Some keep learning new hobbies and developing relationships with family and friends during these later years.

1-9 Adults who choose to become parents must accept the responsibilities of caring for children.

1-10 Keeping physically fit is an important part of preparing for retirement.

1. What are three traits that can be used to describe adults?
2. What is the major goal of early adulthood, and how can it be met during the adult years?

The Main Ideas

The four areas of growth and development are physical, social, emotional, and intellectual. The three stages of growth and development for each individual are childhood, adolescence, and adulthood. Developmental tasks are necessary for a person to develop to his or her fullest potential.

The adolescent years are the time when a young person is moving from childhood toward adulthood. Young adolescents have many needs. The goals of growth and development must be accomplished during adolescence in order to become a healthy adult.

⏭ Apply What You Have Learned

1. Divide a sheet of paper into three columns. In the first column, list the four areas of growth and development. In the second column, write examples of how you've changed during the past year in each area of growth. In the third column, write examples of how you would like to change in each area during the year ahead. Think about how the changes listed in the second and third columns will help you grow toward adulthood.
2. Observe a young child at a playground. Take notes on how the child is working toward achieving the developmental tasks of childhood. (Is the child sharing? Is he or she controlling his or her emotions? What physical skills does the child have?) Compare your notes with your classmates and discuss.
3. Begin a diary or a record that will show your growth and development during the adolescent years. It is helpful to review what you have written and see how you have grown toward adulthood. You might want to write a brief summary every six months. Then discuss how you feel about your progress with a parent or a teacher.
4. Interview three young adults about how being an adult is different from being a teen. Ask each person to describe an activity he or she has mastered. Summarize your findings in a one-page report.

Lesson 1-3
You and Your Family

Objectives

After studying this lesson, you will be able to

➠ *define relationship, family, generation, role, affection, and respect.*

➠ *explain why the relationship between children and parents is important.*

➠ *tell how brothers and sisters can learn to get along with one another.*

➠ *describe how people can stay active and independent as they grow older.*

New Words

relationship: *a link with another person.*

family: *a group of people related to one another by blood, marriage, or adoption.*

generation: *all people who are born and live in about the same time span.*

role: *a person's place in a group.*

affection: *a fondness.*

respect: *a high or special regard for someone or something.*

family structure: *the makeup of a family.*

New Ideas

➠ *Communication among family members is important, especially among children and parents.*

➠ *Brothers and sisters need to learn how to get along with one another.*

➠ *Older relatives living with a family need to be treated with love and respect.*

➠ *Family structures vary.*

A link with another person is called a **relationship.** Relationships are based on many factors. Relationships with your friends may start because you share common interests. Relationships with neighbors form because you live on the same street. Relationships with family members are likely to have the greatest effect on you.

The Family

A **family** is a group of people related by blood, marriage, or adoption. This group may include a mother, a father, and one or more children. Sometimes other relatives are part of the family group that lives together. See 1-11.

1-11 Each family is unique.

Your relationship with your family is important. Family members help you grow and develop. They affect your attitudes, hopes, ambitions, and values. They can offer you support and comfort during times of need.

Family members make up different generations. A **generation** is all the people who are born and live in about the same time span. You and any brother and sisters you may have are part of one generation. Your parents and your aunts and uncles are in a second generation. Your grandparents are part of a third generation. See 1-12.

1-12 This family photo shows three generations.

✔ Check What You Have Learned

1. How is your family different from your best friend's family?
2. How does your family help you grow and develop?
3. How many living generations are there in your family?

Parents

Children are affected throughout their lives by many adults. However, children have a special relationship with their parents. Mothers, fathers, foster parents, and guardians are responsible for the growth and development of their children. They care for and protect their children. They help their children to be the best they can be.

Relationships with their parents affect teens' growth and development. Parents care about their children. They are concerned about what happens to them today and tomorrow. They offer advice based on their life experiences. They hope their advice will be helpful.

Teens may not always agree with their parents. They may feel that their parents do not understand their feelings or friends. They may wonder why their parents act as they do sometimes.

Having these thoughts and feelings is normal. Teens should share them with their parents. Communication with parents is important. By talking to parents, teens can learn to understand and respect their parents' feelings.

Parents and children sometimes disagree. Living in close contact sometimes causes problems. Differences may occur because teens are starting to become more independent. They may not want to follow some of their parents' rules. Teens may have trouble realizing their parents are still responsible for them.

Parents and children can love and care for one another and still have differences. This is part of a normal relationship. Communication can help settle differences and make relationships stronger.

✓ Check What You Have Learned

1. Describe the relationship among parents and children.
2. Why do regular conversations between a parent and a child help build a good relationship?
3. What are some reasons parents and children may disagree?

Brothers and Sisters

As a member of a family, you have several roles. A **role** is your place in a group. You have responsibilities in each of your roles. In your family group, you have the role of son or daughter. In this role, one of your responsibilities is to obey your parents. Other family roles you may have include grandchild, niece or nephew, and brother or sister. Roles in groups outside your family may include student, friend, team member, and worker.

If you have the role of brother or sister, one of your responsibilities is to get along. Brothers and sisters get along differently in each family. In many families, they support each other. However, brothers and sisters sometimes argue. They become jealous. They tease each other.

These actions are normal, but they can still hurt. A child who is teased may develop feelings of resentment. These feelings are not easy to overcome. They create problems in relationships with other people.

Teens should develop a sense of humor. They should learn not to take themselves, or others, too seriously. This will help them ignore some of the teasing that comes from brothers and sisters.

Brothers and sisters should be able to settle their differences. This is part of growing up. Brothers and sisters cannot expect their parents or other adults to always tell them how to handle disputes.

Getting along is based on understanding and respect. Spending time talking and laughing together can help brothers and sisters get to know each other better. This will help them realize they share many of the same needs. It will also help

1-13 Brothers and sisters can care for each other and have fun together.

them develop the patience and understanding needed to form kind, caring relationships. See 1-13.

Brothers and sisters can show love and affection for each other in many ways. (**Affection** is a fondness.) They can offer to help each other. They can give advice. Brothers and sisters can also be willing listeners. This shows they care about each other's problems.

✓ **Check What You Have Learned**

1. Why is it important for brothers and sisters to learn how to get along with each other?
2. What can brothers and sisters do to get along with each other better?
3. How can brothers and sisters show they care for and respect each other?

The Older Generation

Grandparents are often the third generation of a family. Most grandparents want their family members to love and respect them. **Respect** is a high or special regard for someone.

Older people need love and affection. See 1-14. Most people need someone to care about them. Older people have feelings just like you. They appreciate it when family members are thoughtful, considerate, and cheerful toward them. Family members show love and respect if they consider the needs of grandparents when making family plans.

Older people also need to feel useful and wanted. See 1-15. In some families they are not only useful, but also a big help. Some parents depend on grandparents to care for children.

1-15 People can make grandparents feel wanted by including them in family celebrations.

1-14 Spending time with older people is a way to show them love and respect.

Family members may also rely on grandparents to help with other tasks. Family members should not take this help for granted. They should let grandparents know how important they are.

Most older people have many interests besides their families. They may have hobbies. They may take part in community activities. They may plan social gatherings with friends. Interests inside and outside the home help keep older people active, alert, and happy. They enjoy their own lives and feel useful and wanted.

Older people also need to be as independent as possible. They need privacy and time to be alone when they live with other family members. There should be a time and a place where they can take care of their own interests and hobbies. They need a place to keep mail and store personal papers. They need to have their own spending money and not account to anyone for it.

Older people want to be healthy and enjoy life. They want to be able to take care of themselves. However, changes occur in the human body as people age. These changes may be hard for family members to accept.

As people grow older they are not as strong as they used to be. They are no longer able to do what they used to do. Older people sometimes become forgetful. If this happens, family members need to be patient, understanding, and willing to help when needed.

✓ Check What You Have Learned

1. What are some of the needs older people have? How are these different from a younger person's needs? How are they the same?
2. How can younger family members help older people feel useful and wanted?

Family Structures

You learned earlier in this lesson that not all families are the same. You learned about some of the members of the family group. **Family structure** refers to the makeup of a family. Each family structure can give its members the love, support, and attention they need. There are five family structures.

- A *two-parent family* is made up of a married man and woman and their biological or adopted children. Parents share the duties of raising their children. They also share the duties of earning income and caring for the home.

- A *single-parent family* is made up of one adult who is raising one or more children. The adult may be widowed, separated, divorced, or may never have married. The single parent must care for the family and provide income and support.

- When a single parent marries, a *blended*

family forms. Either the husband, the wife, or both have children from other marriages. The blended family type includes stepparents and stepchildren. All family members must adjust to these new family relationships.

- In an *extended family*, several generations of relatives live together. Grandparents, aunts, uncles, and/or cousins might live as part of an extended family. Extended family members must deal with many people in the home. There are also more family members to help care for children, earn money, and complete home tasks.

- A *childless family* is another type of family. A childless family is a couple without children. Some couples choose not to have children. Others are not able to have children. They may focus their life on each other and their careers. They also may be able to spend time with the children of friends and relatives.

1. Describe the two-parent family and the single-parent family.
2. To what kinds of changes might members of a blended family need to adjust? List some examples.

 ## The Main Ideas

Families vary in size. They include people from different generations. They have a big effect on who you are. Family members need to support one another.

Parents care for, and are responsible for, the growth and development of their children. It is important that parents and children talk to one another about how they feel.

Brothers and sisters sometimes have disagreements and tease one another. Learning to get along depends on caring for and respecting one another.

Consider older people's needs as family members. They need to feel useful and loved. They also need to be independent, healthy, and respected. Family structure describes the makeup of a family. Each family structure must meet the needs of its members.

▶ Apply What You Have Learned

1. Think about a holiday your family celebrates together. How does that time together help you get to know one another? Think of examples and share them with your family.
2. Think about factors that affect teens' relationships with their parents. Make a poster or write a poem about how parents and children can get along better.
3. Role-play a situation in which a brother and sister are arguing and teasing one another. Discuss how the brother and sister can be more respectful in their behavior. Also discuss the changes they can make. Role-play the situation again following some of the suggestions made.
4. Look in magazines for pictures of people from the older generation. Cut out some of these pictures. Notice the interesting looks on their faces. Share your pictures with the class and discuss the types of activities they are doing.
5. List the five family structures on a separate piece of paper. Think of a family you know that fits each structure. Write a few sentences to describe each family.

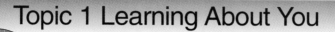
Topic 1 Learning About You

Lesson 1-4
Family Problems

Objectives

After studying this lesson, you will be able to

➡ *define problem, crisis, unity, solution, family counseling agencies, shelter, hotline, and support group.*

➡ *list some problems families have.*

➡ *explain how problems affect family members differently.*

➡ *name sources of help for family problems.*

New Words

problem: *source of difficulty or distress.*

crisis: *an emergency situation.*

unity: *a state of being in agreement, not being divided.*

solution: *an answer.*

family counseling agencies: *groups that work with family members to help them deal with problems.*

shelter: *a place that offers housing and food to people who have nowhere else to go.*

hot line: *a telephone service that offers immediate information to people who need help.*

support group: *a group of people with a similar problem who provide support and help each other cope.*

New Ideas

➡ *Every family has problems.*

➡ *Problems affect each family member in a different way.*

➡ *Families can solve many problems together.*

➡ *Help from outside the family is sometimes needed to solve problems.*

A **problem** is a source of difficulty or distress. All families have problems. Sometimes they are little ones, such as arguing about picking up dirty clothes off the floor. Sometimes they are big ones, such as drug abuse, death, unemployment, or illness. A big problem may be called a **crisis**. For each family, the problems are real and must be faced. See 1-16. Otherwise, they may get worse, or people may be hurt.

1-16 A family problem, such as dealing with a disability, requires family members to make adjustments.

Different Points of View

When things go wrong at home, each person may be affected differently. Young children, adolescents, and adults may each see the same problem from a different point of view.

For instance, young children have little understanding of money problems. Unless they lack food, shelter, and clothing, they may not even know a problem exists. Adolescents, on the other hand, need more than food, clothing, and shelter. They need supplies for school. They also want to have some of the items their friends have. They may feel angry if there is not enough money to buy these items. Adults are responsible for providing for the needs of their entire families. Money problems can cause adults to feel worried.

✔ Check What You Have Learned

1. Why do similar problems affect young children, adolescents, and adults differently?
2. How can you become more aware of the problems your parents have? What can you do about it?

Problem Solving

Families can use several methods to deal with problems. These problem-solving methods include working together and talking openly. Sometimes families will need to seek outside help to deal with serious problems

Unity means to agree, without being divided. When problems occur at home, family unity makes them easier to face. Family members can agree to work together to deal with their problems.

When family members share their feelings, problems do not seem so bad. To young people, problems sometimes seem bigger than they really are. Talking with parents may help young people see problems more realistically. Parents may be afraid to show their fear about family problems. Sharing their concerns with their children gives the children a chance to offer emotional support.

Some family problems have very simple **solutions**, or answers. It may just be a matter of talking the problem over and deciding what to do. See 1-17. Other problems are harder to solve. Finding the answer may not be so easy. Family members may have to think and talk about the problem for hours, days, or even weeks before a decision can be reached.

1-17 Families often gather together to discuss problems and find solutions.

✔ Check What You Have Learned

1. What can help make family problems easier to face?
2. How can sharing feelings help when dealing with problems?

Seeking Help

For many young people, serious problems are those they do not understand. Divorce or death, for instance, changes the basic structure of the family. These changes may be hard to accept. People need to adjust without hurting themselves or others. It takes time and effort to understand and adapt to a problem.

Some families share their problems with one another. The family members find solutions together. Relatives, friends, and neighbors may provide support. Other families sometimes need help from people outside the family.

When family troubles arise, it can be hard to think clearly. Talking to someone outside the family may help. Someone who is not affected by the problem can give a neutral viewpoint.

It is important to discuss family problems with someone who will understand. There are many people who can help. Family doctors and religious leaders may be able to help. See 1-18. Teachers, school nurses, or guidance counselors also may be able to help.

Community resources are other sources of help for troubled families. Community resources include family counseling agencies, shelters, hot lines, and support groups.

Family counseling agencies are groups that work with family members to help them deal with problems. Counselors teach families problem-solving skills.

A **shelter** is a place that offers housing and food to people who have nowhere else to go. Some shelters provide protection for people who are victims of abuse or violence.

A **hot line** is a telephone service that offers immediate information to people who need help. Hot lines often help people who are facing a crisis like drug or child abuse. Most hot lines have toll-free numbers.

A **support group** is a group of people with a similar problem who help each other cope. Some communities have a wide range of support groups. The groups may help people cope with drug abuse, physical and mental illness, obesity, or grief. Some groups are for adults; others are for teens.

When problems occur at home, the greatest source of strength for each family member should be the family itself. Family members should not waste time and energy finding fault and placing blame. This often doesn't help or make people feel better. Instead, they should try to find the best solution for the problem. They need to be patient and understanding and help one another.

1-18 Counselors can help young people sort out some of their problems.

1. Why should you discuss problems with someone who will understand?
2. Who could you turn to for help if you needed someone to talk to about a problem?
3. How can a positive outlook help when trying to solve a family problem?

The Main Ideas

All families have problems. Family members often see the same problem differently. They need to talk so they understand one another. This can help them solve the problem together. Sometimes a family is faced with serious problems that one or more family members cannot handle. The family or individual should seek help from people who can offer help. Community resources include family counseling agencies, shelters, hot lines, and support groups.

Apply What You Have Learned

1. Think of a family situation that might cause problems. Write down how you would react to the problem. Ask a parent, and a brother or sister how they would react. Take notes and compare the answers. Share your findings with your family. Discuss how you can learn to understand one another better when family problems occur.
2. Watch three different television programs about families. Identify how each of the families solve their problems. Discuss with your classmates how television and real-life families differ in how they solve problems.
3. Make a list of the organizations in your community that offer help to families who have problems. Include in the list information on how families can best use these organizations.

Lesson 1-5
Friends

Objectives

After studying this lesson, you will be able to
➡ *define friend, trust, share, peers, peer pressure, reputation, and group dating.*
➡ *explain what it means to be a good friend.*
➡ *explain how your peers influence you.*
➡ *tell why your family cares about the friends you choose.*
➡ *describe how you can help your family and friends get to know one another.*

New Words

friend: *someone you care about, trust, and respect.*
trust: *to believe a person is honest and reliable.*
share: *to experience or enjoy with others.*
peers: *people in the same age group.*
peer pressure: *the influence people's peers have on them.*
reputation: *how others think of a person.*
group dating: *when several people of both sexes meet for an activity.*

New Ideas

➡ *A good friend is someone you care about, trust, and respect.*
➡ *Peers can provide you with a sense of belonging.*
➡ *You can learn skills to manage peer pressure.*
➡ *Skills for making new friends can be used throughout your life.*
➡ *You can find ways to help your family and friends know and like each other.*

A **friend** is someone you care about, trust, and respect. When you **trust** someone, you believe he or she is honest and reliable. Having friends is part of your growth and development. See 1-19. They help you grow. They are part of your support system.

1-19 Friendships can start when you are young and continue throughout your life.

Being a Friend

A good friend is someone with whom you share ideas, thoughts, and dreams. (**Share** means to experience or enjoy with others.) Good friends talk with one another. They laugh and have fun together. You can enjoy both being a friend and having friends.

Good friends have certain qualities. They are understanding. They share the good times and the bad. They are able to help one another with problems. Friends are considerate. They think of each other instead of themselves. Friends are also dependable. You can count on your friends to be there when you need them. You should also be there when they need you.

Good friends like to spend a lot of time together. However, sometimes they need time apart from one another. Most people need time alone to do what they want. Let your friends know you respect their need for privacy by giving them time to themselves.

Another quality of a good friend is being *trustworthy*. Friends often share secrets. If your friend tells you a secret, do not tell others. Your friend trusts you to keep that information private.

✔ **Check What You Have Learned**

1. How do you share with your friends? Give examples.
2. What qualities do good friends have? Give examples.

Making Friends

When you were a young child, your friends were often chosen by your parents. They may have been from families your parents knew. They may have lived in your neighborhood.

As you grow older, you become more independent. You join new social groups. You begin making your own friends. This can be an exciting time. See 1-20.

You will meet many new people during your life. You may meet them at school, social events, or when you visit friends. You will meet some people and become good friends with them. Other people you may like, but you will not become good friends.

Someday you may find yourself in a situation where you do not know very many people. You may want to introduce yourself to people. Do not wait for them to make the first move. This is a good skill to have. You will find it helpful when you meet new people at school, club meetings, or on the job.

1-20 Smiling lets people know that you are interested in them. This may make them want to talk to you.

Being open and friendly with people makes them more friendly toward you. You should greet people with a warm smile. This is important when making new friends.

You should also get to know people before you form an opinion about them. People sometimes change after you get to know them better. First impressions aren't always correct.

✔ **Check What You Have Learned**

1. Where can you meet new people?
2. How can you show someone you want to be friends?
3. What should you do when you meet people for the first time?

Peers

Peers are people who belong to the same age group. They have similar experiences and interests. Your peer group includes your classmates and close friends.

Peers serve an important purpose in your life. They provide you with friendships and good times. They make you feel wanted and give you a sense of belonging.

This feeling of belonging is important, especially during your school years. You feel secure having friends your own age. You and your friends can go places together. You can listen to each other's problems and plans. You can talk about your opinions, ideas, likes, and dislikes with your peers.

You may want to look and act like your peers. See 1-21. This helps you make friends, and gives you a sense of belonging. You fit into a group if you look and act like the other members. Some of your peers may feel that they have to buy certain clothes or have certain hairstyles to be "in." This is part of being a young person.

There is nothing wrong with wanting to look and act like your peers. This can give you a feeling of security. Sometimes, however, peers try to

1-21 Many teens enjoy dressing like their friends.

influence you to make decisions. This influence is called **peer pressure**. If the influence is not good for you, it is called *negative peer pressure*. An example might occur if a friend tells you to ignore the time your parents told you to be home.

If peers influence you to do something that is good for you, it is called *positive peer pressure*. An example might occur if a friend prods you to get home on time to show respect for your parents.

It is not easy to handle negative peer pressure. The way others act may not reflect your beliefs. Teens must stand up for what they believe is right. They must think about what actions are right for them. You can talk to adults you trust about peer pressure you feel from friends.

Being honest with your feelings is a good way to deal with peer pressure. Sometimes friends disagree. See 1-22. If your friends say yes, you can say no. Tell them about your beliefs. Tell them how yours may be different from theirs. Good friends respect each other's differences.

1-22 Friends do not always agree. Talking about their differences can help.

Families and Friends

When your friends visit your home for the first time, introduce them to your family. Your family is interested in meeting your friends. See 1-23. Family members care about the friends you choose because they care about you.

Let your family and friends have a chance to talk to each other. Getting to know your family may help your friends relax. They may feel more at home when they visit you. If your parents know more about your friends, they will feel better when you go out with your friends.

Sometimes you may invite a person to your home who does not act as you expected. After the person has left, let your parents know how you feel. Tell them you are disappointed in this person's behavior. This shows your parents you are learning to use good judgment about people. Your parents like to know you can make these judgments.

Talking with your parents is important. Conflicts may arise over choices of good friends. When you and your parents have a good relationship, the conflicts can be discussed. You can help your parents understand your friends better. Your parents can let you know about their concerns.

If you have a friend who does not get along with your family, try to find out why. It could be that you are wrong about your friend. Perhaps you have not tried to help your family understand your friend. Talk and try to reach an understanding. Respect each other's opinions.

A **reputation** is how others think of a person. If you are friends with someone who does not have a good reputation, your family may object. People do not always see a person the same way. Your family may not see your friends the way you see them.

1-23 Invite your friends to your home to meet your family.

You may also think your family criticizes your friends unfairly. This may be true. However, your family may just be trying to help you. Observe how your friends behave. Are they disrespectful toward others? Are they destructive? Do they use profane language? Do they smoke, or put their feet on the furniture? Do they act in other ways that might upset your family? These are concerns that may cause your family to worry about the friends you choose.

Friendships also produce dating experiences. Group dating often is a teen's first dating experience. **Group dating** occurs when a number of people of both sexes meet for an activity. Each member of the group has a good time. Each teen can get to know all the members of the group. There is no pressure to be close to just one person. After feeling comfortable in a group, most people are ready to date as part of a couple.

Spending time with dating partners helps you learn about yourself. You learn how to give and take in personal relationships. You learn about members of the opposite sex. Spending time with dating partners helps to prepare people for marriage.

✓ Check What You Have Learned

1. Why should you introduce your friends to your family?
2. Why is it good for you to talk to your parents about your friends?
3. What may make your family worry about your choice of friends?

💡 The Main Ideas

Having friends is an important part of growth and development. A good friend is someone you care about, trust, and respect. You will make many new friends during your life. Being open and friendly is helpful. Peers can give you a sense of belonging. You can learn skills to manage peer pressure. You need to help your family and friends know and understand each other. Group dating often is the first kind of dating experience.

➡ Apply What You Have Learned

1. Make a list of the qualities you look for in a friend. List them in order of importance. Compare with your classmates. See which qualities your class considers the most important.
2. Make a poster showing how you can say "no" to peer pressure. Include ways to stand up for yourself and make your own decisions. Display this in your classroom.
3. Interview two students. One should be a student whose family has moved a lot, and the other should be a student who has never moved. Ask how each of them makes friends. Ask what each of them does when he or she meets someone new. Compare the answers.
4. Role-play a situation in which you are visiting a friend's home and do not behave properly. Discuss how you can change your behavior. Role-play the situation again showing the correct behavior.

Lesson 1-6
Communicating with Others

Objectives

After studying this lesson, you will be able to

→ *define communication, verbal communication, nonverbal communication, and feedback.*

→ *tell how you can develop effective communication skills.*

→ *explain the importance of using feedback when communicating.*

→ *describe healthy communication among individuals.*

New Words

communication: *giving or receiving information, signals, or messages.*

verbal communication: *using words to give or receive information.*

nonverbal communication: *sending and receiving messages without using words.*

feedback: *repeating what a speaker says to be sure you understand it correctly.*

New Ideas

→ *Relationships depend upon good communication.*

→ *Communication is both verbal and nonverbal.*

→ *You can communicate effectively.*

→ *Healthy communication helps you get along with others.*

Communication is giving or receiving information, signals, or messages. See 1-24. Developing good communication skills is important. These skills can help you enjoy life. You can resolve conflicts better. You can also communicate in healthy ways and be an effective listener and speaker.

1-24 Giving someone a kiss communicates affection.

How You Communicate

Relationships depend upon communication. People use both verbal and nonverbal communication to share their feelings and ideas. See 1-25. **Verbal communication** is using words to give and receive information. This includes both speaking and writing. **Nonverbal communication** is sending and receiving messages without using words. Facial expressions, gestures, and appearance are examples of nonverbal communication.

Sometimes frowns or hand motions can say more than words.

You are always communicating how you feel. What you say and do lets people know how you are feeling. For instance, sometimes you tell people that you are happy or sad. Other times, people can tell by your facial expressions or actions how you are feeling. You don't just need words to communicate.

As a child, you learned how to communicate. What you learned then affects how you communicate as you grow older. The way you communicate with friends and coworkers may be similar to the way you've communicated with brothers or sisters. If you marry, communication with your partner will be based on how you've seen your parents communicate.

1-25 By talking and holding hands, this mother and daughter are using verbal and nonverbal communication.

✓ Check What You Have Learned

1. Why is communication important in relationships?
2. What is the difference between verbal and nonverbal communication? Give examples.
3. How can the ways you learned to communicate as a child affect you as an adult?

Communicating Effectively

To communicate effectively you need to be able to speak clearly and listen carefully. When you speak clearly, you correctly communicate your message. When people listen carefully, they understand the message. When people communicate effectively, they can understand one another better. They get along better with others.

To speak clearly, there are a few tips you should follow. First, you should always completely pronounce words. Fast, mumbled speech is hard to understand. Do not drop the endings of words. Second, keep your comments brief and to the point. Do not make long, wordy statements. People may lose interest in what you are saying. Third, pause before you speak. This will give you time to know what you are going to say and you will not mumble or stutter.

You should also think before you speak with other people. Always choose your words carefully to avoid hurting others. If people ask you for your opinion, tell them the truth. However, do not tell them in a way that may hurt their feelings or discourage them. Instead, tell them what you think in a positive manner. Try to make other people feel good.

Another part of communicating effectively is listening. Good listeners have many qualities. One is giving **feedback**. After people speak, repeat what you think they said. This lets them know if you understood correctly.

Paying attention is also important. Let the speaker know you are listening. Smile or nod as he or she talks. You should ask questions if something is unclear. However, do not interrupt. If you are patient, the speaker might cover what you want to know.

✓ Check What You Have Learned

1. Why should you think before you speak with other people?
2. What are the qualities of a good listener? Give examples.

Positive Behavior

Behavior is another form of communication. Some people behave in a negative manner. They are more concerned with themselves than others. They are rude, hurt others, or put them down. If you treat people like this, they may not like you and may avoid you.

Other people are the opposite. They don't stand up for themselves. They let others hurt them and treat them badly.

You can behave in a positive manner that communicates you care about others. You should always be polite and never hurt other people.

Also show that you care about yourself. Stand up for what you believe. People will respect you if you do. You will not always agree with everybody. However, you can disagree with them without being afraid of making them angry.

✓ Check What You Have Learned

1. How can people who don't stand up for themselves get hurt?
2. How can your behavior communicate that you care about other people?

Healthy Communication

Living successfully with others depends upon good communication skills. This is true in your daily life with your family and friends. This will also be true in your career when working with bosses and coworkers.

Having good communication skills is healthy. When you communicate well, you feel like a valued person. You enjoy being with other people. See 1-26. Healthy communication means letting people know how you really feel. When you do, they can understand you better.

You should express good thoughts and feelings about other people. Do not assume that people know you care about them. There are many ways

1-26 This friendship is based on good communication skills.

to let them know. You can tell them in person. You can write a letter or poem. You may want to show how you feel by using nonverbal communication. You can make a drawing or give someone a hug or a smile. See 1-27.

Healthy communication often occurs when you feel good about yourself, and you share that with others. However, there are times when you do not feel good about yourself. You may take this out on other people. You may use harsh words to hurt them. You may ignore them. You may act like a bully. These are all unhealthy forms of communication. You need to avoid unhealthy communication. It can hurt people.

When people feel bad, healthy communication can still be present. If people are aware of others' moods, they can help. For instance, your mother may sense when you feel hurt and respond lovingly. Your teacher may know you worked hard in class and praise you.

You should talk about any negative feelings you have. For instance, when your parents buy you new clothes, thank them. If you do not like the clothes, let them know. Ask your parents if you can return them and choose what you like. Explain why you do not like the clothes. Your parents should try to understand. They may also tell you why they chose the clothes. Then, you may understand them better.

1-27 A feeling of love is shared by this mother and child through a hug.

✔ **Check What You Have Learned**

1. What are some benefits of healthy communication?
2. How can you let people know that you care about them?
3. What are some signs of unhealthy communication?

The Main Ideas

Relationships depend upon communication. Feelings and thoughts are shared by people through verbal and nonverbal communication. Communicating effectively includes speaking clearly and listening carefully. Having good communication skills is healthy.

Apply What You Have Learned

1. Watch a television show with the sound turned off. Observe what kind of nonverbal communication was being used. Try to decide what the story line of the show was. Discuss this with your classmates.

2. Write a poem about a parent and child trying to improve how they communicate with each other. Include some of the communication skills discussed in this lesson. Share the poem with your family.

3. Play the "telephone game." As a class, sit in a circle. Your teacher will give a student a phrase. This student will whisper it to the next student. Continue until it has been passed around the circle. The last student will repeat the phrase aloud. Have the first student read the original phrase aloud. Compare the two versions. Discuss the importance of feedback and communicating effectively.

4. On a sheet of notebook paper, write two lists. In the first list, write words that make you feel good about yourself. Put a star by the five words you would most like others to use when describing you. In the second list, write words that can hurt your feelings. Discuss in class how people might use the complimentary words more often. Discuss how people could avoid using the hurtful words.

Case Study

Read the story below and look at Lesson 1-5 again.
Then answer the questions below.

Being a Friend

Tony and Dan are walking part of the way home from school together. Before they each go their way, they take a few minutes to talk.

"I don't know what to do," Tony said. "Pete wants me to go to the video arcade with him Saturday to play this new game. But my parents won't let me go to arcades. I also really need to study for the big history test Monday. Pete says I shouldn't tell my parents we're going there. He said I could tell them that I'm studying at his house. But what if somebody my parents know sees me? Then my parents would find out. They'd be really mad at me. What should I do?"

Dan could tell Tony was upset. "I see where you're coming from. It sounds like you think that if you don't go to the arcade, Pete won't be your friend."

"Yes. I would like to be as popular at school as Pete is. If we are not friends, though, maybe no one else will want to hang out with me either."

"Hey, Tony, you won't have trouble finding friends or being popular. You just need to decide what kind of friends you want to have. If Pete is telling you to lie, is he really your friend?"

Tony asked Dan, "But how do I tell him no?"

Dan looked at Tony. "Remember when I had to tell my friend B.J. that I couldn't lie to my parents?"

Tony glanced at his watch. "Hey, I've got to get home. Can I call you later?"

"Sure!" Dan replied. "Why don't you call about seven?"

To Discuss

→ 1. What factors should Tony consider when making his decision?
→ 2. How does it help Tony to talk over his problem with Dan?
→ 3. What do you think Tony's decision will be? Explain your answer.

Topic 1 Review

Topic Summary

No one else is exactly like you. Your physical traits and personality make you unique. As you grow from a child into an adult, your personality develops and changes. You grow physically, socially, emotionally, and intellectually. During this time, which is called adolescence, you also learn to become more independent from adults.

As you grow and develop, your family supports you. When family members support each other, the family becomes stronger. Families can be many different sizes and include many different members. Understanding and caring for members of your family can help build better relationships. This also helps when family problems occur. The problems are easier to solve.

Friends are also part of your support system. You can laugh and have fun with your friends. You can care about, trust, and respect your friends. Your peers can make you feel like you belong. Being open and friendly helps you make new friends and get along with your peers.

Your relationships with your family and friends depend upon how you communicate. Feelings and thoughts are shared by people through both verbal and nonverbal communication. Having good communication skills means letting people know how you really feel. This is both important and healthy.

To Review

Write your answers on a separate sheet of paper.

1. List four personality traits that you have.
2. The way a person feels about his or her self-concept is called _____-_____.
3. Being able to understand a science formula represents which type of growth?
   a. Physical growth.
   b. Social growth.
   c. Emotional growth.
   d. Intellectual growth.
4. List three developmental needs of young adolescents.
5. List three ways brothers and sisters can get along.
6. How can you show respect for an older person?
7. When faced with problems, why is it sometimes helpful for families to talk to someone outside the family?

8. List community resources that can help families when problems occur.
9. When your friends can be counted on to keep your secrets, they are considered _____.
10. When your friends influence you to make decisions that are not good for you, that influence is called _____ _____ _____.
11. Use V for verbal and N for nonverbal to identify the different types of communication listed below.
    a. _____ Writing a note.
    b. _____ Wearing nice clothes.
    c. _____ Smiling.
    d. _____ Giving a dirty look.
    e. _____ Talking on the phone.

Vocabulary Quiz

Match the definitions in Column A with the terms in Column B.
Write your answers on a separate sheet of paper.

Column A

1. A person you trust, respect, and care about.
2. Giving and receiving information, signals, or messages.
3. A source of difficulty or distress.
4. Gradual changes that take place as the result of growth.
5. The group of traits that make you a unique individual.
6. All people who are born and live in about the same time span.
7. People in the same age group.
8. Repeating what a person has said to be sure you understand correctly.
9. A state of being in agreement.
10. People who are related to one another by blood, marriage, or adoption.
11. The freedom to decide, act, and care for yourself.
12. Stage of development when a person grows from childhood to adulthood.
13. The way a person sees himself or herself.
14. Something a person is expected or trusted to do.
15. When several people of both sexes meet for an activity.
16. A place that offers housing and food to people who have nowhere else to go.
17. A group of people with a similar problem who provide support and help each other cope.
18. The makeup of a family.
19. A telephone service that offers immediate information to people who need help.
20. Groups that work with family members to help them deal with problems.
21. A link with another person.
22. A person's place in a group.

Column B

a. Feedback.
b. Development.
c. Responsibility.
d. Communication.
e. Adolescence.
f. Heredity.
g. Family.
h. Independence.
i. Role.
j. Self-concept.
k. Personality.
l. Generation.
m. Problem.
n. Relationship.
o. Unity.
p. Friend.
q. Peers.
r. Group dating.
s. Family structure.
t. Shelter.
u. Hot line.
v. Support group.
w. Family counseling agencies.

Lesson 2-1
Baby's First Year

Objectives

After studying this lesson, you will be able to
➡ *define* infant, dependent, *and* reflex.
➡ *tell why each child develops at a different rate.*
➡ *explain why babies are completely dependent at birth.*
➡ *describe how babies grow and develop during the first year of life.*

New Words

infant: *a child under one year of age.*
dependent: *relying on another for support.*
reflex: *a natural, unlearned behavior.*

New Ideas

➡ *Babies grow and develop at different rates.*
➡ *Babies need lots of love and care.*
➡ *Infants are constantly growing and changing.*
➡ *Babies grow from dependent infants to active one-year-olds.*

Someday you may work with or care for children. To do a good job, you need to know how they grow and develop. In this lesson, you will learn about infants. **Infant** is the term used to describe a child under one year of age. Children grow and develop in many ways during the first year.

Each Child Is Special

Every child is unique. Each develops at a different rate. Some start to walk, talk, and teethe earlier or later than others their age. Even brothers and sisters develop at different rates. See 2-1. A

2-1 Mothers with more than one child need to remember that their children may grow and develop at different rates.

younger brother may put a puzzle together at an earlier age than his brothers or sisters did. These differences are normal. Each person has a built-in "time clock." This controls when the person is ready to begin performing certain tasks.

Although children grow and learn at different rates, they all achieve developmental tasks in a certain order. The development of one skill leads to the development of the next. For instance, children first learn to crawl. Then they learn to walk. Soon they are also able to run, jump, and skip. One skill builds upon another.

✓ Check What You Have Learned

1. What does the statement, "Each person has a built-in 'time clock,'" mean to you?
2. Why do children achieve developmental tasks at different rates?

Infants

When babies are born, they are completely **dependent**. They rely on others for support. For instance, infants need someone to feed them and to cover their bodies to keep them warm. They cannot perform these simple tasks for themselves.

At birth, a baby's body has a narrow chest and large abdomen. The arms and legs are skinny and curled close to the body. The skin may look wrinkled. The head may seem large and oddly shaped. The eyes are usually blue. Within a few months, the wrinkles disappear, and the arms and legs fill out. The head seems to fit the body better, and the eyes may change color.

Infants do not have strong muscles. They have trouble controlling their actions. They cannot hold up their heads by themselves. Their heads should be supported at all times. Infants' bodies need to be held firmly and securely for many months. Figure 2-2 shows how to support a baby's body.

Although their muscles are not strong, infants are still able to perform some tasks. They use reflex movements. A **reflex** is a natural, unlearned behavior. Some reflexes are grasping, sucking, and rooting. The *grasping reflex* occurs when infants grasp any object placed in their hands. When you touch babies around their mouths, their heads turn, and their mouths search for food. This is called the

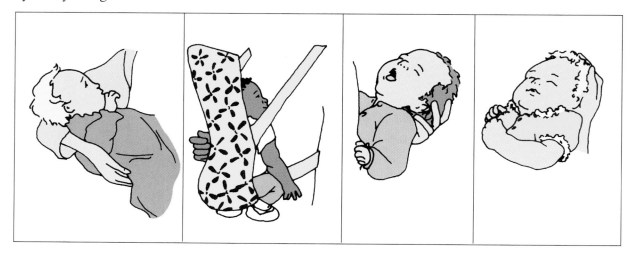

2-2 Infants' bodies need to be supported along the back and neck, until their muscles become stronger.

rooting reflex. After finding objects with their mouths, sucking begins. This is the *sucking reflex.* The rooting and sucking reflexes help infants survive. These reflexes disappear within three to four months, when the muscles become stronger.

Infants are aware of their surroundings. They can see, hear, feel, smell, and taste at birth.

However, their senses are weak. An infant's senses develop and become stronger as the baby matures.

People should keep this in mind as they care for infants. Babies like to be touched and spoken or sung to softly. They like to look at brightly colored objects. They do not like bad smells or tastes.

✓ **Check What You Have Learned**

1. How are babies dependent upon others at birth? Give examples.
2. How do the rooting and sucking reflexes help infants survive?
3. When caring for babies, why should you be aware of the development of their senses?

Two to Three Months

As babies grow, they become more demanding. The number of hours they spend awake increases from when they were infants. They need constant attention, both day and night. They have not learned how to wait. They want their needs met right away.

Crying is how babies communicate. They cannot tell you with words what they want or need. They cry when they are hungry, wet, sick, cold, scared, or bored. They cry when they want to be held and loved.

People caring for infants need to find out why they are crying. If babies' needs are not met during their first few months, babies may quit trying to communicate their needs and become withdrawn. Their emotional and physical health may suffer.

Babies need a lot of love to grow and develop well. Love helps them learn to trust other people. They should be soothed when they are upset. They should also be held and touched when they are happy. Babies like to hear a calming voice.

2-3 During the first few months of life, babies need a lot of love.

See 2-3. This is not spoiling them. This makes them feel warm and secure.

If babies' needs are met during the early months, they can learn to perform many physical tasks. They can smile. They can move their heads to follow sounds or look up for a few seconds. They can kick their legs when lying down. They can reach for objects that attract their attention. They can learn to roll from their sides to their backs.

✓ **Check What You Have Learned**

1. What are some reasons that babies cry? Give examples.
2. What happens if babies' needs are not met during the first few months?
3. What are some tasks that three-month-olds can perform?

Four to Eight Months

Infants' muscles become stronger at four or five months of age. They may hold their heads up for a few minutes without support. They may begin rolling over by themselves. If they have trouble rolling back over, you may need to help them. They are still dependent on other people.

At this age, babies also start reacting more to people and their environment. They enjoy being held in a sitting position, so they can look around. They smile more and may laugh out loud. See 2-4. They begin to babble and coo. Most babies will lie for a while, playing with their hands or reaching for their toes. They also begin exploring their clothes, blankets, and other objects they can reach.

When placed in a sitting position, six-month-olds may sit alone. At this age, they learn to tell the difference between familiar and strange faces. They may become upset around strangers. However, it should not take them too long to become familiar with new people. If people smile and talk to babies, they may smile or "talk" back.

Around seven or eight months of age, babies seem to be in constant motion. This is how they strengthen their muscles and learn to control their actions. When placed on the floor, they may kick their legs and wave their arms. They may also begin to move about and explore. They may kick and push themselves on their stomachs to get to objects beyond their reach. They may also roll over to get to objects. They can no longer be counted on to stay in one place.

Babies are curious at this age. They enjoy seeing, holding, and touching objects. They like toys

2-4 Babies four to eight months of age start interacting more with other people.

of various sizes, shapes, and textures. They like to bang objects together to make noise. They may drop their toys on the floor to see what happens. If their toys are hidden, they will look for them.

✓ Check What You Have Learned

1. What tasks can four-month-olds perform that infants can't?
2. Why may six-month-olds become upset around strangers?
3. How do eight-month-olds strengthen their muscles? Give examples.

Nine to Twelve Months

During the last two or three months of their first year, infants develop in many ways all at once. At this age, many babies go from crawling to walking. They may also begin talking. Some babies learn to walk and talk at the same time. Others may not develop either skill until later. Each baby learns at a different rate. See 2-5.

By 9 or 10 months of age, most babies can move on their own. They can sit up without help. They are no longer content to lie down and play. Most begin crawling to get from one place to another. Each baby has his or her own special way of crawling. For instance, Phyllis pulls herself along on her stomach. Alex crawls on his hands and knees. Rosa keeps her legs fairly straight and walks on her hands and feet. Each way is normal.

Babies this age like to touch objects. They learn how certain objects feel and taste. They want to put everything into their mouths. This means you need to keep small and sharp objects out of their reach. Otherwise, they could swallow something or hurt themselves.

Also during this time, babies start learning the difference between right and wrong. They can tell when their parents approve or disapprove. They are learning how to act when someone says no. People taking care of babies should teach them not to stick their fingers in electric sockets, eat plants, or play in garbage. These are all harmful to babies. Babies should learn that these actions are bad.

By 11 months of age, babies begin to move around more. They may learn how to roll a ball to you. They may take a few steps, while holding onto someone. They may even learn to stand alone, stoop, and stand back up again.

At this age, babies learn to drink from a cup. They also feed themselves with their fingers. (They have not learned to use flatware yet.) Oftentimes, as much food gets in their mouths as on themselves and the floor. Meals can become very messy.

At one year of age, babies may weigh three times as much as they did at birth. Most babies also grow one and one-half times in length during this first year. This is usually 9 to 10 inches.

One-year-olds seem to be busy all the time. They like to watch objects move. They watch cars, people, animals, and anything else that passes by. They are fascinated by other children. They like to play and be held. They enjoy simple games and music. They laugh and throw toys around. They like to explore their surroundings. See 2-6.

2-5 Each baby learns to crawl at a different age.

2-6 Although babies like to explore their surroundings, they feel secure when they are held.

One-year-olds usually sleep through the night and take morning and afternoon naps. Babies need a lot of rest to grow and develop properly.

During this time, babies may become shy with people outside the family. They may cry at the sight of friends or relatives. This is normal. It is a phase most children go through. It passes in a few months.

✔ Check What You Have Learned

1. Why should you keep objects, such as buttons and safety pins, out of the reach of babies 9 to 12 months old?
2. At what age do babies start to learn the difference between right and wrong?
3. What activities do one-year-olds enjoy? Give examples.

The Main Ideas

The first year in a baby's life is very important. Babies grow and develop in many ways. Each grows at a different rate. As infants, they are dependent on others to take care of all their needs. By their first birthday, they are able to move around and take care of simple needs. They are not as dependent on other people as infants.

Apply What You Have Learned

1. Observe two infants who are the same age. Compare their abilities to move about, sit up, grasp objects, and communicate. Make a chart showing how they are alike and different.
2. Cut pictures out of magazines showing babies from birth to one year old. Use these pictures to make a bulletin board display. Write a few words under each picture describing what each baby is doing. As a class, discuss how babies change during the first year.
3. Interview two sets of parents with young children. Ask them about how their children started crawling, and when they started walking. Share your findings with the class and compare.
4. Make a simple mobile for a three-month-old infant. Keep in mind how infants have developed up to this point. Use colors and shapes that will attract their attention. Make sure the objects are safe for them to handle. Remember that the infant will be lying in a crib, looking up at the mobile.

Lesson 2-2
The Toddler Stage

Objectives

After studying this lesson, you will be able to
- *define toddler, confident, separation anxiety, and parallel play.*
- *describe how children grow and develop in the toddler stage.*
- *explain how people can help toddlers gain confidence in themselves.*

New Words

toddler: *a child between the ages of one and three years.*
confident: *being sure of yourself.*
separation anxiety: *a fear that if parents leave, they will not return.*
parallel play: *when toddlers play near, but not with, one another.*

New Ideas

- *Toddlers grow and develop in many ways.*
- *Toddlers need love and support as they discover and explore the world around them.*
- *People who care for toddlers should create a safe environment for them.*

A **toddler** is a child between the ages of one and three years. Toddlers often learn to walk between one year and 18 months. As they start to walk, they begin exploring their environment. They start communicating more. They express more emotions and behave in new ways. You should support their freedom to grow and develop. However, you must also protect them from harm. Caring for toddlers can be fun, but it is also a responsibility.

Physical Development

Toddlers' physical development is slower than that of infants. They do not gain weight as quickly as infants. Their bodies begin to lose some baby fat and become longer and straighter.

Toddlers are always in motion. They spend a lot of time and energy moving about. See 2-7. This

2-7   Toddlers find many ways to move about, including riding toys.

helps their bodies develop. This also lets them explore. They touch, feel, and taste objects. They may empty toy boxes, drawers, and kitchen cupboards to find out where objects are kept. However, they rarely put objects away. They move quickly from one activity to another.

As their muscles develop, toddlers are able to do more for themselves. They learn to use their fingers for tasks, such as using flatware to feed themselves and stacking building blocks. They place big pegs in pegboards. They turn the pages of books made from heavy paper. They turn on the radio to dance to music. They also kick and throw balls. They may grab pets and hold on tight. They may even move furniture to reach objects they want. They are becoming more independent.

As toddlers become more active, you need to reduce the chances of accidents occurring. Remove any items toddlers should not touch. Always watch where they go and what they do. This lets them safely explore and be independent. It also reduces the number of times you have to say no.

✓ Check What You Have Learned

1. Why are toddlers able to do more for themselves than infants?
2. Why do you need to be concerned about the safety of a toddler?

Intellectual Development

Learning to communicate is part of how toddlers grow intellectually. Speech usually begins during the toddler stage. Toddlers learn new words by listening to others. Then they repeat these words over and over. You should always speak correctly when talking to children. Do not use baby talk or profane language.

Toddlers begin speaking by repeating one-syllable words, like "da-da" and "ma-ma." Soon their vocabularies grow to include names of objects with which they are familiar. They may be able to name parts of their bodies, such as "hand," "foot," "nose," and "ear." They may begin to tell others what they want, such as "juice," "cup," "up," and "down." Toddlers learn that they can make actions happen by talking.

People find toddlers easier to care for when they begin to talk. For the first time, toddlers can express themselves by using words. See 2-8. People no longer have to guess what children want.

Being able to walk also adds to toddlers' ability to communicate. They can walk to objects they want.

Toddlers also understand what is being said to them. They can follow short directions. "Give me a hug," "Roll the ball," "Let's go out," and "You can swing now," are examples.

2-8 This three-year-old expresses himself with both words and actions.

✔ Check What You Have Learned

1. Why should you speak correctly when talking to a toddler?
2. Why are toddlers easier to care for when they begin to talk?

Emotional Development

Toddlers are still developing emotionally. Sometimes they are scared. They may be scared of strange people or places. They may not know how to do something. To feel confident, or sure of themselves, they need love and support. People should encourage toddlers to feel free to grow. They should keep toddlers safe but not worry about them too much.

Toddlers like to be near their parents. They may be afraid parents will leave and not return. This is called **separation anxiety**. Toddlers may even become upset when separated from parents for a short amount of time. Toddlers can act upset in many ways. For instance, when their parents leave, toddlers may cry, act angry toward their baby-sitters, or refuse to eat. Often toddlers can be distracted by involving them in activities they enjoy. This may help them feel less lonely. Separation anxiety is normal in toddlers. They grow out of it.

Toddlers can become frustrated. They may not be able to perform certain tasks. They may want objects they cannot have. Often toddlers do not know how to act when they feel that way. They may become angry. A temper tantrum may result. They may fall to the floor, kick, and scream. This is the only way they know how to express their feelings.

If this happens, toddlers need to be treated calmly and gently. Scolding them does not help. Toddlers should be shown good ways to express their anger. You may tell them to use words. You may suggest that they pound on a pounding toy. You may provide a pillow for them to hit. However, do not let them hurt themselves or others.

✔ Check What You Have Learned

1. What should you do if children start crying after their parents leave?
2. How can you help toddlers express anger without hurting themselves or others?

Social Development

As toddlers grow, they begin interacting more with others. They become more aware of their abilities and environment. As a result, they respond to situations differently than they did as infants.

Toddlers do not like to hurry. They do not understand the concept of time. They like to perform tasks by themselves, such as dressing and eating. This may take time. Adults should be patient. If toddlers are forced to dress or eat more quickly, they may become discouraged and quit trying. Let toddlers do as much for themselves as possible. See 2-9. This helps them learn to be independent.

Toddlers do not always act the same from day to day. For instance, Rob may fasten all the buttons on his sweater today. Tomorrow, he may not be able to fasten any buttons. Maria may feed herself easily and without a lot of mess on one day. The next day she may squeeze her food, mash it with her fingers, or drop it on the floor. Manuel may dress himself each day, then suddenly demand that you do it for him. Changes in behavior can be caused by tiredness or desire for attention. See 2-10. This is normal. It is a part of the growth process.

The way toddlers play reflects their social development. One-year-olds mainly play by themselves. After two years of age, toddlers enjoy playing near other children. However, they do not play with one another. This is called **parallel play**. They also have not learned how to share. They may take what they want from other children. Show toddlers other toys to divert their interest. Explain that toys should be returned to their owners.

Toddlers are curious. They like to pick up a toy or book and inspect it. Toddlers like to taste, throw, and pull apart objects. This type of play helps them explore their surroundings.

2-10 When toddlers become tired, they may refuse to do as they are told.

2-9 Toddlers should be allowed to feed themselves, despite the time and mess involved.

Toddlers often have a hard time choosing a favorite toy. You may need to offer only one or two playthings at a time. Choose toys carefully with children's safety in mind.

Toddlers like books, and they enjoy having others read to them. Another favorite play activity is imitating adults. Toddlers enjoy dressing up in adults' old clothes. They also like playing with toy dishes, cars and trucks, and stuffed animals to act out adult experiences.

The toddler stage is often called the no stage. Toddlers answer no to almost everything. They may say no because they hear it a lot. They may say no because people react when they say it.

You should tell toddlers what they can do, instead of what they can't do. This will keep toddlers from hearing no so often. For instance, Sam keeps standing on a chair. You could say, "No, Sam! Don't stand on the chair." However, a better response would be, "Sam, you need to sit when you're on the chair."

Giving toddlers choices gives them less chance to say no. For instance, Dorothy needs to wear a sweater. You should ask her whether she wants to wear the blue sweater or the red sweater. This gives her a choice. If you ask her whether she wants to wear a sweater, she may say no. Then you will still have to convince her to wear a sweater.

✔ Check What You Have Learned

1. What can happen if you encourage toddlers to hurry?
2. What can cause toddlers to act differently from day to day?
3. If a toddler answers no to a question, how should you respond?

💡 The Main Ideas

The toddler stage is a time of growth and exploration. A toddler's world grows as he or she learns to walk. Toddlers can move about and perform more tasks. They become more independent. Talking lets them communicate more easily. Sometimes toddlers become scared. People should give them love and support to help them gain confidence in themselves. Their behavior may change from day to day.

▐▐▐▶ Apply What You Have Learned

1. Observe a toddler once while playing, once while eating, and once while dressing. Take notes on how the behavior of this toddler compares to the toddler behavior described in this lesson.
2. Divide into small groups. Brainstorm ideas for distracting a child with separation anxiety. As a class, discuss your ideas. Make a list for everyone to use when baby-sitting toddlers.
3. Write a short story about a situation between a toddler and a baby-sitter in which the toddler keeps saying no. Explain in your story how the baby-sitter deals with this situation.
4. Plan a dramatic play corner for a toddler. List the play items and dress-up clothes you would choose for the child to use in imitating adult activities. Make notes about precautions you should take to keep the child safe during dramatic play.

Lesson 2-3
Preschoolers

Objectives

After studying this lesson, you will be able to
- *define preschooler, stutter, and cooperate.*
- *describe how children grow and develop in the preschooler stage.*
- *explain how people can help preschoolers develop their independence.*

New Words

preschooler: *a child between the ages of three and five or six years.*

stutter: *to repeat a word or parts of a word several times.*

cooperate: *to act or work together with others.*

New Ideas

- *Preschoolers continue to grow and develop with the help of other people.*
- *Preschoolers are more independent than infants and toddlers.*
- *Preschoolers learn skills that prepare them for going to school.*

Preschoolers are children between the ages of three and five or six years. This stage lasts until children start first grade. During this time they change from dependent babies into independent children. Their bodies grow and develop in many different ways. See 2-11. They learn new words and tasks. They express their emotions better.

2-11 During the preschooler stage, children grow taller.

58

Physical Development

Preschoolers do not grow as fast as infants and toddlers. They gain weight slowly while growing taller. This makes them look slimmer.

The larger muscles of the arms and legs grow stronger during the preschool years. This allows preschoolers to enjoy active play. Preschoolers can climb trees or run up and down sidewalks. They can ride tricycles and use swings. These activities help preschoolers learn to control use of their large muscles. See 2-12.

After they learn to control their large muscles, preschoolers learn to use and control the smaller muscles of their hands and fingers. These muscles allow them to thread beads on a string and play with pegboards. Doing simple puzzles, cutting with scissors, and drawing with crayons also helps develop small muscle skills.

2-12 Playing in the pool gives preschoolers a chance to develop their large muscles.

✓ Check What You Have Learned

1. Why do preschoolers appear slimmer than toddlers?
2. What can preschoolers do to develop their smaller muscles?

Intellectual Development

Preschoolers learn new words quickly. They practice by talking a lot. They enjoy listening to themselves. At first, you may not be able to understand them. However, as preschoolers grow, they begin to speak more clearly. You can help by speaking clearly to them.

Preschoolers often use words they hear, because they like the way the words sound. They may find that some words get your attention quickly. They may not know what these words mean. You should ignore any words you do not want them to use. Always use proper language around preschoolers. This is how they learn which words to use.

Some preschoolers have trouble talking. They **stutter**. They may repeat words or parts of words several times. This is often because their minds work faster than their tongues. Children usually grow out of this. Their brains and tongues develop and begin to work together. You can help stutterers by listening to them. Give them time to finish talking. Do not point out the stuttering or make fun of it. This will not help them quit stuttering. It may make it worse.

✓ **Check What You Have Learned**

1. Why should you use proper language around preschoolers?
2. How can you help preschoolers who stutter?

Emotional Development

As preschoolers grow, they learn how to express their emotions better. However, they still need people to guide and support them. You should tell and show preschoolers how you expect them to express themselves. You should also make them feel loved and wanted. This helps them develop good self-concepts.

Preschoolers' moods may change quickly. One minute they may be playing happily. The next, they may start throwing toys or hitting people. You should tell them right away that this is wrong. You should tell them what they can and cannot do. You may say, "Blocks are for stacking. You may not throw them." You may tell them, "You must not hit people. It hurts." You may want to give them a pillow to hit or a foam ball to throw. This way they can't hurt anyone or break anything. See 2-13.

2-13 Give children a soft toy to play with when they are upset. This can help prevent them from hurting themselves.

✓ **Check What You Have Learned**

1. What helps preschoolers develop good self-concepts? Give examples.
2. What should you do when preschoolers' moods change?

Social Development

Preschoolers are more independent than toddlers. However, they still need love and support. As preschoolers learn to do more, you should praise them. This helps give them confidence in themselves and their actions.

Preschoolers like to perform tasks by themselves. "I want to do it," is a common request. They want to dress and feed themselves. They want to help adults. They may ask to help set the table, feed the dog, or empty the wastebasket. They should be allowed to do these tasks. This is how they learn to perform bigger tasks and develop independence.

Often, it is hard for preschoolers to switch from one task to another. For instance, Mickey does not like to stop playing when it is time for a bath. However, he agrees after a while. Soon, he is having fun playing in the water. Then, he refuses to get out of the tub, because he is enjoying his bath. People who care for preschoolers have to be patient. Preschoolers are still learning.

Preschoolers do not say "no" as often as toddlers. However, they sometimes have trouble making up their minds. You can help by making your directions simple. When you ask Gwen if she wants to go to the store, she may quickly decide to go. Other times, she may take a long time to decide. If this happens tell her, "Let's go to the store." Be sure to still let preschoolers make decisions when they don't affect other people.

Children need to know how they are expected to behave. They also need to know what will happen if they do not meet those expectations. For instance, you may tell children they should play nicely with their toys. You may tell them if they throw their toys, you will take the toys away.

You must follow through on warnings you give to children. In the example above, you must take the toys away if the children throw them. If you do not, children will not learn the consequences of their actions. They will not learn to believe what you say either.

When you correct children's behavior, they may become upset. If this happens, try removing them from the activity. See 2-14. Watch them until they calm down. Do not yell. This will only upset the children more. Try to be patient and calm.

Preschoolers play and share with other children. They learn to **cooperate**. They act or work together with others. Sometimes, they may fight. However, they often make up quickly. They may need help learning how to be a friend. You should set good examples for them. Let them know how they should or should not act.

2-14 When children are upset, they need time by themselves to think.

✓ Check What You Have Learned

1. How can praise help preschoolers become more independent?
2. When should you let preschoolers make decisions?
3. Why should you always follow through on warnings you give children?

The Main Ideas

The preschool years extend from age three to first grade. Preschool children learn many new physical, intellectual, emotional, and social skills. This helps them develop their independence. They need lots of love and support during this time.

Apply What You Have Learned

1. Look through child care books for games that you can play with preschoolers indoors on a rainy day. Choose games that can help them develop physically, intellectually, emotionally, and socially. Make a list of the games you might use when baby-sitting.
2. Cut out pictures of toddlers and preschoolers from magazines and bring them to class. You may also bring pictures of yourself as a toddler or preschooler. Make a bulletin board with captions discussing how the preschoolers in the pictures differ physically from the toddlers.
3. Create a game for preschoolers who stutter. In this game, have them practice speaking clearly. While making this game, keep in mind what you have learned about helping people who stutter.
4. Observe a group of preschoolers. Take notes on how they practice saying new words. Notice the similarities and differences in how their language skills develop.

Topic 2 Learning About Children

Lesson 2-4
How Children Learn

Objectives

After studying this lesson, you will be able to
- → define learning.
- → give examples of activities that help infants learn.
- → explain how toddlers and preschoolers learn.
- → describe how communicating with children helps them learn.

New Word

learning: *gaining information or skills through instruction or practice.*

New Ideas

- → *Children need learning experiences.*
- → *Communication between children and adults helps children learn.*
- → *Children can learn how to behave in ways acceptable to themselves and others.*

Children learn an almost endless amount of information during their first six years of life. **Learning** is gaining information or skills through instruction or practice. Learning is very important, especially during the early years. Infants, toddlers, and preschoolers learn by exploring the world around them. All children need praise and encouragement to learn.

Infants

Infants learn by using their senses. They learn when they touch, see, hear, smell, and taste. For instance, Aretha's parents have given her a rattle as her first toy. Aretha grasps the rattle and learns what it feels like. She learns what it tastes like as she puts it in her mouth. She learns what it sounds like when she shakes it.

Playing also helps infants learn. They can learn new concepts and how to control their bodies. Peekaboo teaches them that objects or people can disappear and return again. Waving good-bye and playing pat-a-cake helps them control their hands and arms. Games like these can teach infants a lot.

Infants learn to speak by making sounds. You should let them know that you enjoy the sounds they make. This encourages them to make more sounds. You can also help infants learn to speak by talking to them. They imitate how people talk. The more words they hear people use, the more they learn. They can also learn that people express their thoughts and feelings by using words. See 2-15.

Infants need love and attention in order to learn. As people around infants love and care for them, the infants respond by wanting to learn more. For instance, Rudy's parents hold him close and talk to him. They stroke his cheek and rub his body. They feed and bathe him. As a result, Rudy feels loved and secure. He feels free to learn by exploring the world around him.

As adults hold, feed, bathe, and play with infants, they communicate emotions. For instance, when an adult is nervous about holding a baby, the infant can sense the adult's anxiousness. The infant may respond by crying more than usual. On the other hand, when an adult holds a baby securely, the baby senses love. This helps the infant develop trust in the adult.

2-15 Encouraging infants to make sounds helps them learn about speech.

✔ Check What You Have Learned

1. How can infants learn through play? Give examples.
2. How can talking to infants help them learn to speak?

Toddlers and Preschoolers

As toddlers and preschoolers learn new skills, their behavior may swing from independence to dependence. Dirk may try jumping from a step but hold on to his father's hand. Nina may run after a pigeon in the park. Then she may return suddenly and want to be held by her mother. Understanding the growth and development of children can help you be sensitive to these swings of behavior.

When you help children learn, they enjoy childhood more. This also makes it easier for them to learn when they start school. You should give toddlers and preschoolers the chance to explore their surroundings and try new tasks. Let them see and talk about new events and objects. See 2-16. Let them feel objects that are safe to touch.

2-16 Children are often fascinated by objects like bubbles.

Young children learn many skills and concepts. They learn how to count. They can identify shapes and colors. They learn how words and sounds are used. You should provide opportunities for children to learn these skills and concepts.

Children can learn about numbers through many daily activities. You can play counting games with children, such as counting toes, fingers, or blocks and other toys. You can use numbers when talking. You may hold out an apple and say, "Here is one apple." You may offer crackers and say, "You may have two crackers." Let the children count and decide how many to choose. Letting children use measuring cups or spoons to prepare simple recipes can also help them learn number skills.

You can help children learn about concepts like size, shape, and texture. Use descriptive terms when talking to children about objects they see and use daily. You might say, "That building is *tall*," "Your cookie is *round*," or "Sandpaper is *rough*."

You can also help children learn about colors by talking to them. Talk about the red sweater, the blue ball, the yellow sun, and the green grass. Show children these objects as you talk about them.

Reading to children can help them learn how words and sounds are used. See 2-17. Nursery rhymes help them learn about sounds and rhythms. Identifying pictures in books helps them learn the meaning of words. They can also learn to match words with real objects. For instance, they learn from a picture book what an orange looks like. When you ask them to choose an orange from a fruit bowl, they can identify which piece of fruit to choose.

Learning to care for themselves is another skill children need to learn. For instance, they should

2-17 Children can learn about words and objects when parents read to them.

learn how to dress themselves and decide what colors to wear. This may not be easy for them at first. They may need your help. Children may have to practice these tasks many times. You should be patient. When children succeed, they feel good about themselves.

Children like to help adults. For them, learning to pour milk and sweep floors are often fun tasks, not work. Adults and children can have fun together doing laundry or setting the table. Children can also have fun and learn by caring for plants or pets. Doing household tasks helps children learn responsibility. If children enjoy doing these tasks, their feelings toward work later on in life may be better.

✔ Check What You Have Learned

1. How can you help children learn about concepts like size, shape, and texture?
2. How can reading to young children help them learn?
3. Why may children need your help learning to care for themselves?

Communicating with Children

When you talk to children, speak correctly. In order for them to learn to use the right words to describe objects, you need to set an example. This will help them when they start school. If you use the wrong words to describe objects, children will also use the wrong words. When they start school, they will have to learn to use the right words. This can be hard.

Children need to feel that you care for and understand them as they are learning. They like to be praised when they learn to behave correctly or perform tasks for themselves. See 2-18. For instance, when children tie their shoelaces for the first time, you should praise them. Say, "You did a good job tying your shoelaces!" Smile and encourage them to do it again. Such rewards are important for children as they are learning.

When you care for children, you should encourage them to try new tasks. Show interest in what they do. This encourages them to keep learning and trying. When children make mistakes or do not succeed, they become discouraged. You should not criticize them. This does not help them learn. When they are discouraged, they need patience and understanding. They need to know that they are loved and accepted.

2-18 Children should receive lots of encouragement when learning new tasks.

✔ **Check What You Have Learned**

1. Why do you need to speak correctly to children?
2. How can you let children know you care for and understand them?

Behavior

Children need to act in ways acceptable to themselves and others. They need to learn right from wrong. They need to know how to behave in different situations. See 2-19. Good behavior helps children get along with others. It gives them confidence.

Telling children what they can do is a positive way to teach good behavior. This lets children learn what they can do instead of what they can't do. This also lets them decide how they want to behave. Children need encouragement. Too many no's and not enough praise may make them afraid to try new tasks.

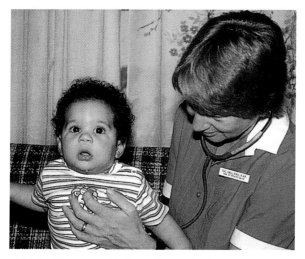

2-19 Children need to learn how to behave during physical exams.

Sometimes children do need to be told no. They may be doing something that is harmful or unacceptable to others. If you show them how to behave correctly and praise them, they will learn acceptable behavior. Also, when children learn that some types of behavior are unacceptable, they can say no to other people. This can help them avoid being taken advantage of or hurt.

✓ Check What You Have Learned

1. Why should you tell children what they can do, instead of what they can't do?
2. How can you help children learn acceptable behavior?

The Main Ideas

Children learn a lot during the first six years of their lives. They learn by using their senses. They also learn by playing. Communicating with children helps them learn. You can praise them and encourage them to try new tasks. This helps children learn how to behave acceptably.

Apply What You Have Learned

1. Observe two or three infants at play. Notice what kinds of games they are playing. Take notes on what each infant is learning through play.
2. Choose a task you would like to help a young child learn. Select games to teach this task. Give a demonstration to your classmates on how you would use these games to help teach the child the task.
3. Visit a family with a child who is learning to talk. Talk to the child. Note what words the child can say and whether or not the child repeats words you say. What is the child's reaction when you repeat words he or she says? Share your observations with the class.
4. Recall examples from your toddler and preschool years of when you had behavior swings from independence to dependence. Share these examples in a small group. Discuss ways in which you and your classmates feel you still exhibit swings of behavior.

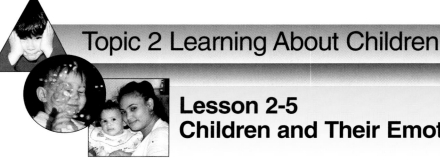

Topic 2 Learning About Children

Lesson 2-5
Children and Their Emotions

Objectives

After studying this lesson, you will be able to

⇒ *define* emotions, love, caregiver, *and* time-out.

⇒ *give examples of ways children can learn to express their emotions.*

⇒ *list the basic elements of love.*

⇒ *describe how people can show love for children.*

New Words

emotions: *feelings about people and events.*

love: *a strong feeling of affection for someone or something.*

caregiver: *a person who takes care of children.*

time-out: *a technique used to improve a child's behavior by moving the child to a place where he or she must sit quietly.*

New Ideas

⇒ *Children need to learn how to express their emotions in good ways.*

⇒ *Children need to give and receive love to become mature adults.*

⇒ *The basic elements of love are care, responsibility, respect, and understanding.*

⇒ *Time-out is a way to help correct a child's behavior.*

Emotions are feelings about people and events. Learning to understand and express emotions is an important part of a child's development. One emotion that is especially important for children to learn about is love. **Love** is a strong feeling of affection for someone or something. This lesson will explain how you can help children learn about love and their other emotions.

Learning to Express Emotions

You can learn to understand children by the emotions they express. They act in certain ways to show how they feel. For instance, Steve shows love when he hugs his mother or father. He shows anger and frustration when he cries and throws or breaks objects.

You may enjoy being around children more when they are expressing feelings of love and happiness. When children are angry or frustrated, they may annoy or upset you. Some people scold or punish children who are angry or upset. This does not help children. The angry feelings do not go away.

When you care for children you need to remember that children are not "little adults." They cannot express their emotions as adults do. They need help expressing and understanding their emotions. You should allow children to express how they feel. Children can learn how to express their emotions in good ways through experience and example.

Children need to express their emotions. However, they need to learn that talking is better than throwing objects when they are angry. They need to learn words to describe their emotions. If they are acting happy, you can say, "You are happy." If they are upset, you can say, "You seem angry." When you talk about emotions, children learn that it is okay for them to talk about how they feel and why. They also learn what words to use to talk about their emotions. See 2-20.

2-20 Expressing emotions is an important part of being a healthy person.

✔ Check What You Have Learned

1. Why should people remember that children are not "little adults"?
2. Why shouldn't people punish children who are angry or upset?
3. How does talking help children learn to express their emotions?

Helping Children Handle Their Emotions

Children express their emotions in different ways at various ages. Two-year-olds are trying to be independent. They have strong feelings. They want to try new skills and do more for themselves. When they can't do things their way they may yell or kick. Trying to do a task that is too hard may make toddlers feel angry.

When you are around children, you may need to help them handle their emotions. You may be able to help a two-year-old find appropriate ways to handle anger. For example, you can help a child learn that kicking and screaming is not acceptable conduct. Talk to the child to find out what is wrong. Anger often results from the frustration of not being able to do something. You may be able to help the child reach his or her goal.

Help a child feel more independent by encouraging him or her. Tell the child, "You can do it." Be

a role model by showing a child how to play a game or use a toy. A child can build his or her confidence by watching you or learning from you.

Four- and five-year-olds want to help others to show their love. You can allow children to help you with safe tasks. Four- and five-year-olds tend to express anger with words. They are less likely to yell or kick because they have learned that adults do not accept this. Listen to four- and five-year-olds when they feel angry. You also may set an example by expressing your anger in words.

As children grow older they become more aware of the world around them. This causes fears to develop. Some children fear the imagined, such as monsters and burglars. They may fear pain caused by doctors. They also may fear physical injury from what they believe can hurt them, such as dogs or water. You can help a child handle fear through play. For example, a child might pretend to be a doctor to help work out fears of an upcoming checkup.

Some people use time-out to help correct a child's conduct. **Time-out** is a technique used to improve a child's behavior by moving the child to a place where he or she must sit quietly. Let children know ahead of time what behaviors will result in time-out. When you see one child upsetting another child, say firmly, "time-out." Then move the child to a place to sit quietly for three minutes.

During the time-out tell the child why you are not happy with his or her conduct. You may say, "When I see you punching John, I am unhappy because you are hurting him." If the child does not sit quietly, start the time period again. You must make sure the child obeys the time-out rules. Otherwise, the child will not take you seriously.

✔ **Check What You Have Learned**

1. What may cause a two-year-old child to yell or kick?
2. How can you help a child to feel more independent?
3. How does time-out work? Why do some people feel it is effective?

Learning to Love

Love is an important emotion. It provides meaning and purpose to people's lives. All children need to give and receive love to become mature adults. See 2-21.

Children are not born with the capacity to give love. They learn about love by being loved by other people. During the toddler and preschooler years, children grow in their relationships with others. However, they focus on receiving love, rather than giving it.

As children grow older, their capacity to love develops. This capacity does not begin at any specific age. Each child grows and develops individually.

Showing love for others often begins in the form of giving. For instance, a preschooler may give his or her parent a drawing. The child's desire to give is a feeling related to the need to love. Parents and other caregivers need to show they are happy to receive items children give them. This helps children learn to feel good about giving and loving.

2-21 Giving kisses helps children learn about love.

✔ **Check What You Have Learned**

1. Why do all children need to give and receive love?
2. How do infants differ from toddlers and preschoolers in their capacity to love?

Elements of Love

The most important people during the first six years of a child's life are the parents and caregivers. A **caregiver** is a person who takes care of children. Caregivers can be brothers, sisters, relatives, or baby-sitters.

In healthy relationships between children and the people who care for them, certain elements of love can be found. They are care, responsibility, respect, and understanding. When you care for children, you can show these elements of love.

When taking care of children, you can show caring love in many ways. For instance, you show caring love when you play with children. Children are happy when you read them stories or take them for walks. Spending time with children and paying attention to them is needed for them to feel cared for and loved.

Parents show responsibility for their children in many ways. They take their children to a doctor or nurse for medical care. See 2-22. They work to provide shelter and food for their children. When you care for children, you can also show responsibility. You can watch children to make sure they do not harm themselves. When children know that someone is responsible for them, they feel secure.

Parents show respect by letting their children grow and develop in their own ways. You show respect when you talk to children. You show respect when you take time to listen to children and answer their questions. See 2-23.

2-23 Giving children a chance to talk about a story shows your respect for them.

Loving children requires understanding them. You should learn about children before you begin caring for them. This will help you understand the children better and build healthy relationships with them. Your understanding will also help you show caring, responsibility, and respect for children.

Your relationships with children can bring you pleasure and satisfaction if the elements of love are present. You can give as well as receive love. You can learn about yourself and children. You can benefit through giving of yourself and seeing children respond. You can help children feel happy, secure, and loved as you care for them. These are good feelings for them to have.

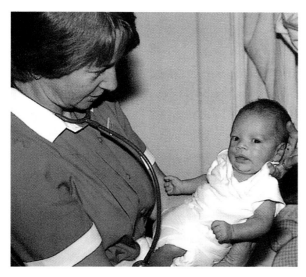

2-22 Parents use medical care to protect their children's health.

✓ **Check What You Have Learned**

1. How can you show caring love for children? Give examples.
2. Why does loving children require understanding them?

The Main Ideas

Children need to learn to express their emotions in good ways. Talking helps children express their emotions. Children's greatest need is to be loved. As children grow older, their capacity to love develops. There are four basic elements of love. They are care, responsibility, respect, and understanding.

Apply What You Have Learned

1. Find pictures of children in magazines and newspapers. Look at what kinds of emotions they express. Share these pictures with the class. Discuss what might have caused these emotions. Also discuss times when you felt like that and how you expressed your emotions.
2. Watch a television program about a family with young children. Observe how the children show that they need to be loved. Observe how the parents show love for their children. Write a one-page paper, discussing whether or not the family is acting realistically.
3. Think about parents and a child. Write a poem about how the parents use the four elements of love when caring for their child.
4. In a small group, talk about the ways you could use time-out to correct a child's behavior when you are baby-sitting.

Lesson 2-6
Baby-Sitting

Objectives

After studying this lesson, you will be able to
- ⇒ *define baby-sitting, limit, physical disability and mental disability.*
- ⇒ *list some of the responsibilities baby-sitters have.*
- ⇒ *explain how you can prepare to be a good baby-sitter.*
- ⇒ *describe the tasks you need to perform when baby-sitting.*
- ⇒ *tell how children with special needs differ from other children.*

New Words

baby-sitting: *caring for children, usually during a short absence of the parents.*
limit: *a boundary or restriction.*
physical disability: *a condition that limits a person's ability to use part of his or her body.*
mental disability: *a condition that limits a person's ability to use his or her mind.*

New Ideas

- ⇒ *Baby-sitters are expected to treat children as their parents treat them.*
- ⇒ *Keeping children safe and happy should be the main concern of a baby-sitter.*
- ⇒ *Being a good baby-sitter takes a lot of preparation.*
- ⇒ *Children with special needs should be treated like other children as much as possible.*

You may take care of younger brothers and sisters, cousins, or neighborhood children when their parents are gone. This is called **baby-sitting**. Baby-sitting gives you a chance to learn about children. It also gives parents the chance to get away for fun, to relax, or to handle emergencies.

Responsibilities of Baby-Sitting

When you baby-sit, you are responsible for the children. You are a substitute for the parents. You are expected to treat children as their parents treat them.

Parents show their love by setting **limits**, which are boundaries or restrictions. Parents set limits to help children learn proper behavior. Discipline may be needed to enforce some limits. In relationships with children, limits and discipline are used with love. As a baby-sitter, you need to find out what the limits are. You also need to find out what kind of discipline the parents want you to use to enforce them.

You are also expected to keep children safe and happy when you baby-sit. Keeping them safe is an important and serious responsibility. See 2-24. Keeping them happy is sometimes as hard as keeping them safe. Following parents' instructions will help you keep children safe and happy.

Never leave babies and young children alone, unless they are asleep in their beds. As they explore the world around them, accidents may occur. See 2-25. Stay with children and watch them. Play games and talk with them.

Keeping Children Safe

★ Never leave infants alone on a changing table or bed.

★ Never leave infants or toddlers alone in the bathtub.

★ Keep medicines, cleaning products, poisons, and matches in cabinets, out of the reach of children.

★ Keep dangerous and breakable items, such as plastic bags and glass decorations, out of the reach of children.

★ Do not let small children touch ranges, radiators, space heaters, sharp objects, or electric cords.

★ Do not let small children play with toys that are small, have removable parts, or have sharp edges.

★ Use gates to keep children from climbing up and down stairs.

★ Never leave children alone in the house, even for a short time.

★ Check children often while they are sleeping and playing.

★ Keep first aid supplies and a flashlight handy in case of emergencies.

2-24 To keep children safe, you should follow these tips.

2-25 If you do not watch children, they may get themselves into harmful situations.

If an accident or illness does occur, you may need help. Call the parents or the doctor. Good baby-sitters are not afraid to ask for help. Keep the emergency telephone numbers beside the telephone for easy reference.

Do not give children medicine without the parents' or doctor's consent. If you think children may have taken medication on their own, call the parents at once and tell them.

Keeping children happy may require extra patience. They may have separation anxiety after their parents leave. You should try to distract them. You could talk to them and hold them. You could play games and read stories to them. See 2-26. You could ask them to show you their favorite toys. Most children will become calm within a short period of time.

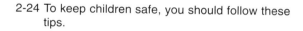

✓ Check What You Have Learned

1. How can parents help their children learn proper behavior?
2. What are two responsibilities that you may have as a baby-sitter?
3. What can baby-sitters do to keep babies and young children from hurting themselves?

2-26 Interacting with children is a good way to keep them happy after their parents leave.

Preparing to Baby-Sit

Some people are good baby-sitters. Others are not. To be a good baby-sitter, you need to be prepared. You need to know how children grow and develop. You should like children and enjoy being with them. You also need to be patient with them. You should be able to handle emergencies and act responsibly.

It is important to learn how children behave at each age. Read books about children. Observe children around you. Think about how what you read relates to what you've observed. Remember this when baby-sitting.

Before baby-sitting children for the first time, visit their homes to meet them and their parents. See 2-27. Let the parents know what baby-sitting skills you have. Find out what duties they expect you to perform. Decide how much you will charge to baby-sit. Be sure the parents agree that this is a fair amount.

Ask for any special instructions about the children. What are their eating and sleeping habits? Do you need to feed them while you are there? If so, what foods should they eat? What time should they

be put to bed? What are their favorite toys? When you know and respect the rules, children cannot talk you into breaking them. Talk to the parents about the ways you try to guide children's behavior. See 2-28.

Before the parents leave, have them give you a telephone number where they can be reached. Ask for telephone numbers for the doctor, the police, the fire department, and the local poison control center. Find out when you should call the doctor before calling the parents. Certain emergencies need to be taken care of quickly.

2-27 It is important to meet with the family and discuss the job before you begin baby-sitting.

 Guiding Children's Behavior

★ Give children time to change from one activity to another. Play is important. Children do not like to be interrupted. Warn a child 5 or 10 minutes ahead of time.

★ Use distraction to focus a child's attention on something else. If a child wants a book that he or she cannot have, offer another toy or book that the child likes and can have.

★ Smile when a child's behavior is good. Also, tell the child that you approve of his or her behavior. Smiles and words help a child feel good about pleasing you.

★ Use questions to help a child know what you expect. If you expect a child to pick up the toys when playtime is over, ask the child, "What are you supposed to do when you are finished with your toys?"

★ Plan enough activities to keep a child busy. Try to have activities that will interest the child. A child may misbehave if he or she is bored. Remember that a child's attention span varies with different activities.

2-28 Follow these tips to reduce behavior problems.

✓ **Check What You Have Learned**

1. Why should baby-sitters visit the family before they baby-sit children for the first time?
2. What information should baby-sitters gather before the parents leave?
3. What kind of an emergency might require a baby-sitter to call the doctor before the parents?

On the Job

Following a few simple guidelines can help you be a successful baby-sitter. When you baby-sit, take a notebook and pencil to write down instructions. Wear comfortable clothes that will let you move around with the children. You may want to take some books and games that you think the children might enjoy.

Take reading material or homework to keep you busy after the children are asleep. However, don't get so involved in your reading or homework that you forget to check on the children. If you have permission to use the telephone, make only necessary calls. This is not the time to be chatting with friends, even when the children are in bed. If you expect to get hungry, take along a sandwich or fruit. Do not eat the family's food unless you have been invited to do so.

Make sure that you respect the family's home. Handle dishes, decorations, and other breakable items very carefully. Take care of furnishings. If an object gets broken or damaged, you need to fix or replace it. Leave the house as clean as when you arrived. Help the children pick up their toys before they go to bed or their parents arrive home.

You also need to respect the family's privacy. Do not look through rooms, closets, or personal belongings unless you have been told to do so. Do not repeat anything the children say about the family. This is private information. However, if you find out about an action that may endanger the health or safety of the children, tell an adult whom you trust. The adult will help you get help for the family, if needed.

✓ **Check What You Have Learned**

1. What reasons are there for not talking on the telephone when baby-sitting?
2. How can you show respect for a family's privacy when you are baby-sitting?

Children with Special Needs

All children share certain basic needs. They all need food, clothing, and shelter. They all need to feel safe and secure. They all need love and support.

Some children have special needs that go beyond basic needs. Some children need special tools to help them perform everyday tasks. Some may need special programs to help them learn or develop skills.

Someday you may baby-sit or work with children with special needs. The more you learn about these children, the better you will be able to care for them.

Children with physical disabilities have special needs. A **physical disability** is a condition that limits a person's ability to use part of his or her body. Children with physical disabilities may be blind, deaf, or paralyzed. These children may use guide dogs, hearing aids, wheelchairs, or crutches to help meet their special needs. See 2-29.

Children with mental disabilities also have special needs. A **mental disability** is a condition that limits a person's ability to use his or her mind. Children with mental disabilities may have emotional problems. Some have trouble learning. Others may have brain damage due to an injury. These children may take part in special programs that address their specific needs.

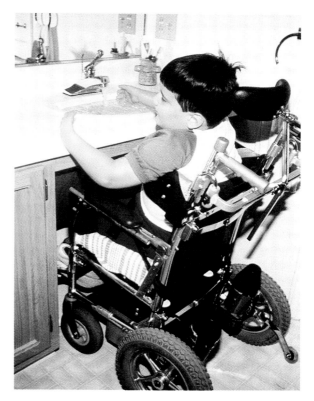

2-29 This boy uses a wheelchair to move around his house.

Children with outstanding skills have special needs, too. These children may be skilled in English, math, art, music, or sports. These children may participate in special programs that help them develop and use their skills.

✓ Check What You Have Learned

1. What are three needs all children share?
2. How can you learn to take care of children with special needs better?

The Main Ideas

Good baby-sitters are responsible for children. They keep children safe and happy. They prepare for their job by visiting the home and talking with the parents. They ask for instructions and follow them. They can learn to help and care for children with special needs.

Apply What You Have Learned

1. On the chalkboard or in your notebook, list the qualities of a good baby-sitter. Using this list, rate yourself on each qualification.
2. Suppose you are baby-sitting five-year-old Stacia who says she has a headache. She asks you to give her "baby" aspirin. As a class, take turns role-playing how you would handle this situation.
3. Suppose you have agreed to baby-sit for three hours for a certain amount of money. When you arrive, the parents ask you to wash dishes and iron clothes. This was not part of the agreement. Write a paragraph describing what you will say to the parents. As a class discuss each of your responses.
4. Suppose you have been asked to care for Wesley for two hours on Saturday morning. Wesley is six years old, and his mother says he enjoys active play. You planned outside activities because sunny weather was forecast. When you get up in the morning, it is raining. Brainstorm with a classmate a new plan for indoor activities.
5. Interview the parents of a child with special needs. Find out what special help and care they have to give their child.

Case Study

*Read the story below and look at Lesson 2-6 again.
Then answer the questions below.*

Preparing to Baby-Sit

Emily is planning to baby-sit four-year-old Dustin for two hours this Saturday morning. However, she first met with Dustin's mother, Mrs. Goodwin. Emily asked Mrs. Goodwin for the information she will need to perform her job.

"What would you like me to do while I'm taking care of Dustin?" Emily asked.

"I would like you to start playing with Dustin before I leave. If you do this, he won't mind my leaving so much," said Mrs. Goodwin. "He likes to play in the TV room. I think that is because we all seem to like that room. However, I do not want Dustin to watch TV while you are here. Please do not turn it on. I prefer that Dustin play games. He learns more that way."

Then Emily asked, "What kinds of games does he like to play?"

"He loves puzzles. I will show you a couple of his favorite ones. He likes to play with his building blocks. He also loves it when people read to him. I would like you to read a book to him," said Mrs. Goodwin. "He thinks it's fun to repeat words when you are reading. He also knows the stories from his favorite books."

"I have a book at home about turtles that my little sister likes," said Emily. "She laughs and laughs every time I read it to her. Could I bring it over and read it to Dustin?"

"I think that's a great idea, Emily," Mrs. Goodwin answered. "It is nice of you to offer to share your books with Dustin."

"Mrs. Goodwin, I want to write down in my notebook the telephone numbers where you can be reached if I need to call you. I already have the numbers for the police and fire departments and your home telephone number. Are there any other numbers you want to give me?" Emily asked.

To Discuss

➡ 1. What other telephone numbers should Mrs. Goodwin give Emily?
➡ 2. If Dustin cries when his mother leaves, what should Emily do?
➡ 3. If Dustin wants to watch television, how might Emily distract his attention?

Topic 2 Review

Topic Summary

During the first six years of their lives, children grow and develop in different ways and at different rates. At birth, they are dependent on others to take care of all their needs. By the time they reach six years of age, children are ready to attend school all day on their own.

Each year children become more independent and learn new skills. They learn by using their senses. They learn by playing. They also learn from other children, teens, and adults.

During this time, children need a lot of love and support to gain confidence in themselves. They also need help learning how to properly express their emotions.

Learning about children can help you when you baby-sit. You will know how to keep children safe and happy. You will also be able to help them grow and develop.

To Review

Write your answers on a separate sheet of paper.

1. Use + to identify the traits that describe infants at birth. Use - to identify the traits that do not describe infants at birth.
   a. Wrinkled skin.
   b. Strong muscles.
   c. Large head.
   d. Fat arms and legs.
   e. Large abdomen.
   f. Large chest.
2. How do babies communicate their needs?
3. What do toddlers need to feel confident?
4. What are two reasons that toddlers may say no a lot?
5. How can you help a preschooler who stutters?

6. List three ways you can calm pre-schoolers who become upset when you correct their behavior.
7. How do infants learn to speak?
8. Give an example of how you can help a child learn about numbers.
9. Which element of love is described in each sentence?
   a. Pay close attention to children so that they are safe.
   b. Spend time with each child.
   c. Take time to listen to children and answer their questions.
   d. Know how children develop.
10. What are three ways you can prepare to baby-sit a child for the first time?

Vocabulary Quiz

Match the definitions in Column A with the terms in Column B.
Write your answers on a separate sheet of paper.

Column A

1. A fear that if parents leave, they will not return.
2. A child under one year of age.
3. A child between the ages of three and five or six years.
4. A child between the ages of one and three years.
5. Caring for children, usually during a short absence of the parents.
6. Strong feeling of affection for someone or something.
7. A natural, unlearned behavior.
8. When children play near one another but not with one another.
9. Relying on another for support.
10. To act or work together with others.
11. Feelings about people and events.
12. Gaining information or skills through instruction or practice.
13. A condition that limits a person's ability to use his or her mind.
14. A technique used to improve a child's behavior by moving the child to a place where he or she must sit quietly.
15. A condition that limits a person's ability to use part of his or her body.

Column B

a. Infant.
b. Toddler.
c. Preschooler.
d. Dependent.
e. Reflex.
f. Separation anxiety.
g. Parallel play.
h. Baby-sitting.
i. Mental disability.
j. Limit.
k. Love.
l. Cooperate.
m. Learning.
n. Emotions.
o. Physical disability.
p. Time-out.

Unit 2
You — A Manager

You must make decisions about how to use your time and skills to meet basic needs.

Topic 3 Making Decisions

Lesson 3-1
Your Needs and Wants

Objectives

After studying this lesson, you will be able to
- *define needs and wants.*
- *list basic physical and emotional needs.*
- *explain how wants are different from needs.*

New Words

needs: *the basic items you must have to live.*

wants: *the extra items you would like, but can live without.*

New Ideas

- *You have basic physical and emotional needs.*
- *Wants can make your life more satisfying.*

Your needs and wants affect your life. **Needs** are the basic items you must have to live. **Wants** are the extra items you would like but must not have to live. Needs and wants affect how you use your time, skills, and talents. They affect your feelings. They even affect how you get along with others.

Physical Needs

Each person has the same basic *physical needs.* These needs include having enough food, clothing, shelter, and sleep to stay alive. See 3-1. They must be met before any other needs and wants can be met. For instance, in disasters, such as floods and tornadoes, these needs must be met first. You need to have clean food and water, dry clothes, and a safe place to sleep.

3-1 Food is a basic physical need.

Most adults are able to meet their basic physical needs on their own. They earn money to pay for food, clothes, and shelter. Other people, such as babies, children, and sick people, depend on others to help them meet their basic physical needs. People who have been in disasters also depend on others for help.

Helping people who are not able to meet their basic physical needs is everyone's responsibility. For instance, part of your tax money is used to help meet other people's basic physical needs. When you give money to a charity, it is used to help people. Volunteering your time is a way you can help people without spending any money. See 3-2.

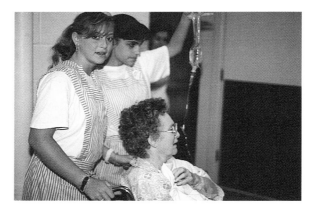

3-2 These candy stripers volunteer their time as nurse's aides.

✓ Check What You Have Learned

1. Why must the basic physical needs be met first?
2. How can you help other people meet their basic physical needs?

Emotional Needs

There are other basic needs besides physical needs. They are called *emotional needs*. They include being liked by others, feeling secure, gaining recognition, and having new experiences. Emotional needs are related to living and getting along with others. They are also related to peace of mind and happiness. All people have these basic emotional needs.

Everyone needs to feel that they are liked by others. To meet this need, you make friends and work to maintain these friendships. See 3-3. You join clubs and sports teams to meet new people. When you are assigned tasks, you try to do well.

You also need to feel secure. You need to feel safe from harm. Knowing that your belongings are safe can also make you feel secure. When you feel secure, you are more relaxed and happy.

You need to be noticed and feel special. You may like to have people pay special attention to you. When people have high needs for recognition,

3-3 Being friends with someone can help meet your emotional need to be liked by others.

they may excel in certain areas, such as sports, school, or the arts.

If you are like most people, you like some change in your life. You have an emotional need to have different experiences. This can be fun and help you learn more about the world around you.

Joining different after-school groups and sports teams is one way to try different experiences.

There are both good and poor ways to meet these basic emotional needs. Good ways meet needs without preventing other needs from being met. Poor ways meet one need and prevent another from being met. For instance, being president of an after-school club is a good way to gain recognition and help others. On the other hand, if you like to gossip to gain recognition, you may lose friends in the process. This would be a poor way to meet your need for recognition. See 3-4.

3-4 Gossip can keep you from meeting your need for friendship.

✔ **Check What You Have Learned**

1. How do you meet your need for recognition?
2. How do you meet your need for new experiences?

Wants

Wants are different from basic needs. Basic needs are limited. Wants, however, can be unlimited. Most people are not able to fulfill all of their wants. See 3-5.

When you fulfill your wants, your life can be more satisfying. For instance, you may want a musical instrument so you can join a band. You may believe that if you belong to a band, your life will be more fun. You may think about the friends you can make.

The basic need for food can be met with simple foods that provide good nutrition. However, for many people, these foods do not fulfill their wants. They want foods they enjoy eating and that taste good. They want to try different foods away from home.

Clothes are another example of the difference between needs and wants. The basic need for clothing may be taken care of with a few simple items.

However, most people want more clothes than they need. Some want clothes that show their status. They want to gain recognition by having clothes in the latest fashions.

3-5 Going to an amusement park is a want rather than a need.

Check What You Have Learned

1. How are wants different from needs? Give examples.
2. What is something you may want to eat but do not need to eat?

The Main Ideas

Everyone has needs and wants. Basic physical needs are those needs that must be met before any other needs and wants. Emotional needs are related to peace of mind and happiness. Wants are items you would like to have but do not need. Needs must be met before wants can be fulfilled.

Apply What You Have Learned

1. Survey six students in your school. Ask them if they consider the following items to be needs or wants:

blue jeans	sleeping bag
chewing gum	lunch in the cafeteria
haircut	stereo system
bicycle	

   Compare the answers and discuss them with your classmates.
2. Make a list of volunteer organizations in your community that help other people meet their basic physical needs. Find out how you can join one of these groups.

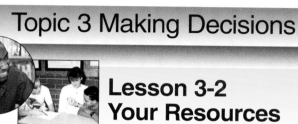

Lesson 3-2
Your Resources

Objectives

After studying this lesson, you will be able to

⟹ *define resource, human resource, nonhuman resource, private resource, public resource, and scarce.*

⟹ *list the different types of resources.*

⟹ *explain how resources can be developed.*

⟹ *describe ways in which resources can be used.*

New Words

resource: *assets that can be used to meet needs and fulfill wants.*

human resource: *what people have within themselves to get what they need or want.*

nonhuman resource: *objects and conditions available to people to help them meet needs and fulfill wants.*

private resource: *a resource owned and controlled by a person or a family group.*

public resource: *a resource shared by everyone and paid for through taxes.*

scarce: *a resource that is limited in supply.*

New Ideas

⟹ *Resources help you meet needs and fulfill wants.*

⟹ *Resources can be identified as human, nonhuman, private, or public.*

⟹ *You have the ability to develop your resources.*

Resources are assets that can be used to meet needs and fulfill wants. Without resources, you cannot do what you want to do. You need resources to reach your goals now and in the future. There are many different types of resources available to you.

Types of Resources

Resources can be grouped as human and nonhuman. **Human resources** are what people have within themselves to get what they need or want. Your human resources are yours alone. They are like no one else's. They are a part of you. Human resources include knowledge, skills, talents, creativity, health, work habits, energy, ability to use time, and personality. See 3-6. Human resources are also called *personal resources.* Your human resources make you special.

As a student, you use your human resources daily. Your ability to learn and how you learn are human resources. Knowing how you learn best can help you be a better student.

Nonhuman resources are objects and conditions available to people to help them meet needs and fulfill wants. Nonhuman resources are also called *material resources.* They include money, equipment, housing, schools, and fuel. Objects you own are considered nonhuman resources.

Resources can also be grouped as either private resources or public resources. **Private resources** are owned and controlled by a person or a family group. One example of a private resource is income. Others are houses or cars owned by a family. Human resources are also private resources.

3-6 Your personality and ability to make friends are human resources.

3-7 When you study in the library, you are using a public resource.

The use and cost of **public resources** are shared by everyone. Public resources are paid for through taxes. If you are sitting in a public school reading this book, then you are using public resources. Other examples of public resources include roads, parks, and fire and police protection. See 3-7. Public resources are nonhuman resources.

✔ Check What You Have Learned

1. How do you use your human resources as a family member? Give examples.
2. How do communities pay for public resources?

Using Resources

You can use resources in a variety of ways. You can trade one resource for another resource. For example, Tracy's neighbor, Mr. Topper, is paying Tracy to walk his dog while he is on vacation. Tracy is trading her time and skills for money. When you walk to the store instead of riding in a car, you are trading your energy for gas.

It is important to use resources without wasting them. Some resources are **scarce**, which means they are limited in supply. Scarce resources can run out. For example, many communities experience water shortages when the supply of clean water becomes scarce. People can cope by reducing their use of water. They can shut off the faucet when brushing their teeth. They can take showers instead of baths. See Lesson 6-2 for other ways to conserve scarce resources.

✓ Check What You Have Learned

1. How can one resource be traded for another resource?
2. Why is it important to avoid wasting resources?

Developing Your Resources

Developing your resources is important. The more resources you develop, the more goals you can reach. There are many ways to develop your resources, especially your human resources. You can increase your knowledge, learn new skills, and improve the skills you already have. You can also develop new interests, learn more about yourself, and improve your health.

Families are the main influence in helping young children develop their human resources. In fact, a major responsibility of families is helping all members develop their human resources. (A discussion on how young children develop is included in Topic 2, "Learning About Children.")

As you grow older, you begin taking responsibility for your own development. You become the only person who can choose how to develop your human resources. As a student, you can develop your intelligence by reading, going to school, and meeting new people. You can develop any skills you have through practice. You can improve your health through diet and exercise.

How you choose to develop your resources is an important decision that you must make for yourself. Everyone develops their resources differently. It depends on what their needs and wants are. Also, some people are born with more resources than others. They may be rich or live in an area where there are many chances to explore new interests and develop skills. No matter what, all people should work toward improving themselves.

Everyone has special skills they can develop as resources. You may be good at sports, schoolwork, or dancing. You may be artistic or get along well with other people. You may not have discovered your special skills yet. Many famous people did not discover their special skills until they were older. Some skills need practice to be developed. Others occur naturally.

Developing your human resources will help you make better use of your nonhuman resources. For instance, you may like working with computers. These skills may help you earn an income in your future career. See 3-8. You use the human resources of skill and knowledge to earn money, which is a nonhuman resource.

3-8 Learning to use computers can help you develop your human resources.

✓ Check What You Have Learned

1. How can you develop your human resources? Give examples.
2. How can developing your human resources now help you develop your nonhuman resources in the future?

The Main Ideas

You use your resources to meet needs and fulfill wants. Resources can be human or nonhuman, and private or public. You can choose how to develop your resources. Developing your human resources lets you use your nonhuman resources better.

Apply What You Have Learned

1. Look in your local telephone book for five public resources your city or town offers. Make a poster illustrating these resources. Your title might read: "Look what (name of your city or town) has to offer!"
2. Interview an adult who is taking a college class or who has gone back to school. Ask the adult what motivated him or her to take the class. Find out how he or she expects to benefit in the future from taking the class. In small groups discuss your findings.
3. Look in the library for biographies or magazine articles about a famous person who did not develop his or her talents until he or she was older. Write a one-page report about this person.

Topic 3 Making Decisions

Lesson 3-3
Your Values and Goals

Objectives

After studying this lesson, you will be able to
- *define values, goals, priorities, and standards.*
- *give examples of values and goals.*
- *tell how values and goals are related.*
- *give examples of how values affect priorities.*

New Words

values: *strong beliefs or ideas about what is important.*
goals: *what you want to achieve.*
priorities: *important goals that must be met before less important goals.*
standards: *a means of measuring how well goals are achieved.*

New Ideas

- *Values and goals affect your wants, how you make decisions, and how you use your resources.*
- *Values affect the goals you try to achieve.*
- *Priorities are important goals that must be met first.*
- *Standards help you judge how well you have met your goals.*

What is most important to you in life? What do you hope to do today and tomorrow? The answers to these questions are determined by your values and goals. **Values** are strong beliefs and ideas about what is important. **Goals** are what you want to achieve. Your values and goals affect the life you lead.

Values

Your values are a part of you. They serve as guides for how you live your life. They give direction to your actions. See 3-9. Knowing what your values are can help you make satisfying decisions.

You can have many different values. A few examples are freedom, service to others, and strong family ties. Religion, education, beauty, and security are also values. Values affect what you want and how you act. They also affect how you use

3-9 Participating in community service projects with FHA/HERO reflects your values.

your resources and the decisions you do and do not make. For instance, you may value being in good shape. To stay in good shape you choose to exercise regularly and eat right.

You learn values from what others say and do. For instance, young children are strongly affected by their parents' values. They notice how their parents act and what they say. When parents volunteer to help with the community food drive, children learn to value community involvement. See 3-10. Children are also influenced by the values of their religious training.

As children get older, they have more experiences outside the home. Their friends and teachers may have values different from their parents. Children may try out these values, accept some, and reject others.

You also learn values from how your experiences affect you. Throughout your life, you continue to have new experiences. You learn about other places and people. These experiences may strengthen your values. They may also cause you to change some of your values. For instance, you may become friends with a student from another country. As you learn about his or her country and language, you begin to value learning about different people.

Values vary among people. People from different backgrounds may have different values. Countries often have different values. For instance, in the United States, women are valued for their contributions in business and politics. However, people in some other countries do not value women in such public roles.

3-10 You learn values from your family.

✓ **Check What You Have Learned**

1. What are some of the values you have? How do they affect the decisions you make?
2. How can other people affect your values? Give examples.

Goals

Goals are what you are striving to achieve. Your values affect the goals you decide to set for yourself. If you value a good education, you will make finishing homework a goal. If you value having a nice bike, you may set a goal to save enough money.

Goals can be short-term or long-term. *Short-term goals* are what you plan to get done soon. For instance, you may want to earn money to go to a movie this weekend. *Long-term goals* are what you hope to accomplish at a later date. A long-term goal may be saving money to buy a stereo. Long-term goals often take time to plan and are reached one step at a time.

Short-term goals are related to long-term goals. You may not reach your long-term goal if you do not reach your short-term goals first. See 3-11. For instance, your long-term goal may be to go to college. Your short-term goals should include getting good grades and saving money. Otherwise, it may be hard to reach your long-term goal.

3-11 By setting several short-term goals, this boy was able to meet his long-term goal of winning an FHA/HERO trophy.

✓ **Check What You Have Learned**

1. How do your values affect your goals? Give an example.
2. How are short-term goals related to long-term goals?

Priorities

Some goals are more important to you than others. They are called **priorities**. See 3-12. They must be met before less important goals. The goals most important to you are considered your top priorities. They must be met first. For instance, Dana has to complete her homework tonight. She also wants to learn how to play her new video game. She needs to choose the goal that is most important to her and complete it first. That goal she chooses is her priority.

3-12 Graduating from college is a priority for many people.

Your values may affect the priority you place on your goals. The more values you have related to a goal, the better your chances are of reaching that goal. For instance, if you value having good friends and being well-liked, you will make getting along well with others a priority.

Check What You Have Learned

1. What are top priorities?
2. How do values affect your priorities?

Standards

Standards are a means of measuring how well you achieve your goals. Each person has a different set of standards.

Many standards come from your family. Krista's family has high standards for grades. To meet those standards, Krista set a goal to get an A in math. When she does poorly on a math test, Krista feels she has not met her standards.

Some standards are based on scientific knowledge. For instance, research shows that food choices affect health. Therefore, you may set a goal to follow healthful eating guidelines. Reviewing your daily food choices can tell you if you have met your standard for good eating.

Check What You Have Learned

1. What are two factors that affect standards?
2. What are some of your standards?

 ### The Main Ideas

Values are beliefs and ideas about what is important. They affect your decisions, goals, actions, and priorities. They are learned from people and events that affect you. Values may change as you grow and develop. Goals are what you hope to achieve. Goals can be both short-term and long-term. Priorities are important goals that must be met before less important goals. Your standards can help you judge how well you have met your goals.

 ### Apply What You Have Learned

1. Observe parents with their children. Note any comments and actions from the parents that may be shaping the children's values. Write a one-page report based on your observations and share it with the class.
2. Write three goals you would like to achieve by this date next year. Make a list of the resources you will need and the steps you will take to achieve these goals. Think about how your needs, wants, and values affected the goals you chose. Consider the standards you will use to measure how well you achieve your goals.

Lesson 3-4
It's Your Decision

Objectives

After studying this lesson, you will be able to
- ⇒ *define* decision, decision-making process, alternatives, trade-off, conflict, conflict resolution, family council, leadership, *and* integrity.
- ⇒ *apply the decision-making process.*
- ⇒ *list hints for resolving conflicts.*
- ⇒ *give suggestions for making group decisions.*
- ⇒ *explain qualities of effective leaders.*

New Words

decision: *a choice made about what to do or say in a given situation.*

decision-making process: *steps followed to help make a decision, solve a problem, or reach a goal.*

alternatives: *options available to choose from when making a decision.*

trade-off: *the giving up of one thing for another.*

conflict: *a disagreement between two or more people.*

conflict resolution: *when a disagreement among two or more people is settled.*

family council: *an informal meeting called to talk over issues concerning family members.*

leadership: *the ability to inspire others to meet goals.*

integrity: *a commitment to do what is right.*

New Ideas

- ⇒ *You are responsible for the decisions you make.*
- ⇒ *There are six steps in the decision-making process.*
- ⇒ *When problems occur in group decision making, they need to be resolved.*
- ⇒ *You can develop leadership skills.*

To make the best use of your resources to meet your goals, decisions must be made. A **decision** is a choice made about what to do or say in a given situation. There are steps you can follow to make good decisions. There are also skills you can use when making decisions that affect a group.

3-13 Ask for advice from family members when learning to make important decisions.

Decisions

As you grow from a dependent infant into an independent adult, you will make many decisions. See 3-13. As an adolescent, you are already making some decisions about your life. You must accept what happens as a result of your decisions. You are responsible for your decisions, whether they are wrong or right. Accepting the consequences of your decisions is called *personal responsibility*. You need to learn to make decisions carefully.

Adults can help you learn how to make good decisions. They can guide you and let you know which decisions are good. Some adults think it is easier to make decisions for children than to let children decide for themselves. However, adults cannot always be with you. They should let you practice making your own decisions.

✓ Check What You Have Learned

1. Why do you need to learn to make decisions carefully?
2. Why should adults let you practice making your own decisions?

The Decision-Making Process

You have already made many decisions on your own today. See 3-14. Some of your decisions may have been easy ones. You had to decide what to wear to school. You may have decided what to eat for breakfast. You make these kinds of decisions without a lot of thought. They are almost habit. Other decisions are harder to make. They could be what after-school activity to join or what sport to play. They take more thought.

When you make decisions, there are six basic steps to follow. These steps are called the **decision-**

3-14 You make simple decisions every day, such as what to have for lunch.

making process. They help you make decisions, solve problems, or reach goals.

   1. *Identify the problem.* The first step is to clearly identify the problem to be solved. A problem may include a decision to be made or goal to be reached. For example, Kayla has just made the soccer team at her school. Practice takes up a lot of after-school time. In the past, she studied during this time. She takes part in other activities such as scouts and her church youth group in the evenings. She identifies the problem by asking, "When can I complete my homework?"

   2. *List the alternatives.* **Alternatives** are the options available to choose from when making a decision. You need to consider all the alternatives you have. Kayla considers her alternatives. They include *(a)* quitting the soccer team or *(b)* giving up some of her evening activities.

   3. *Research the alternatives.* When you make major decisions, list the advantages and disadvantages of your alternatives. *Advantages* are the good points. *Disadvantages* are the bad points. Kayla thinks about her alternatives. Playing on the soccer team takes up a lot of time during the week and on the weekends. She really enjoys playing soccer, however, and being a member of the team. She knows the exercise is good for her. Kayla also enjoys her evening activities, which take time. She has been a part of these groups for several years now. She likes to spend time with her friends and do worthwhile projects.

   4. *Make a decision based on your resources, needs, wants, values, goals, standards, and priorities.* Your friends and family can give you advice. Only you, however, can decide what is best for you. No one else has the same values, wants, needs, resources, goals, standards, and priorities as you have. Kayla wants to go to a good college someday. To do this she needs to study and get good grades. By quitting the soccer team, she will have time to study. She also will be able to stay involved in her other activities. She has been a member of these groups for many years and has lots of friends. Soccer is important to her, however, and she has worked hard to make the team. She is making new friends and improving her soccer skills. Kayla decides to give up scouts during the soccer season. She only meets with her church group once a week, so she decides to continue this activity.

   5. *Act on the decision.* You need to take responsibility for the decisions you make. When Kayla made her decision, she gave up some of her evening activities for soccer. This is called a **trade-off.** She told her scout troop that she had to take time off during soccer season. When she made her decision, Kayla knew she would miss being with her friends from the troop. She decided to accept this as a result of making her decision.

   6. *Evaluate the decision.* The last step of the process is to evaluate your decision. People often make the same decisions over and over again without thinking. By evaluating your decision, you may avoid repeating a bad one. After the soccer season ended, Kayla evaluated her decision. She decided that she had made a good one. Her grades were good because she was able to do homework in the evening. She also ended the season with some new friends and improved soccer skills. In addition, she still was in touch with her friends from her scout troop. She became active in this group again.

✓ Check What You Have Learned

1. What are the six steps of the decision-making process?
2. Why do you need to be able to make your own decisions?

3-15 Making a group decision takes extra effort.

Group Decisions

You can use the decision-making process when you are part of a group. Group decisions can be harder to make than personal decisions. See 3-15. This is because group members may have many different ideas based on their needs, wants, values, goals, priorities, and standards. They may have a conflict about what is the best decision. A **conflict** is a disagreement between two or more people.

Conflict resolution occurs when a disagreement between two or more people is settled. In Lesson 1-3, you learned about methods families can use to solve problems. Some of these problem-solving methods can also be used to resolve conflicts in a group.

Like family members, group members should use good communication skills to resolve conflicts. Communicating well helps people understand you better. It also makes it easier to get along with others.

Use good communication to clearly express your feelings. Be polite and avoid yelling or arguing. Attack the problem, not the person. For example, you may say, "I feel frustrated when my ideas are not considered." This is more effective than saying, "You never pay attention to my ideas."

Good communication also involves talking with other people, not to them. It is important to listen carefully to others to understand their point of view. Group members need to share ideas, opinions, and feelings. This helps them find solutions to their problems.

Find the right time to settle a disagreement. Consider a compromise.

Family decisions. At home, you are part of a family group. Families make many decisions. Sometimes members may disagree with each other. When this happens, a family council can be helpful. A **family council** is an informal meeting called to talk over issues concerning family members. Every member should be included, even younger children. They may not understand all that is said. However, they are still a part of the family. See 3-16.

Discussing family issues gives members a chance to express their views. Discussing feelings can help them understand one another. Sometimes families may discuss serious issues, such as money problems. Other times, they may discuss simple issues, such as which movie to see. Many families find that when all family members share a problem, they can reach a solution more easily.

✓ **Check What You Have Learned**

1. List three hints for resolving conflicts within a group.
2. How can family councils help solve family problems?

3-16 Family members should be given a chance to express themselves.

Contributing to Group Decisions

You may belong to after-school groups. In these groups, decisions are often made. One after-school group is Future Homemakers of America/Home Economics Related Occupations (FHA/HERO). FHA/HERO is offered through the family and consumer sciences department. FHA/HERO helps teens develop leadership skills for life through projects that address family issues, career exploration, and community involvement. Members of the organization use a five-step planning process to reach group goals. See 3-17. The steps in the planning process are as follows:

1. Identify concerns.
2. Set your goal.
3. Form a plan.
4. Act.
5. Follow up.

Other after-school groups you may belong to can include sports teams, bands, youth groups, and scouts. Each of these groups makes decisions, too. Others elect leaders to make decisions.

You also are part of a group in your classes. Class discussions give you and your classmates a chance to talk about different topics and make decisions. By taking part in class discussions, you can find out what your classmates are thinking and feeling. You also can express your thoughts and feelings. Discussing current events, school policies, and important social issues with your classmates can help you understand your decisions about these issues.

When making decisions, you need good information. It is better to discuss topics or subjects when you know the facts. This is why reading and doing research are a part of your schoolwork. Although what you think is important, you need to be able to support your ideas with facts.

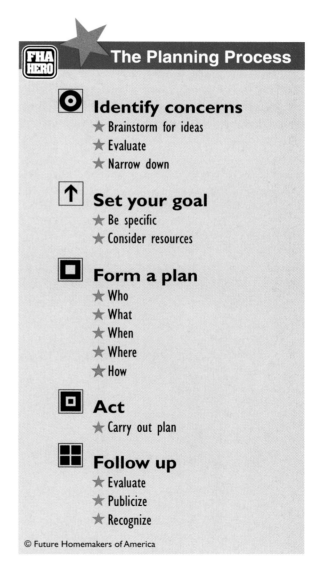

3-17 The FHA/HERO Planning Process can help you reach your individual as well as group goals.

The group decision-making skills you learn now will help you in the future. In your city or town, you will be able to help make group decisions. On the job, you will be better able to help solve group problems. Decision making can help you as a member of any group.

✓ **Check What You Have Learned**

1. How can you benefit by taking part in group decisions?
2. Why do you need to have good information when making decisions?

Leadership

Working with groups, such as FHA/HERO, can help you develop leadership skills. **Leadership** is the ability to inspire others to meet goals. Leaders value the needs and interests of others. They set examples for others to follow. They guide group decisions.

Effective leaders have certain qualities that help them influence group members. Leaders need to be knowledgeable about group issues. Leaders must be wise to make good decisions. They need courage to do what needs to be done. Leaders need enthusiasm to get group members excited about achieving goals. They need friendly, caring personalities. Leaders must be organized. They need good time management skills to meet obligations. Effective leaders also have **integrity.** They are committed to doing what is right.

✓ **Check What You Have Learned**

1. Which traits of an effective leader would you like to develop?
2. How can you be a leader in your school?

The Main Ideas

It is important for you to learn to make decisions carefully. Following the six steps in the decision-making process will help you make decisions. When problems occur in group decision making, they need to be discussed. Becoming involved in school groups can help you develop the qualities of an effective leader.

Apply What You Have Learned

1. Write a story about a teen who has an important decision to make. Outline the steps of the decision-making process in your story. Be creative.
2. List suggestions for successfully making group decisions at school. Share your suggestions in class. Then, as a class, use the suggestions to make a group decision.
3. Survey students at your school about the qualities they use to describe an effective leader. Write an article for the school newspaper reporting the results of your survey.

Case Study

Read the story below and look at Lesson 3-3 again.
Then answer the questions below.

Setting Goals

When Vicky Garmon was in the third grade, her father died. Her mother had to get a job to support Vicky and her younger brother and sister. Mrs. Garmon made just enough money to support the family.

When Vicky was in eighth grade, she decided that she wanted to go to college. However, she knew that her mother wouldn't be able to pay for her college expenses.

Therefore, Vicky decided to make plans to reach her long-term goal of going to college. First, she talked to her guidance counselor. She learned about different ways to earn money for college. She then set several short-term goals. While in high school, she worked part-time at the public library. She saved most of the money she earned. During this time, she also studied hard to make good grades. When she graduated from high school, she won several scholarships.

While Vicky was in college, she worked part-time at the college library. After four years, she graduated from college. Through careful planning and reaching many short-term goals, Vicky's long-term goal was reached.

To Discuss

➡ 1. How did Vicky's short-term goals help her reach her long-term goal?
➡ 2. What other short-term goals could Vicky have set for herself?
➡ 3. What might have happened if Vicky hadn't set short-term goals?

Topic 3 Review

Topic Summary

As a teen, you learn to make decisions. To make good decisions, you need to know about needs, wants, resources, values, goals, priorities, and standards. These factors play an important part in the decision-making process.

Your needs and wants affect your life in many ways. They affect your feelings, how you get along with others, and how you use your time and skills. You often make decisions based on your needs or wants.

Resources are what you use to meet needs and fulfill wants. The types of resources that are available to you often determine how you will make a decision.

When you make a decision, you are often trying to reach a goal. Your goals are based on your values or what you believe is important.

There are six basic steps to follow in the decision-making process. The first is to identify the problem to be solved. The second is to list the alternatives. The third step is to research the alternatives. The fourth is to make a decision based on your needs, wants, resources, values, goals, standards, and priorities. The fifth step is to act on the decision. The sixth step is to evaluate your decision.

To Review

Write your answers on a separate sheet of paper.

1. Use a *P* to identify physical needs. Use an *E* to identify emotional needs.
   a. Food.
   b. Friendship.
   c. Security.
   d. Shelter.
   e. Sleep.
   f. New experiences.
   g. Recognition.
   h. Warm clothes.
2. Give an example of a good way to meet an emotional need. Give an example of a poor way to meet an emotional need. Explain your answers.
3. True or false. When you want people to notice you, you have a need to be liked by others.
4. How can you meet the need for new experiences?
5. What type of need is the need to feel liked by others?
6. Give examples of three human resources and three nonhuman resources you have.
7. Planning to go to a baseball game this weekend is a _____-term goal.
8. Jim wants to teach small children. He believes that education is very important. He thinks that he could make a difference as a teacher.
   a. What is Jim's goal?
   b. What does Jim value?
9. List the six steps of the decision-making process. Next to each step, give an example of an action that could be taken to help make a specific decision.
10. When families meet together to discuss decisions, it is called a _____ _____.
11. List three hints for making good group decisions.

Vocabulary Quiz

Match the definitions in Column A with the terms in Column B.
Write your answers on a separate sheet of paper.

Column A

1. A choice made about what to do or say in a given situation.
2. What people have within themselves to get what they want or need.
3. The extra items you would like but can live without.
4. The basic items you must have to live.
5. Objects and conditions available to people to help them meet needs and fulfill wants.
6. Strong beliefs or ideas about what is important.
7. Options available to choose from when making a decision.
8. Important goals that must be met before less important goals.
9. A resource shared by everyone and paid for through taxes.
10. What you want to achieve.
11. A resource owned and controlled by a person or a family group.
12. A disagreement among two or more people.
13. When a disagreement among two or more people is settled.
14. A resource that is limited in supply.
15. The ability to inspire others to meet goals.
16. A means of measuring how well goals are achieved.

Column B

a. Needs.
b. Wants.
c. Human resource.
d. Nonhuman resource.
e. Public resource.
f. Private resource.
g. Values.
h. Goals.
i. Priorities.
j. Standards.
k. Decision.
l. Alternatives.
m. Trade-offs.
n. Scarce.
o. Conflict.
p. Conflict resolution.
q. Leadership.
r. Integrity.

Good management starts with paying attention to details.

Lesson 4-1
The Management Process

Objectives

After studying this lesson, you will be able to

➡ *define* management, management process, schedule, implement, evaluate, time management, habit, *and* procrastinate.

➡ *identify the steps in the management process.*

➡ *explain how you can manage your time.*

New Words

management: *using resources to reach goals.*

management process: *a series of steps for reaching a goal. They are setting goals, planning, implementing, and evaluating.*

schedule: *a written plan for reaching goals within a certain period of time.*

implement: *to carry out a plan of action.*

evaluate: *to judge an entire plan of action.*

time management: *the skill of organizing your time so you can accomplish what you need to do.*

habit: *a repeated pattern of behavior.*

procrastinate: *to put off difficult or unpleasant tasks until later.*

New Ideas

➡ *The management process helps you set and reach goals.*

➡ *You can learn to manage your time.*

Do you ever feel that you are not in control of your life? Does time seem to fly by? If so, you need to learn more about the management process. Understanding the management process and how it works can help you get the most from your resources.

The Management Process

Management is using resources to reach goals. See 4-1. Goals can be reached through the **management process**, which is a series of steps for reaching a goal. The steps are setting goals, planning, implementing, and evaluating.

Setting goals. The first step in the management process is setting a goal. Sometimes people set unrealistic goals, which are goals that are impossible to reach. You need to learn to set realistic goals, which are goals that can be reached. Reaching goals is easier if you set priorities and focus on one goal at a time.

For instance, Desmond is an overweight teen who wants to lose 20 pounds. When he first decided to lose the weight, he wanted to lose it before the school dance, which was two weeks away. Desmond decided to ask his family and consumer sciences and his physical education teachers for advice. After doing so, he realized that he had set an unrealistic goal. His teachers told him that losing more than one or two pounds a week is unhealthy. They also told him that it is very unlikely that he could lose ten pounds in one week.

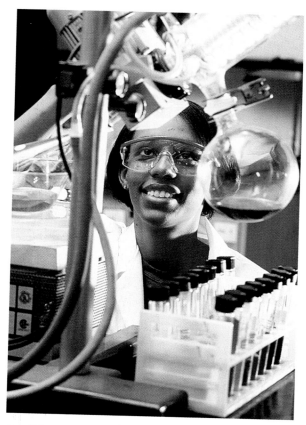

4-1 The management process can help you to reach your career goals.

information on nutrition. He talked to his family doctor about planning a healthy diet. He also talked to his physical education teacher about a good exercise program. After gathering all this information, Desmond planned what foods he would eat and when. He also made a schedule of when he would exercise.

Implementing. When your plans have been made, you must implement them. **Implement** means to carry out your plan of action. During this step, you need to check your progress. You need to make sure that you are following your plan. After checking, you may need to make changes in your plan. See 4-2.

4-2 You can use a calendar to check the progress of your plan and make needed changes.

Therefore, Desmond changed his goal. He decided to lose 20 pounds by following a healthy diet over a period of time. This way he would be able to keep the weight off by eating sensibly.

Planning. After you set a goal, plans must be made. Begin by asking yourself, "What do I have to do to reach this goal?" Look at the resources you have and decide which actions you need to take. Then, make a schedule for meeting your goal. A **schedule** is a written plan for reaching goals within a certain period of time. It should tell you when you will perform your actions and in what order.

Desmond made a list of the resources he could use to reach his goal. These resources included his family and consumer sciences teacher, his family doctor, and his physical education teacher. He asked his family and consumer sciences teacher for

In order to follow his plan, Desmond made some changes. Instead of buying lunch at school, he got up a little earlier each morning to make his own lunch. This way he would be sure to eat only the foods on his diet. He would avoid going over to a friend's house and having snacks after school. Instead, he would stay at school and exercise in the gym and weight room. At first, this was hard for Desmond. He wanted to spend time with his friends. However, he soon got used to it. He made plans to see his friends on the weekends.

Evaluating. The last step of the management process is to evaluate. **Evaluate** means to judge the entire plan of action. After you have completed your plan, evaluate whether or not it was a good plan. You also need to evaluate your goals. Evaluating plans and goals can help you improve your management skills. If you find that your plans were weak or your goals were unrealistic, you can make changes in the future.

After Desmond lost 20 pounds, he evaluated his weight loss plan. Although it had taken a long time to lose the weight, he felt good about his plan. It taught him to eat right and get enough exercise. Now that he had lost the weight, he knew that he would be able to stay at the weight he wanted.

✓ **Check What You Have Learned**

1. What are the steps of the management process?
2. Why do you need to set realistic goals? How do you go about doing this?
3. Why do you need to check the progress of your plan?

Time Management

Time is a limited resource. There are only 24 hours in each day for you to use. Sometimes you may not have enough time to do all you want. Some people may be able to do more than you. You may wonder how you can better use your time. Using the management process can help. **Time management** is the skill of organizing your time so you can accomplish what you need to do.

To improve your time management, start by analyzing how you spend your time. For one day, keep a record of everything you do each hour. See 4-3. Your record may include sleeping, going to school, reading, listening to music, visiting with friends, or watching TV. By keeping a record of how you spend your time, you will be able to see where you waste your time.

Next, plan how you want to spend your time. Set goals for what you want to do each day. Goals that are the most important should be your top priorities. Try to meet these goals first.

To implement your plan, set up a schedule. Write down everything you want to do that day and plan a time to do it. Following your schedule will help you do what you want to do. Write down important appointments on a calendar so you remember them.

Making a daily "to do" list can also help you manage your time. The list reminds you of what you want to do each day. As you complete each item, cross it off the list. This can make you feel good about yourself.

Be sure to evaluate whether your schedule or list has helped you better manage your time. If it has not, analyze what you have done. See what improvements you can make, then try again.

Scheduling can also help you better use your study time. Set aside a certain time and place to study each day. See 4-4. Plan to study during the time of day you work best. Some people work better in the morning, while others work better at night. Make sure you allow enough time to complete your assignments. Some projects may take days or even weeks to complete. Do not try to finish a big project all at once. Instead, plan to spend an hour or two each night on it. This will make it seem easier, and you will do a better job.

Keeping track of how you spend your day can identify ways in which you waste time. Some common time wasters include habit, clutter, and procrastination. A **habit** is a repeated pattern of behavior. Watching TV for long periods of time can be a habit. Other habits that can hurt your time management include talking on the phone and

Time	Activity
6:00 am	wake/shower
7:00 am	eat breakfast
8:00 am	school
9:00 am	↓
10:00 am	
11:00 am	↓
12:00 pm	lunch
1:00 pm	school
2:00 pm	↓
3:00 pm	↓
4:00 pm	soccer practice
5:00 pm	↓
6:00 pm	eat dinner
7:00 pm	homework
8:00 pm	homework/TV
9:00 pm	go to bed

4-3 Keeping an hourly record of your activities can help you better manage your time.

4-4 Scheduling a quiet place to study is important.

playing a computer or video game. Habits can also be helpful. For instance, Jamal does his homework every afternoon when he gets home from school. When he is finished, he plays video games. This habit allows him to finish his work before playing.

Clutter occurs when your personal belongings are unorganized. If your closet is cluttered, it may take you more time to get dressed in the morning. If your locker is messy, it may take you a long time to find your books and important papers. Organizing your belongings can help you save time.

Sometimes you may procrastinate. To **procrastinate** is to put off difficult or unpleasant tasks until later. Instead of doing your weekly chores,

you watch TV or talk on the phone. People often procrastinate if they are scared of doing a task. For instance, Kara wants a good grade on her book report, but she is afraid she will not do well. Therefore, she procrastinates until there is not enough time to do a good job on the project.

It is important to tackle areas in which you are procrastinating. If you have two projects to do, do the one that you dislike first. For instance, you may have both math and English homework to do tonight. Start with the one that you dislike the most. Once it is done, you'll feel good. Then do your other homework. This will help you avoid wasting time.

Just as you value your own time, it is important to respect other people's time. Be on time for appointments. This way other people do not have to waste time waiting for you.

Gaining control over your time will help you meet your goals in life. You can plan time to do all the things you want to accomplish.

✓ **Check What You Have Learned**

1. Why do you need to analyze how you use your time?
2. How does making a schedule help you manage your time?
3. Why do you need to respect other people's time?
4. What are three common time wasters?

The Main Ideas

The steps of the management process are setting goals, planning, implementing, and evaluating. Following these steps will help you reach your goals and get the most from your resources. You can also learn to manage your time better by following the steps of the management process.

Apply What You Have Learned

1. Write a short story about a teen who has a goal to reach. Show how this teen uses the steps in the management process to reach this goal.
2. For one day, keep a record of all your activities. Then analyze how you spent your time. Look at how much time you spent sleeping, eating, attending school, doing homework, and relaxing. Based on this record, make a schedule for yourself to follow the next day. Allow time for your priorities. Also, allow time to relax. Try following your schedule. As a class, discuss how this did or did not help you manage your time better.

Lesson 4-2
Managing Your Health and Appearance

Objectives

After studying this lesson, you will be able to

- ⇒ *define lifestyle, appearance, wellness, addiction, image, posture, self-confident, and stress.*
- ⇒ *give examples of ways to promote wellness..*
- ⇒ *explain why exercise and rest are important to appearance.*
- ⇒ *show how to use good posture when standing, walking, and sitting.*
- ⇒ *explain how to manage stress.*

New Words

lifestyle: *the continuing way in which a person lives.*

appearance: *how you look.*

wellness: *state of physical, emotional, and mental well-being.*

addiction: *a physical dependency on a substance.*

image: *the mental picture of a person.*

posture: *how you hold your body when standing, walking, or sitting.*

self-confident: *to be sure of yourself.*

stress: *emotional, mental, or physical tension felt when faced with change.*

New Ideas

- ⇒ *Health habits can affect the way you look.*
- ⇒ *Good nutrition, rest, and exercise are important to your health and appearance.*
- ⇒ *Good posture makes you look and feel better.*
- ⇒ *Stress can be both good and bad.*

When you feel good about yourself, you manage your life better. You have an improved lifestyle. A **lifestyle** is the continuing way in which a person lives. Managing your health can make you feel better and give you energy. It can improve your **appearance,** or how you look. You need to care for your body on the inside as well as on the outside.

A healthy lifestyle promotes wellness. **Wellness** is a state of physical, emotional, and mental well-being. Eating nutritious foods and avoiding unhealthy habits can improve your health. Exercising, resting, having a positive image, and managing stress can also contribute to wellness.

Eating Right

Eating the right foods in the right amounts helps improve your health. Good food gives you energy for daily activities. Eating right can also help you improve your appearance.

Meat, fish, poultry, and other foods contain protein. Protein helps build and repair body cells. Protein is also needed for proper growth and muscle development. You need to eat good sources of protein for shiny hair and strong nails.

Milk and milk products are also a good source of protein. Besides protein, they provide calcium and phosphorous, which you need for strong bones and teeth.

Fruits and vegetables help keep your skin smooth and glowing. They also provide energy and important vitamins and minerals. Fresh fruits and vegetables are good for almost every part of your body. The chewing action helps keep teeth and gums strong and healthy.

Grains such as wheat, oats, and rice help give you energy. These grains can be found in breads and cereals. They promote digestion. They help keep your blood and nerves healthy.

Eating too many foods that have little or no nutritional value can affect your health. Many snack foods do not provide nutrients. Foods such as chips, soft drinks, candy, cakes, and pastries should not be eaten often. They can lead to weight, skin, and health problems. See 4-5.

4-5 Snack foods, such as cookies and chips, can detract from your appearance.

✔ Check What You Have Learned

1. Why is it important to include milk and milk products in you diet?
2. Why should you limit the amount of candy, chips, and soft drinks you consume?

Avoiding Drugs, Alcohol, and Tobacco

Many substances can be harmful to health. Drugs can keep the body from functioning normally. Drugs can affect the mind. Alcohol is classified as a drug. It can slow reflexes and cause loss of muscle control. Alcohol can also cause lasting damage to the body if used too much. The liver, stomach, and heart may be harmed. People who give up eating to drink may even starve themselves.

Cigarette smoking is the largest cause of preventable illness. Many people die each year because of tobacco use. As smoke is inhaled, the nose, throat, and lungs are irritated. The lungs and heart are damaged. Cigarettes can harm nonsmokers through passive smoke.

Drugs, alcohol, and tobacco can have lasting effects on health. They often cause **addiction,** which is a physical dependency on a substance. Addictions are very hard to overcome. People with addictions often need a lot of help and support to recover. Many adults developed unhealthy addictions during their teen years. You should avoid using drugs, alcohol, and tobacco now and in the future.

✓ **Check What You Have Learned**

1. How can drugs, alcohol, and tobacco affect your health? Give examples.
2. What are the dangers of an addiction?

Exercising

Regular exercise is another way to improve your health and appearance. It can help you control your weight and feel more energetic. Exercise can build your muscles and endurance. Exercise helps you resist diseases. You will feel more alert and learn better when you exercise.

When you do not get enough exercise, you may feel tired. For instance, you may stay home all day and watch TV. Then you may feel tired from sitting all day. If you go out and exercise, you will have more energy. You will not feel tired anymore.

For exercise to benefit you the most, it should be part of your daily routine. This helps keep your muscles strong, healthy, and flexible. Your posture will be improved and you will look better. If you do not exercise on a regular basis, you may hurt yourself. You may try doing too much at once and strain your muscles.

Exercise can help you manage stress. Physical sports such as jogging and tennis are great ways to

4-6 Roller hockey is a fun way to exercise.

work off steam. Working out can make you sleep better at night. You will feel more relaxed.

You can exercise alone. You can walk, jog, hike, bicycle, or skate by yourself. You take part in team sports such as football, soccer, basketball, and volleyball. See 4-6. Exercising with friends can be fun. Swimming, tennis, skiing, and aerobics are other activities that provide good exercise.

✓ **Check What You Have Learned**

1. What are three benefits of exercise?
2. What types of activities would you enjoy doing to get more exercise?

Establishing Your Image

Regular exercise and healthy muscles can contribute to your appearance. You project a healthy image. **Image** is the mental picture that others have of you. Your image is influenced by your posture and your attitude.

Posture is how you hold your body when standing, walking, or sitting. Your posture can reflect how you feel about yourself. See 4-7. Good posture makes you look and feel better.

Good posture when standing means that your chin is up. Your head is held high. Your legs, shoulders, and back are straight. You should always hold your body straight. When you round your shoulders and slump forward, you look sloppy. When you have good posture, your clothes will look better on you. Whether you are tall or short, you appear **self-confident**, or sure of yourself.

Sitting up straight will help you feel rested. You become tired when you slump. If you sit at a computer, it is important to support your back. Your muscles tire when you slip down in a chair.

Your attitude can also affect your image and your energy level. Positive people reflect self-confidence. Bad feelings can decrease your energy. Good feelings can make you feel energetic. For instance, you may not want to go out with your friends because you feel too tired. After you go, you may start to have a good time. Your energy level will increase. When you are excited about something, you will have more energy.

4-7 Good posture can make you look and feel self-confident.

✔ **Check What You Have Learned**

1. What good health habit is important for good posture?
2. How can your posture reflect your self-confidence?
3. How can your energy level affect your image?

Getting Enough Rest

When you have enough rest, you look fresh and feel energetic. See 4-8. You add to your good health. When you are tired, your appearance, attitude, and health are affected. You may get dark circles under your eyes. You may feel grouchy. You may not have enough energy. This can keep you from reaching your goals.

Many teens need eight to ten hours of sleep each night. If you stay up late at night and get up early in the morning, you will not get enough sleep. You cannot make up lost sleep by sleeping late on the weekends. You should try to get enough sleep every night.

4-8 Getting enough sleep is important to look your best.

✔ **Check What You Have Learned**

1. How can getting enough rest affect your appearance?
2. Why is it important to get enough sleep every night?

Handling Stress

Some people set too many goals. They do not have enough time and energy to meet their goals. This can cause stress. **Stress** is emotional, mental, or physical tension felt when faced with change. You can feel stress when you are in a new setting. Stress can also be caused by having too much to do.

When you are under stress, your hands may become sweaty. Your heart may beat rapidly. You may even feel dizzy. These are all physical signs of stress. There are also emotional signs of stress. They include crying easily or acting bored, cranky, or depressed. People react differently to stress.

The leading cause of stress is change. When you are in a new setting, it is normal to feel uncomfortable. Moving to a new school or neighborhood is very stressful for many teens. See 4-9. Divorce, death, and illness can also cause stress. They can cause changes in your family. A change in your family can be very hard to accept.

Following good health habits can help reduce stress. You will be able to cope with problems and changes better if you feel your best. When you are tired, do not have enough energy, or do not eat right, situations may seem worse than they really are. Everyday problems may seem out of proportion. They may not be as easy for you to handle. For instance, if you are tired, you may think that you don't have anything nice to wear to school. When you have had enough sleep, you can be creative and make up new outfits.

Talking with someone can also help you feel less stressed. Your family members and friends can often help you find ways to deal with your stress. School counselors are trained to help teens learn to deal with stress. See 4-10. Listening to others can reduce your stress and make you feel better about your problems.

There are other actions you can take to manage your stress. You can practice good time management skills. Review Lesson 4-1. You can prepare ahead. If getting ready for school is stressful, choose your clothes the night before. If you are worried about being in a new place, learn as much about it ahead of time as possible.

Take time to relax and have fun. Petting animals can reduce stress. Many people tell their problems to their pets. Exercise can help you cope with stress. Solving puzzles, playing games, and reading can take your mind off your stress. Sometimes, just taking a walk will make you feel better. Many teens like listening to music when they are under stress. Hobbies can be relaxing.

Not all stress is bad for you. Without a certain amount of stress, you would not get up and go to

4-9 Meeting new people can cause stress.

4-10 Seeing a counselor can help you relieve stress.

school. Stress can make you study for a hard test. The stress of meeting new people can make you care more about how you look. The stress of a new job can make you work harder.

Stress in life cannot be avoided. The secret in handling stress is to learn how to recognize it in your life. Then, it is important to learn ways to cope with it.

✔ Check What You Have Learned

1. What are some signs that you are under stress?
2. How can following good health habits help you reduce stress?
3. How can you manage your stress? Give examples.

💡 The Main Ideas

Good eating and exercising habits are needed to keep your skin, hair, teeth, and nails in good condition. These habits plus getting enough sleep and having correct posture can help you look and feel your best. Following good health habits can help you manage stress better.

▐▐▐➤ Apply What You Have Learned

1. With one of your classmates as a partner, check your posture when you are standing, walking, and sitting. Take notes on your posture. After you have checked your posture, write down what you can do to improve it. Help your friend do the same. Then make an agreement with your friend to keep checking your posture habits. Make a note each time one of you has to be corrected. At the end of a few days, compare notes to see how well you remembered to practice good posture.
2. Prepare a list of questions to ask a guest speaker about how to manage stress. Compile your questions with those of your classmates to form a master list.

Lesson 4-3
Managing Your Looks

Objectives

After studying this lesson, you will be able to

➡ *define* grooming, pores, deodorant, antiperspirant, dermatologist, manicure, *and* pedicure.

➡ *explain the importance of keeping your body clean.*

➡ *list the steps in keeping your hair and scalp clean.*

➡ *explain how to care for teeth.*

➡ *tell how to care for hands and feet.*

New Words

grooming: *cleaning and caring for your body.*

pores: *tiny openings in the skin.*

deodorant: *a product that helps destroy or cover unpleasant body odors.*

antiperspirant: *a product that helps control wetness and covers unpleasant body odor.*

dermatologist: *a doctor who specializes in treating the skin.*

manicure: *a method of caring for hands and fingernails.*

pedicure: *a method of caring for feet and toenails.*

New Ideas

➡ *Good grooming adds to your health and appearance.*

➡ *There are steps you can follow to care for your body.*

Grooming is cleaning and caring for your body. Good grooming habits help you look attractive and feel good about yourself. They help prevent illness. Being well-groomed can help you get and keep a job.

It is important to form good grooming habits while you are young. You will probably keep some of the habits you form now for the rest of your life. Part of managing your daily living includes making plans to care for your appearance.

Keeping Clean

Your skin has **pores**, or tiny openings. Pores give off oil and sweat that collect on your skin. Dirt and dust from the air also collect on your skin. You need to wash often to remove these substances. If you don't, your body may have an unpleasant odor. Blemishes may develop on your skin.

When you shower, bathe, or wash your face or hands, be sure to rinse away all traces of soap. Soap left on your skin can cause it to become dry and irritated.

Bathing and showering regularly can help prevent body odor. However, these grooming habits cannot do the job alone. You need a deodorant or antiperspirant. A **deodorant** is a product that helps destroy or cover unpleasant body odors. An **antiperspirant** is a product that helps control wetness and covers unpleasant body odors. These products are applied to the underarm area. They work best when used right after a bath or shower.

As a teen, you are growing in many ways. This growth causes chemical changes in your body. Some of these chemical changes may cause blemishes such as blackheads and pimples. These often occur around the nose and on the chin and forehead. They may also occur on the back and chest. When pimples develop, they should not be squeezed. This can cause infection and scarring.

If you have blackheads or pimples, wash the affected areas often with soap. See 4-11. Eating right, exercising, and getting plenty of rest may also help clear up your skin. Doctors also suggest drinking at least eight glasses of water a day. For severe skin problems see a **dermatologist**. This is a doctor who specializes in treating the skin.

4-11 Wash your face thoroughly at least twice a day.

✓ Check What You Have Learned

1. What is the difference between a deodorant and an antiperspirant?
2. What can happen if pimples are squeezed?

Hair Care

To keep your hair and scalp clean and healthy, you need to wash your hair regularly. How often people wash their hair varies. You should wash your hair when it gets dirty. People with oily skin often have oily hair. Oily hair needs to be washed more often than dry hair.

Some flaking of skin cells from your scalp is normal. Excessive flaking is a condition called *dandruff*. Some shampoos and rinses are made to treat dandruff. If you have an extreme case, you may need to see a doctor. Also, do not use other people's combs or brushes. This can transfer dandruff and other scalp conditions.

When you wash your hair, use your fingertips to rub your scalp. See 4-12. This will help loosen any dirt or dandruff. Be sure to get your scalp clean. This is where the oil comes from that

4-12 Gently massage your scalp when washing your hair.

causes dirty hair. Be careful not to rub with your fingernails. If you scratch your scalp, you may get an infection. Also, if you rub too roughly, your hair may become tangled. This may cause strands of hair to break or split.

Rinse your hair thoroughly to remove all traces of shampoo. You may want to use a special rinse that helps condition your hair. After washing your hair, use a comb instead of a brush to gently comb out the tangles.

Brushing your hair between shampoos helps remove lint and dust that collect in your hair. It can also help make your hair soft and shiny. When brushing your hair, be careful. Brushing too hard can damage your scalp and hair.

After you wash your hair, you can let your hair dry naturally. You can also use a blow dryer. If you use a blow dryer, be careful. Heat can cause your hair to break and split. Keep the blow dryer at least six to eight inches from your hair. Keep it moving constantly, so that your hair doesn't get too hot.

Let your hair cool from the heat before brushing it. Make sure that it is completely dry before using a curling iron or electric curlers. Hair that has been permanently waved, straightened, or colored is easily damaged by heat.

Your hairstyle is a frame for your face. A good hairstyle can help you look attractive by accenting your good features. See 4-13. The shape of your face determines how a hairstyle will look. Have a friend, parent, or hairstylist help you choose a style that makes you look good.

When choosing a hairstyle, you should also consider the type of hair you have. You may have

4-13 A good hairstyle can show off your best features.

fine hair or coarse hair. You may have straight hair or curly hair. Some hairstyles are better for different types of hair. Also, think about your activities. Decide how much time you are willing to spend caring for your hair. For instance, you may be in sports and need hair that can be cared for easily.

✓ Check What You Have Learned

1. Why should you use your fingertips instead of your fingernails when washing your hair?
2. How can you help prevent your hair from being damaged by heat?

Caring for Your Teeth

Healthy teeth and gums are important to your health. It is important to care for your teeth properly. You should visit your dentist every six months. See 4-14. Your dentist will examine your teeth and give you advice on how to care for them.

Removing food from your teeth is important. Regular brushing will help keep teeth clean and your gums healthy. You should brush your teeth after each meal. This helps remove food from around and between your teeth. If you are not able to brush, rinse your mouth out with water.

You should also use dental floss at least once a day. Dental floss is used to remove food from between the teeth and at the gums. Using dental floss is as important as brushing. Many cavities are caused by pieces of food that cannot be removed

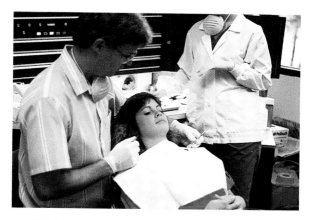

4-14 Visiting your dentist regularly can help prevent problems with your teeth and gums.

with a toothbrush. Your dentist can show you the correct way to brush and use dental floss.

✓ **Check What You Have Learned**

1. How often should you brush and floss your teeth?
2. What should you do if you can't brush your teeth after each meal?

Caring for Your Hands and Feet

You should wash your hands thoroughly several times a day to keep them looking good and prevent spreading germs. Always wash your hands before meals and after using the toilet.

When you wash your hands, use warm water and soap. Lather the soap on your hands and wrists. Use a nailbrush to remove dirt under your nails and around your cuticles. Remove all traces of soap with warm water. Dry your hands thoroughly. This helps prevent rough, chapped hands, which can be very painful.

Well-groomed people take care of their nails. However, many people have formed a habit of biting their fingernails. If you bite your nails, you may want to start breaking this habit now.

To keep your nails attractive and in good condition, you may want to start giving yourself a manicure and a pedicure. A **manicure** is a method of caring for hands and fingernails. A **pedicure** is a method of caring for feet and toenails. It is important for both males and females to take care of their hands and feet.

To give yourself a manicure or a pedicure, first file and shape or trim your nails. Then soak them in warm, soapy water to soften the cuticles. Finally, push back the softened cuticles. Some girls may want to apply nail polish to their fingernails or toenails.

Constant exposure to the weather or cleaning supplies can dry your skin. Use lotion regularly to help keep your hands soft. When cleaning, you may want to protect your hands by wearing rubber gloves.

Shoes and socks that do not fit right may cause foot and back pain, blisters, and rough spots on your feet. Do not wear shoes and socks that can cause these problems. When you buy shoes, try on both shoes to check the fit. See 4-15. One of your feet may be larger than the other. Make sure both shoes are comfortable.

4-15 It is important to buy shoes that fit properly.

✓ **Check What You Have Learned**

1. What are the steps you should follow when washing your hands?
2. Why is it important to try on both shoes when buying a new pair?

Personal Care

As girls begin to grow into adults, hair growth under their arms and on their legs becomes heavier. Guys start growing more hair on their faces, arms, legs, chests, and under their arms. It is common for girls to shave their legs and underarms. Guys usually shave their faces.

When shaving, choose a razor that is comfortable to hold and easy to use. Wet the area that is to be shaved with warm water. Apply shaving cream or a rich lather of soap. This helps soften your hair. It also helps prevent the razor from cutting or irritating your skin. See 4-16. Shave in the opposite direction from which your hair grows. Rinse off the soap or cream after shaving. Then apply lotion to your face or legs to prevent dryness.

Some teen girls wear makeup. Makeup includes eye shadow, powder, blush, mascara, and lipstick. There are special types of makeup for different skin types and problems. Read the labels on the makeup packages to make sure you have the

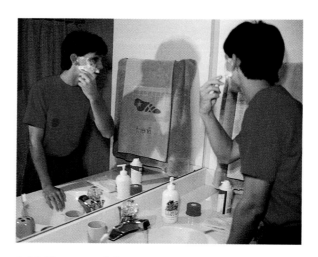

4-16 Shave carefully to keep from cutting yourself.

right type for you. Salesclerks at cosmetic counters can also help you.

If makeup is worn, it should be applied lightly. This helps keep the look natural. Makeup should also be applied to clean skin. It should always be removed before going to bed. Makeup applied to dirty skin, or makeup left on overnight, can lead to skin problems. This can result in blackheads and pimples.

You should not lend makeup or borrow it from other people. Germs can be spread through makeup.

✓ Check What You Have Learned

1. How does applying shaving cream or a rich lather of soap help when shaving?
2. What can happen if you leave makeup on overnight?

The Main Ideas

Keeping your body clean will help you feel and look more attractive. When you take proper care of your skin, hair, teeth, and nails, you will be healthier. This is all part of being well groomed.

Apply What You Have Learned

1. Divide into groups of four to five students. In your groups, prepare a 3-minute skit showing teens how to properly care for their skin. Vote on which skit is the best. Make a videotape of it.
2. Look through fashion magazines for current hairstyles you like. Cut these pictures out and tape them on pieces of paper. Decide which hairstyles would be best for you. Look at each model's face shape and hair texture. See if these are similar to yours. Think about how much time the hairstyles would involve. Write your observations under each picture and make a decision.
3. Prepare a demonstration for first graders on the correct way to brush and floss teeth.

Lesson 4-4
Managing Your Money

Objectives

After studying this lesson, you will be able to

➡ *define* income, money management, budget, fixed expenses, flexible expenses, consumer, unit price, quality, *and* warranty.

➡ *tell how to make a budget.*

➡ *give examples of how you can shop wisely.*

New Words

income: *the money you earn.*

money management: *the process of planning and controlling the use of money.*

budget: *a plan for spending.*

fixed expenses: *regular expenses that cannot be avoided.*

flexible expenses: *costs of goods and services that are not purchased on a regular basis.*

consumer: *a person who buys or uses goods and services.*

unit price: *cost for each unit of measure or weight.*

quality: *how well a product is made.*

warranty: *a written guarantee on a product from the manufacturer.*

New Ideas

➡ *Making a budget can help you control your money better.*

➡ *Good consumer skills can help you save money.*

You may get money as a gift or as an allowance. You may earn money baby-sitting or doing yard work. The money you earn is called your **income.** Your income may be small. However, you can begin developing money management skills that you can use now and in the future when your income increases. **Money management** is planning and controlling the use of money.

Making a Budget

An important part of money management is making a budget. A **budget** is a plan for spending. Before you make a budget, keep a record of all the money you spend in one week. This lets you know where your money is being spent.

The first step in writing a budget is to list all your income. Knowing how much money you earn can help you control your spending. You know how much you have to spend.

Next, list your expenses. Expenses can be both fixed and flexible. **Fixed expenses** are regular expenses that cannot be avoided. They include school lunches, club dues, and music lessons. See 4-17. **Flexible expenses** are costs of goods and services that are not purchased on a regular basis. They may include movies, magazines, clothes, gifts, and snacks.

The money you save should be listed as a fixed expense in your budget. When you save, you are

4-17 Club dues are an example of a fixed expense.

taking money out of your income to set aside for later and unexpected uses. You may also be saving for a special purchase. For instance, Ann is saving money to buy a stereo. Each week, she puts the same amount of money into her savings account.

To keep track of your budget, set up a record-keeping form. See 4-18. This form will show you how well you are following your budget. First add up your income and then your expenses. Then compare the two totals. They should be the same or very close. If your expenses are more than your income, you will need to reduce your flexible expenses, or increase your income. You cannot spend money you don't have. If your income is greater than your expenses, you can spend more money. You may also decide to save more money.

Monthly Budget			
Income		Expenses	
Allowance	20.00	Fixed Expenses	
Baby-Sitting	55.00	Lunch	20.00
Gifts	15.00	Savings	8.00
		Scout Dues	4.00
		Flexible Expenses	
		Movies	15.00
		Snacks	12.00
		Music	10.00
		Clothes and Accessories	12.00
		Books and Magazines	4.00
		Other Expenses	5.00
Total	90.00	Total	90.00

4-18 Following a written budget can help you avoid overspending.

✓ Check What You Have Learned

1. How can a budget help you manage your money?
2. How do record-keeping forms help you keep track of your budget?

Consumer Skills

A **consumer** is a person who buys or uses goods and services. You're a consumer when you shop. You're also a consumer when you use a service. For instance, you're a consumer when you get a haircut.

You may have friends who never seem to have money. You may also have friends who always seem to have enough money. As a consumer, you can learn skills to help you manage your money. You will learn to get the most for your money.

One important skill is *comparison shopping.* When you shop, you may notice that the price of a product varies from store to store. In order to get the most for your money, you should shop at several stores.

You should also learn how to figure out the unit price of the product. The **unit price** is the cost for each unit of measure or weight. To find the unit price, divide the price of the product by the unit of measure or weight. After figuring the unit price, compare the products to see which is really less costly. For instance, one bottle of shampoo weighs 8 ounces and costs $1.20. Its unit price is 15 cents an ounce. Another bottle of shampoo weighs 10 ounces. It costs $2.00. Its unit price is 20 cents an ounce. The first bottle of shampoo is a better buy than the second bottle.

Usually if you buy a large amount of a product, its unit price will be lower than the small amount. However, this may not be the best size for you to buy. If you do not use up the product quickly, it may spoil. Also, if you are trying a new product, you may want to buy the smallest size to test it.

Besides comparing price, you should also compare quality. **Quality** refers to how well a product is made. It also refers to how well a product performs and how long it lasts. A high price on a product does not always mean quality.

Sometimes, a lower-priced product may have better quality.

You can gather information about the quality of products from many sources. For instance, you want to buy a telephone. Ask friends or family members who have bought telephones what they think. Talk to salesclerks who sell telephones. Read about telephones in consumer magazines. See 4-19. Magazines such as *Consumer Reports* report the results of tests done on certain products.

4-19 You can research products you are thinking about buying through the computer.

Also be sure to read the labels on products when you are shopping. Government regulations say what must be included on product labels. Labels can give you information about nutrition, directions on use of the product, package contents, and the warranty. A **warranty** is a written guarantee on a product from the manufacturer. Some information on labels is not important. Companies often put information on labels to help them sell their product. See 4-20.

4-20 What information on these labels is important and what information isn't?

✓ **Check What You Have Learned**

1. Why shouldn't you always buy the lowest priced product?
2. What helpful information should you look for on labels?

The Main Ideas

As a consumer, you need skills in money management. Making a budget and following it can help you learn these skills. You can also learn to shop wisely. These skills will help you get the most for your money.

Apply What You Have Learned

1. You received $50 from your grandparents for your birthday. Make a budget for how you will spend this money. Keep in mind the many different ways you can use your money.
2. Go to a store and find a product that comes in several sizes. Write down the price for each size of the product. When you are back in class, figure out the unit price for each size of this product. Discuss whether or not the product with the lowest unit price would be the best buy for you.
3. Bring labels from several different products to class. Look for information that is helpful to consumers. Look for information that is only trying to sell the product. As a class, discuss what you have found.

Lesson 4-5
Making Consumer Decisions

Objectives

After studying this lesson, you will be able to
➡ *define* consumer decisions, mass media, advertising, impulse buying, *and* redress.
➡ *explain how needs, wants, values, and goals affect consumer decisions.*
➡ *give examples of how peers, mass media, and advertising can affect what you buy.*
➡ *list the six basic consumer rights.*
➡ *tell how you can be a responsible consumer.*

New Words

consumer decisions: *decisions made about how to spend your money.*
mass media: *a means of communicating to large groups of people.*
advertising: *the process of calling attention to a product or a business through the mass media.*
impulse buying: *making an unplanned or spur-of-the-moment purchase.*
redress: *to correct a wrong.*

New Ideas

➡ *Your needs, wants, values, and goals affect your consumer decisions.*
➡ *Peers, mass media, and advertising affect consumer decisions.*
➡ *You have six basic consumer rights.*
➡ *You can be a responsible consumer.*

You make decisions as a consumer every day. Someday others may depend on you for financial support. This will make your money management skills even more important. The way of life for you and your family will depend on your consumer decisions. Knowing your consumer rights and responsibilities can help you make good decisions.

Consumer Decisions

Consumer decisions are decisions made about how to spend your money. When you buy a product, you make decisions. Some of these you may not be aware of. However, they are important. Sometimes your decisions may be affected by outside pressures.

When you shop, you should think about your needs, wants, values, and goals. They affect how you earn money and how you manage it. Many needs and wants can be met by spending money. For instance, the need for food can be met by spending money. You need to learn to make consumer decisions that will let you meet as many needs and fulfill as many wants as possible. See 4-21.

4-21 You cannot always afford to buy what you want.

Your values and goals also affect your consumer decisions. Your values help you decide which products to buy. If you value the environment, you may choose a recyclable product over one that is not recyclable. Your goals affect how you use your money. For instance, your goal may be to buy a new pair of skis. While you are saving money for the skis, you may spend less on other products.

✓ **Check What You Have Learned**

1. How can your consumer decisions affect your family?
2. How do your values help you decide which products to buy?

Outside Pressures

Your consumer decisions are affected by a number of outside pressures. These pressures include peers, mass media, and advertising.

Your peer group can affect your consumer decisions. As a teen, it is normal for you to want to fit in with your peers. You want to look and act like them. You may decide to buy products because your peers have them. This can give you a feeling of belonging. It may also help you fit into the group. However, be careful not to give in to peer pressure when you know it is wrong.

Mass media is a means of communicating to large groups of people. It includes TV, radio, movies, billboards, magazines, and newspapers. Mass media can affect your consumer decisions. You may buy clothes or copy hairstyles you see on TV or in magazines. You may buy music you hear on the radio. Magazines and newspapers have articles telling people what is popular and trendy.

The most powerful pressure from mass media comes from advertising. **Advertising** is the process of calling attention to a product or business through the mass media. Companies pay the media to use their advertisements. They hope the advertisements will make consumers buy their products. See 4-22. The price of products includes the cost of advertising. Thus, consumers really pay for advertising.

Advertisements can be useful when they give information about a product or service. Useful information includes facts about the size and color of the product. The price of the product, the

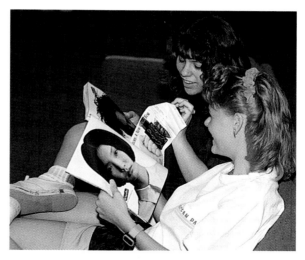

4-22 Magazine advertisements influence many consumer decisions.

method to use it, and the care it needs are also useful information. Advertisements give you information to compare products and services. This helps you make informed decisions.

Advertising can also influence you to buy products that you do not need and may not want. These advertisements only want you to buy. Few, or no, facts are given about the product. Attention is given to emotions or feelings connected to the product. Advertisements use appeals to make you think you need the product. They may say you will be happier with their product. Some ads promise you will be popular. Others say that you will look better if you use their service.

Advertising appeals can lead to **impulse buying**. This is making an unplanned or spur-of-the-moment purchase. Impulse buying is unwise because you may not be sure what you want to buy. You also may not have enough information to be ready to make a good decision. Take time to get the facts about what you want to buy. Do not be rushed into a quick decision by advertisements.

As a responsible consumer, view advertising carefully. Use it to help you gather information about products. Do not be pressured into buying something you do not need or want.

✓ Check What You Have Learned

1. How can peers influence you to buy certain products?
2. How can the mass media affect your consumer decisions?
3. How can you use advertising to make informed decisions?

Consumer Rights

In 1962, the Consumer Bill of Rights was created. It said that consumers have four basic rights. They are the right to choose, the right to be heard, the right to safety, and the right to be informed. Two other rights were added later. They are the right to redress and the right to consumer education. These rights protect you from unsafe products and services. They also give you power as a consumer.

The right to choose. You have the right to choose among products and services. See 4-23. When you shop for a product, you can choose from more than one brand. You have a choice about where to buy products and services. You can choose to buy the products and services that are the best for you.

The right to be heard. You have the right to speak out when you have a complaint about a product or service. You can express your point of view about laws that affect consumers.

4-23 The right to choose gives you the chance to select from different businesses.

The right to safety. You have the right to know that the goods and services you buy are safe. Government agencies test products to make sure they are safe. The agencies keep unsafe products from being sold. These agencies also listen to your complaints about unsafe products.

The right to be informed. You have the right to the facts you need to make informed consumer decisions. This means having the correct information about credit costs, and how to use and care for products.

The right to redress. The right to **redress** means that wrongs done to you will be corrected. If you buy a flawed product, you have the right to return it to the store. See 4-24. The store should listen to your complaint and act upon it. Government and consumer agencies can help you with this.

The right to consumer education. You have the right to information about your consumer rights. The government provides ways for you to learn about your rights. It publishes pamphlets and offers programs to inform you of your rights and the laws concerning them. See 4-25.

4-24 Clearly state the problem when you return merchandise.

4-25 There are government pamphlets that explain the rights of the consumer.

✓ Check What You Have Learned

1. How do you benefit from your consumer rights?
2. How do government agencies help protect your consumer rights?

Consumer Responsibilities

With rights come responsibilities. To keep your consumer rights and have them be meaningful, you need to behave responsibly. You need to take action to make these rights work for you. Think about your responsibilities when you use products and services. The following are tips on how to be a responsible consumer:

- When you shop, comparison shop. Refuse to buy poor quality products. Choose only the services that best meet your needs.

Refuse to buy goods and services that are harmful or cause pollution.

- Write to manufacturers and the government to tell them your concerns and complaints. Share your compliments with them, too.
- Use products safely if you expect them to remain safe. See 4-26. If a product is unsafe, you should report it to the seller, the manufacturer, and the government.
- If you have a problem with a product, talk to the seller. If you are fair and polite, most

4-26 Read use-and-care manuals to learn how to correctly use products.

sellers will listen. However, sometimes you may need to write the manufacturer about the problem. Most product labels include the address of the company. Your local library may also have the company's address.

- Keep informed of new consumer laws. Read government pamphlets explaining your rights. Read findings published by agencies that test new products.

You also have other responsibilities as a consumer. You can help control store losses by handling goods carefully so they do not break or become damaged. See 4-27. You shouldn't shoplift. You should take good care of what you buy. Avoid wasting products. Don't overbuy during shortages. Instead, share limited supplies.

4-27 Responsible consumers handle goods carefully when shopping.

✓ Check What You Have Learned

1. How can you show responsibility as a consumer?
2. What can you do to help control store losses? Give examples.

The Main Ideas

Your needs, wants, values, and goals affect your consumer decisions. Your peers, the mass media, and advertising also affect some of your consumer decisions. There are six basic consumer rights. As a consumer, you also have responsibilities.

Apply What You Have Learned

1. Find out what the phrase "Keeping up with the Joneses" means and how it relates to peer pressure. Write a short story about people trying to "Keep up with the Joneses."
2. Find out the cost of advertising. Call a local TV station and a local radio station to find out the cost of 30-second commercial spots. Then, call a newspaper to find the cost of half-page advertisements.
3. Role-play a situation in which you are returning a product to a store. Show right and wrong ways to do this. As a class, discuss the consumer rights and responsibilities involved in this situation.

Case Study

Read the story below and look at Lesson 4-4 again.
Then answer the questions below.

Making a Budget

Kevin gets up early every morning to deliver newspapers on his paper route. Since he has a large distance to cover, Kevin rides his bike to deliver the newspapers.

"Mom and Dad, I need to talk to you," said Kevin. "My bike is getting old and is starting to fall apart. The chain keeps slipping off and the brakes are getting bad. I want to buy a new bike. I have some money in the bank that I saved from my paper route. However, it's not enough to buy a good bike that I can depend on for my paper route."

"Well, Kevin, your father and I can lend you the extra money," said Kevin's mom.

"We can also help you set up a budget," said his father. "This will help you set aside a certain amount of money each month to pay us back."

Kevin asked, "How do I start setting up a budget? I thought only people who make and spend a lot of money had budgets. I only make one hundred dollars a month."

"No matter how much money you earn, it's important to learn how to budget it," said Kevin's father. "Otherwise, you'll have no control over your money. You won't be able to buy some of the items you want."

"The first step you need to take is to write down all your income," said Kevin's mom. "Remember that besides your paper route, you have an allowance, and you get money when you do yardwork for Mrs. Nix."

"Then, you need to make a list of all the money you spend," she said. "This includes your Boy Scout dues, school lunch, movies, and video games. If you write down all your expenses for two weeks, you will be able to see how you are spending your money."

To Discuss

1. What is the next step Kevin should take when making his budget?
2. What should he do if his expenses are higher than his income?
3. What do you think Kevin will learn from making a budget?

Topic 4 Review

Topic Summary

The management process helps you set and reach goals. There are four steps in the management process. First you set a goal. Then you work out a plan or schedule to meet that goal. The third step is to implement or carry out your plan of action. The fourth step is to evaluate your goal and plan. Was it a good plan? Was your goal realistic?

The four-step management process can help you succeed as you begin making more decisions about your life. You will use the management process over and over again. It will help you make decisions about how to manage your health, appearance, looks, and money.

Your consumer decisions are more important as you become more responsible for spending your money. Your needs, wants, values, and goals affect your consumer decisions. Your peer group, the mass media, and advertising all affect what you decide to buy and when.

There are six basic consumer rights that protect you as a consumer. Along with these rights come responsibilities. Understanding these can help you make good consumer decisions.

To Review

Write your answers on a separate sheet of paper

1. List the four steps of the management process.
2. Why is it important to evaluate your plans?
3. A written plan for reaching goals within a certain period of time is a _____.
4. _____ is a physical dependency on a substance.
5. How can drugs and alcohol affect your health?
6. How can exercise affect the way you feel?
7. What does your posture tell others about you?
8. True or false. Most teens need between six and seven hours of sleep each night.
9. True or false. Stress is bad for you.
10. True or false. Change is the leading cause of stress.
11. How can you benefit from having good grooming habits?
12. The tiny openings of the skin are called _____.
13. What can you do to prevent body odor?

14. Which step should be taken to improve your appearance?
    a. Eat the right foods.
    b. Get enough sleep.
    c. Exercise daily.
    d. Drink water regularly.
    e. All of the above.
15. True or false. Blow dryers should be kept three to four inches from your hair.
16. How can you choose a flattering hairstyle?
17. You should use dental floss at least _____ a day.
18. List the steps in giving a manicure.
19. Which is the best example of a fixed expense?
    a. Magazines.
    b. Movies.
    c. Clothes.
    d. Club dues.
20. True or false. The largest product is always the best buy.
21. How can you learn about the quality of a product?
22. TV, radio, and magazines are examples of _____.
23. Give examples of how advertising can influence your consumer decisions.
24. List the six basic consumer rights and explain what each one means.

Vocabulary Quiz

Match the definitions in Column A with the terms in Column B.
Write your answers on a separate sheet of paper.

Column A

1. A written guarantee on a product.
2. To carry out a plan of action.
3. Cleaning and caring for your body.
4. A doctor who specializes in treating the skin.
5. The money you earn.
6. A plan for spending.
7. How well a product is made.
8. Using resources to reach goals.
9. To judge an entire plan of action.
10. How you look.
11. The process of planning and controlling the use of money.
12. To put off tasks until later.
13. Tension felt when faced with change.
14. A person who buys or uses goods and services.
15. The mental picture of a person.
16. A repeated pattern of behavior.
17. The skill of organizing your time so you can accomplish what you need to do.
18. State of physical, emotional, and mental well-being.

Column B

a. Management.
b. Implement.
c. Evaluate.
d. Dermatologist.
e. Lifestyle.
f. Appearance.
g. Wellness.
h. Procrastinate.
i. Stress.
j. Grooming.
k. Income.
l. Budget.
m. Label.
n. Money management.
o. Consumer.
p. Quality.
q. Warranty.
r. Time management.
s. Image.
t. Habit.

Filing personal papers and storing books neatly on shelves can help you keep your living space looking tidy.

Topic 5 Managing Your Living Space

Lesson 5-1
Your Living Space

Objectives

After studying this lesson, you will be able to
➠ *define home, house, scale floor plan, and traffic pattern.*
➠ *describe ways homes meet needs.*
➠ *give some tips for sharing space in a home.*
➠ *show how to use a scale floor plan.*
➠ *explain how your values, goals, and resources can affect the way you decorate your space.*

New Words

home: *any place people live.*
house: *a freestanding, single-family dwelling.*
scale floor plan: *a drawing that shows the size and shape of a room.*
traffic pattern: *a path people follow as they move within a room.*

New Ideas

➠ *Homes meet physical, emotional, and social needs.*
➠ *Every home has shared space and private space.*
➠ *Carefully arranging your furniture and storage space can help you make the best use of your room.*
➠ *Your values, goals, and resources will affect how you decorate your space.*

Your living space is in your home. A home is different from a house. A **home** is any place people live. A **house** is a freestanding, single-family dwelling. Apartments, mobile homes, and houses are all types of homes.

Homes Meet Needs

Homes meet many needs for people. See 5-1. Your home meets your physical needs for shelter and safety. Having a roof over your head protects you from bad weather. Having locks on your doors helps protect you from crime.

5-1 At home, you can relax and spend time playing with friends.

Homes help meet people's emotional needs. Your home is a place where you are free to express yourself. Having a home gives you a sense of belonging.

Your home can also meet some of your social needs. You can enjoy being with family members and friends in your home. You can treasure moments alone in your home, too.

✓ **Check What You Have Learned**

1. What physical needs can a home meet? How can a home meet these needs?
2. What are some of the emotional and social needs a home can help you meet?

Sharing Space

In every home, there is shared space and private space. *Shared space* is the area you share with members of your family and guests. You need to make shared space comfortable for everyone. You can do this by helping take care of the space.

Private space is an area that is only yours. It can be a bedroom or part of a room. You may read, study, or write letters in your private space. You may just spend time thinking there.

Even if you share a bedroom, you and your brother or sister can both have private space. To avoid problems when sharing a room, you must respect each other's rights. See 5-2. This means respecting your brother or sister's privacy when he or she wants to be alone. If the door is closed, knock before going into the room. You need to respect his or her belongings, too. If you want to

borrow something from your brother or sister, ask first. Make it clear that you would like him or her to show you the same respect.

5-2 Roommates need to respect one another's private property.

✓ **Check What You Have Learned**

1. What are some shared spaces in your home? How can you make these spaces comfortable for everyone?
2. What can you do to help avoid problems when sharing a bedroom?

Arranging Your Space

Even if you share a room, careful planning can help you get the most from your private space. You need to plan how to arrange your furniture and your storage space. If you share a room with your brother or sister, you will need to discuss these plans together.

Using a scale floor plan can help you arrange the space in your room. A **scale floor plan** is a drawing that shows the size and shape of a room. A certain number of inches on the scale floor plan equals a certain number of feet in the room. Special symbols are used to show doors, windows, and closets. The symbols for the room in 5-3 are defined next to the scale floor plan.

You can draw a scale floor plan of your room on graph paper. From colored paper, cut out scale-sized pieces to represent your furniture. Place the furniture pieces on your scale floor plan. Try different arrangements. When you find the best arrangement, glue the pieces down.

Drawing a scale floor plan can save you time and energy. You can find a good arrangement before you move the furniture.

When you arrange furniture, you need to allow space for traffic patterns. **Traffic patterns** are the paths people follow as they move within a room. Leave at least two feet of space between pieces of furniture so people have room to walk. Also leave space to use the furniture. For instance, you need room in front of a dresser to pull out the drawers.

Once you have arranged your furniture, you need to decide how to arrange your belongings. You can use hidden or displayed storage space to store objects in your room. *Hidden storage* is space for storing items out of sight. Hidden storage spaces include closets, chests, or trunks. *Displayed storage* is space for storing items in view. Displayed storage spaces include shelves and tables. Some guidelines for arranging your storage space are listed in 5-4.

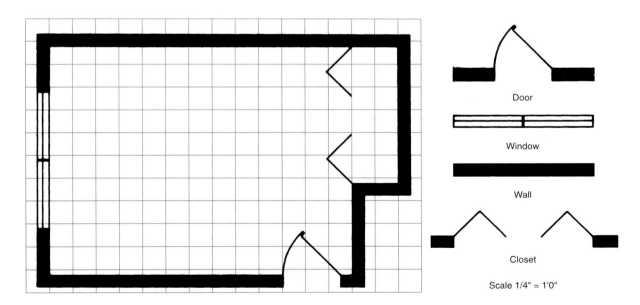

Door

Window

Wall

Closet

Scale 1/4" = 1'0"

5-3   You can save time and energy by arranging furniture on a scale floor plan first.

Storage Guidelines

★ Store items near the area where they are most often used. For instance, keep your alarm clock on your nightstand.

★ Store items that you use often, such as hairbrushes and combs, in easy-to-reach places. Items you only use once a year, such as holiday decorations, can be stored in places that are hard to reach, such as a high shelf.

★ Use all available space. Look for space that is not being used. It is easy to put up nails or hooks in your closet. You can also add extra shelves and clothes rods.

★ Be creative. Use hidden and displayed storage to your advantage. Any hollow object can be used for storage. For instance, baskets, crates, storage cubes, and pottery all make great storage containers and look good.

5-4 These guidelines can help you make the most of your storage space.

✓ Check What You Have Learned

1. How can using a scale floor plan help you arrange furniture?
2. What kinds of items do you store in hidden storage? What kinds of items do you store in displayed storage?

Decorating Your Space

The way you decorate your space can say a lot about you. See 5-5. You can paint your room in your favorite colors. You might hang posters that show your interest in travel. You may display trophies to show your skill in sports.

Your values will affect your decorating decisions. For instance, suppose you value comfort. You may choose to have floor pillows and beanbag chairs in your room. On the other hand, you may value neatness. In this case, you may feel that floor pillows and beanbag chairs look messy.

Your goals for using your room will also affect your decorating decisions. You may choose a desk lamp if your goal is to study in your room. You may choose an accent lamp if your goal is to visit with friends.

Your resources will affect how you decorate your space, too. If you have time, you may decide to paint your room. If you have money, you may decide to buy new furniture. If you have sewing skills, you may decide to make new curtains.

You may not be the only one who will be affected by your decorating decisions. You should get approval from your parents before putting your plans into action. If you share a room, consult your brother or sister first. He or she should also agree to your decorating decisions. You may even decide to decorate your room together.

5-5 The decorations in your room can reflect your different interests.

✓ Check What You Have Learned

1. How does the way you decorate your room say a lot about you?
2. How can your values, goals, and resources affect your decorating decisions?

The Main Ideas

Your living space, or your home, helps meet some of your physical, emotional, and social needs. Some of your living space is shared and some is private. Using scale floor plans and storage can help you arrange your space. Thinking about your values, goals, and resources can help you decorate your space to suit your lifestyle.

⫸ Apply What You Have Learned

1. In a small group, make up a situation that might cause a problem between room-mates. Role-play the situation and show how the roommates avoid the problem.
2. Measure your room and your furniture. Draw a scale floor plan. Arrange the furniture, keeping traffic patterns in mind. Then make a list of three decorating ideas you'd like to try.

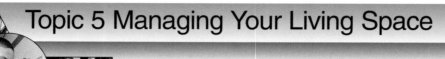
Lesson 5-2
Home Safe Home

Objectives

After studying this lesson, you will be able to

➡ *define* accident, fatal, toxic, *and* appliance.

➡ *describe some common household accidents.*

➡ *list steps that should be taken to prevent household accidents.*

➡ *tell how you can help keep your home secure.*

New Words

accident: *an unexpected event causing loss or injury.*
fatal: *deadly.*
toxic: *poisonous.*
appliance: *a tool run by gas or electricity.*

New Ideas

➡ *Falls, fires, poisonings, and electric shocks are common household accidents.*

➡ *You need to protect your home from break-ins.*

Homes can meet your need to live in a safe, secure place. However, homes can sometimes be unsafe. **Accidents**, or unexpected events causing loss or injury, can happen. Common household accidents result from falls, fires, poisoning, or electricity. Most accidents can be avoided. As a family member, you are responsible for making your home a safe place.

Falls

Falls are the most common accidents that occur in the home. Children and older people are the most likely people to fall. Children need safety gates to protect them from stairs. Older people need handrails in certain areas of their homes, such as in the bathroom.

Bathrooms are common areas for falls to occur. To prevent falls, put nonskid mats and decals in showers and bathtubs. Clean up spilled water quickly. Otherwise, somebody could slip and get hurt.

In the kitchen, use sturdy step stools or ladders to reach high cabinets. Do not climb on top of counters. Clean up all spills right away. Kitchens can be specially designed for people with physical disabilities. See 5-6.

If your home has stairs, make sure they are well lit and have sturdy handrails. Hold on to the handrails when you go up and down stairs. Walk up and down stairs. Don't run. Otherwise, you could fall or trip.

You can also trip on rugs that are not securely tacked to the floor. Nonskid backing should be put on throw rugs and other rugs that can't be tacked down.

If a member of your family has a physical disability, he or she needs to be protected from falling, too. Special features, such as ramps and wider hallways and doors, can be built. These features let people in wheelchairs and on crutches move around safely.

5-6 Specially designed kitchens are safer for people with physical disabilities.

✓ Check What You Have Learned

1. Who is most likely to fall in the home? What can cause falls?
2. How can you help prevent falls from happening in your home?

Fires

Fires are very dangerous accidents. They are often **fatal**, or deadly. Most fatal fires occur at night, while people are asleep. Smoke often kills more people than the actual flames of the fire. All homes should have smoke detectors located near or in the bedrooms and stairwells. See 5-7.

You should sleep with your bedroom door closed in case of a fire. This will give you more time to escape before the smoke reaches you. If you wake up and smell smoke, touch your door. If it feels warm, do not open it. Drop to the floor and crawl away from the door. If you can, wrap a wet towel around your mouth and nose so you can breathe without inhaling the smoke. All families should have day and night fire escape plans.

After you escape, call the fire department. In most areas, the emergency number for fire and police is 911. Find out what the emergency number is in your area. See 5-8. When you call, state your

5-7 Check smoke detectors regularly to make sure they work properly.

name, address, and problem clearly. Don't hang up until you are sure that you have given all the important information.

Fires can be caused by overloading the electrical wires in your home. Do not have too many plugs in one outlet. The wires can overheat and start a fire.

Cigarettes can cause fires, too. If there are cigarette smokers in your home, they should be careful. They should make sure their ashes are cool before they empty their ashtrays. They shouldn't smoke in bed. They could fall asleep with cigarettes in their hands.

To help conserve fuel, many families use space heaters or wood stoves. You should read the instruction booklets for all of your heat sources. Learn how to use them safely. Saving money on fuel bills will not help if your home is destroyed by fire.

5-8   Know where to find local emergency numbers.

✓ Check What You Have Learned

1. What should you do if you wake up and smell smoke?
2. What information should you give if you have to call the fire department?

Poisonings

Toxic, or poisonous, substances can be found in most homes. These substances can be found in household cleaners, insecticides, and medicines. Read the labels on cleaners and insecticides and follow the directions carefully. Most cleaners and insecticides are toxic. If you swallow or inhale them, they can poison or hurt you. Never mix cleaning products because they may produce toxic gases. These can make you sick or hurt your eyes.

Toxic substances should be stored away from young children. See 5-9. Children are the most likely victims of poisoning. They do not understand that poisons are dangerous. They like to explore and often swallow objects that attract their attention. You can buy special latches to keep children out of cabinets and drawers.

Never tell children that medicine is candy. Do not let them see you taking medicine. They like to copy what you do. Many medicine bottles come with childproof caps to protect children.

5-9   If not stored properly, toxic substances can lead to poisoning.

You should also never store toxic substances in food containers. If someone mistakes the substances for food, poisoning could result.

To determine if a product is toxic, check the label. The label should tell you how to safely use the product. It may tell you how to dispose of the container and any unused product when you have finished using it. It should also state what to do if an accidental poisoning occurs. Be sure to read and follow all label directions carefully. See 5-10.

If poisoning occurs, act quickly. Follow the directions on the product label. Then call the toll-free phone number on the label or the local poison control center and calmly state the problem. Have the container with you so you will have complete information.

Reduce the amount of toxic materials you buy. You can substitute nontoxic substances for hazardous ones. For example, you can use baking soda as a cleaner and odor reducer. You can mix it with water to form a paste for cleaning sinks and bathtubs. Vinegar is also a nontoxic substance that can help with many cleaning tasks. It can help cut grease when cleaning windows and floors.

Some general rules for managing toxic household products include the following:

- Select the least toxic product for your home.

5-10 Read the labels of hazardous products to determine how to properly usw them.

- Buy only what you need.
- Read and follow instructions on the label.
- Avoid aerosol spray cans.
- Dispose of toxic waste as recommended.

✓ Check What You Have Learned

1. Why shouldn't you tell children that medicine is candy?
2. What should you do if someone in your home has been poisoned?
3. What are three hints for managing toxic household products?

Electricity

Electricity can cause two major problems in the home. The first is fire. The second is electric shock that a person can receive when using electric appliances. An **appliance** is a tool run by gas or electricity. See 5-11.

You may have received an electric shock. Electricity is always seeking a way to the ground. Dry skin doesn't often attract electricity, but wet skin does. Never touch an electric appliance or cord if you are wet or standing in or near water. This can cause an electric shock that can injure or kill you.

You should always unplug appliances before cleaning them.

When you buy electric appliances, look for the Underwriter's Laboratories (UL) label. Appliances with the UL label meet the latest safety requirements.

You need to use products safely to prevent electric shock. Pull electric cords from outlets by the plug rather than the cord. Never use appliances if they are broken or have frayed cords. Have a repair person fix them.

Young children need to be protected from electric shock. They like to play with outlets, which are often located within their reach. If there are young children in your home, buy covers for your outlets. Also, don't let children play with electric appliances.

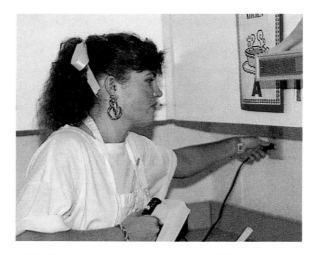

5-11 Always use electric appliances with care.

✔ Check What You Have Learned

1. How can you prevent yourself from receiving an electric shock when using appliances?
2. Why shouldn't you use an appliance that is broken or has a frayed cord?

Securing Your Home

Besides preventing accidents, you also need to protect your home from break-ins. See 5-12. To keep your home safe, always lock your doors and windows. Make sure your locks are secure. Leave a light on when you are gone at night. Burglars do not like to enter occupied homes.

If someone you do not know calls, do not identify yourself. Never tell a caller that you are home by yourself. Do not let strangers into your home. Before you open the door, always ask, "Who is it?"

When your family leaves for a vacation, make your home look like you are still there. Ask a neighbor or friend to collect your newspapers. Have the post office keep your mail until you return. Use a light timer so your lights go off and on at certain times.

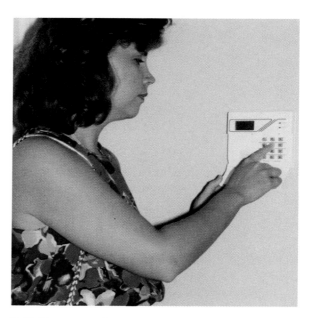

5-12 Homes can be protected by security systems.

The Main Ideas

It takes a lot of effort and care to make your home safe. Most household accidents result from falls, fires, poisons, and electricity. Everyone in your family is responsible for making your home safe against accidents and break-ins.

Apply What You Have Learned

1. Find out if your family has a fire escape plan. If not, make one for each member of your family for both day and night. Hold family fire drills to practice both plans.
2. Look through your home for toxic substances. Be sure they are in a safe place. Then make a chart of the products you found. List what each label tells you to do in case of accidental poisoning. Keep this list near the emergency phone numbers in your home.
3. Prepare a list of questions to ask a police officer about how to secure your home and prevent break-ins.

Lesson 5-3
Caring for Your Home

Objectives

After studying this lesson, you will be able to
- ⇒ *define homemaker.*
- ⇒ *list household cleaning tasks that need to be done on a regular basis.*
- ⇒ *make a family cleaning schedule.*

New Word

homemaker: *anyone who manages or cares for a home.*

New Ideas

- ⇒ *You should clean your home on a regular basis.*
- ⇒ *A cleaning schedule is helpful in caring for a home.*

There are many benefits to having a clean home. When your home is clean, it is a healthier place to live. When you clean up a messy room, you can see your results. This can give you a sense of pride. You can also enjoy your home more when it is clean. You can relax. You can have friends over without being embarrassed.

Why Clean?

If you clean often, cleaning will be easier. See 5-13. You can also avoid waste. Your furniture and carpets will last longer when you take care of them.

5-13 Putting up your belongings will help keep your home clean.

To keep your home clean, there are certain tasks that need to be done. How well each task is done will depend on your family's needs and standards of cleanliness. Some people want very clean and neat homes. Others do not like to spend a lot of time cleaning. Their homes may be less clean and neat. As a family, you need to decide how clean you want your home to be.

There are daily, weekly, and occasional cleaning tasks that need to be done to keep your home clean and neat. Having plants, pets, or a yard means you will have extra tasks to do.

✓ **Check What You Have Learned**

1. What are some benefits of cleaning your home often? Give examples.
2. Why do some families spend more time cleaning than other families?

Daily Tasks

A number of household tasks need to be done daily. Doing these tasks will help keep your home looking neat. Doing daily tasks will also make the weekly cleaning much easier.

Making beds. Making beds can be easy. Put the fitted sheet on the mattress using alternate corners. Then put on the top sheet and smooth out all the wrinkles. Tuck it in. Lastly, put the pillowcases on the pillows.

Cleaning the kitchen. Kitchens need to be cleaned each day to prevent odors and germs. This means wiping tables and counters. You also need to wash the dishes and sink.

Straightening the home. Everybody should pick up his or her belongings. Some families put a basket in the hall for all belongings that are not put away. Some also have a tray or basket near the front door for keys, messages, and mail.

Emptying trash and ashtrays. Trash can be removed easily by using trash can liners. Ashtrays should be emptied to prevent odor.

Cleaning the bathroom. Keep sponges near the sink, bathtub, and shower. Use these to wipe down the sink, bathtub, and shower after each use. This will make the weekly cleaning much easier.

✓ **Check What You Have Learned**

1. What is the order you should follow for making your bed?
2. Why should everybody pick up his or her own belongings?

Weekly Tasks

There are several household tasks that need to be done weekly. Doing weekly tasks will help keep your home clean.

Cleaning the floors. Carpets need to be vacuumed, and floors need to be mopped or swept.

Dusting and polishing the furniture. Feather dusters are good for light dustings. Old tube socks slipped over your hand or reusable rags are good for heavy dusting and polishing. You may want to use wax or dusting spray, too.

Cleaning the bathroom. Clean the toilet, sink, bathtub, and shower with bathroom cleaners that won't scratch the surface. This will keep germs and mildew from growing.

✔ Check What You Have Learned

1. Why should some household tasks be done on a weekly basis?
2. Why do you need to thoroughly clean the bathroom?

Occasional Tasks

There are some household tasks that need to be done occasionally. They may need to be done only once a month or once or twice a year.

Cleaning windows. Use a window cleaner or water mixed with ammonia. Also use lint-free rags, such as old sheets. These can be used again and again.

Cleaning woodwork and walls. Wipe down woodwork and walls that have fingerprints and other dirt on them. Hard-to-reach cobwebs found in corners and around the ceiling can be removed with a pillowcase over a broom.

Cleaning the oven and refrigerator. These should be cleaned once a month. Read the instruction booklet for your oven. Your oven may have special features, such as removable doors, that make cleaning easier. (More hints for cleaning ovens and refrigerators will be given in Lesson 9-2, "Safety and Sanitation.")

✔ Check What You Have Learned

1. Why may some household tasks only need to be done occasionally?
2. How can you clean hard-to-reach areas of walls and woodwork?

Working Together

More women are working outside the home than in the past. Not as many are full-time homemakers. A **homemaker** is anyone who manages or cares for a home. Women have less time to spend cleaning their homes. Therefore, it is important that each family member help care for the home.

To help share cleaning tasks, your family should make a cleaning schedule. More work will get done when everybody helps. No one will feel like they are doing all the work.

To make a schedule, first list all the tasks that need to be done. After that, decide who is responsible for each task. Be sure to divide the tasks evenly among the family members. See 5-14. Keep in mind how long it takes to do each task. Rotate the tasks that people dislike.

When making a cleaning schedule, think about the amount of time each family member has available. Parents who work outside the home may have less time to clean on weekdays. They may want to do all their cleaning on the weekend. When you are out of school for the summer, you may have more time for cleaning.

You should also think about the tasks you like to do. You may like to work indoors instead of outside. You may prefer to clean the bathroom instead of doing laundry. Volunteer to do the tasks you like most.

Let everyone in the family help, especially young children. Find tasks they can do well. For instance, Allison is a five-year-old. She likes to help on cleaning days. Her task is to dust. This makes her feel needed.

Task	Monday 3/5	Tuesday 3/6	Wednesday 3/7	Thursday 3/8	Friday 3/9	Saturday 3/10	Sunday 3/11
Set kitchen table	Mom	Dad	Suzanne	Izzy	Joel	Mom	Dad
Clean off kitchen table	Dad	Suzanne	Izzy	Joel	Mom	Dad	Suzanne
Clean and put away dishes	Suzanne	Izzy	Joel	Mom	Dad	Suzanne	Izzy
Straighten living room	Izzy	Joel	Mom	Dad	Suzanne	Izzy	Joel
Feed pets	Joel	Mom	Dad	Suzanne	Izzy	Joel	Mom

5-14 Every member of the family needs to help keep the home clean. Writing down your family's cleaning schedule lets everyone see what his or her tasks are for the week.

 Check What You Have Learned

1. Why should all family members share in the care of the home?
2. What factors should be considered when making a cleaning schedule?

 The Main Ideas

Having a clean home is important. It can make you feel better and help you enjoy your home more. Cleaning tasks need to be done on a regular basis. A cleaning schedule helps divide these tasks fairly among all family members.

Apply What You Have Learned

1. Invite a person from a cleaning service to speak to your class. Ask him or her to share some hints for doing cleaning tasks well.
2. List the responsibilities you have for caring for your home. With other family members, make a schedule to care for your home.

Case Study

Read the story below and look at Lesson 5-1 again.
Then answer the questions below.

Planning Your Living Space

The Gomez family is going to be moving into a new home soon. The Gomez children, Lily and Juan, want to decorate their new bedrooms. Lily and Juan have spread out the scale floor plans their mother helped them make on the kitchen table. Mrs. Gomez also helped them cut out scale-sized pieces of colored paper to represent their bedroom furniture.

"This is like a game," Juan said. "I can move the bed and dresser around like toys. I wish I could move that window that looks out over the street. I would rather have it close to the tree."

"You can't move windows, doors, or closets," said Lily. "You can only move furniture. I think it's fun to move the bed around so easily. I like the bed against this wall. I wonder how much space I should leave between the bed and the dresser."

"Mom said that we need to leave two feet of space between pieces of furniture," said Juan.

"She showed me how to measure that. One quarter of an inch equals one foot. You need to move the dresser over one inch."

Lily said, "That looks good. I also have a big poster that I want to look at from my bed. There's only one wall that seems right."

"I have a lot of toys and books," Juan said. "I may need to get a storage chest and desk to put some of them in to keep my room from getting messy."

"I can't wait until Dad paints and wallpapers my bedroom. I've always wanted a blue and yellow room. Mom is going to buy me a new rug and bedspread. I get to choose the colors. My animal collection will look neat against the blue and yellow wallpaper," Lily said.

"Navy blue is my favorite color," said Juan. "I want a blue striped bedspread. Mom said that she will let me have white walls if I help keep them clean."

To Discuss

1. What arranging and decorating concepts are Lily and Juan using from this lesson?
2. What else should Lily and Juan consider as they arrange and decorate their bedrooms?
3. How has using a scale floor plan helped Lily and Juan arrange their bedrooms?

Topic 5 Review

Topic Summary

Your home helps meet some of your physical, emotional, and social needs. Managing your home, or living space, can help you enjoy it more. Some living space is shared. Keeping this space clean and comfortable lets you and your family enjoy it more. Each family member should help keep it clean and comfortable.

Private space is an area that is only yours. By planning carefully, you can use and decorate your private space wisely. Use a scale floor plan to arrange the furniture in your room. Use hidden and displayed storage to store your belongings. You should discuss your decorating plans with your parents. If you share a bedroom with a brother or sister, you also need to discuss this with them.

To feel safe and secure in your home, you need to help prevent accidents and break-ins. Most household accidents result from falls, fires, poisonings, and electricity. You need to follow safety rules to prevent these accidents from happening. Certain steps can also be taken to protect your home from break-ins.

To Review

Write your answers on a separate sheet of paper.

1. What is the difference between a house and a home?
2. List three types of needs that a home can meet.
3. True or false. Shared space is the area that belongs to one person in a home.
4. List at least three hints for sharing space in a home.
5. Draw the housing symbols for a door, window, and wall.
6. True or false. Allow at least two feet of space between pieces of furniture.
7. Which of the following is an example of hidden storage?
   a. Bookshelves.
   b. Tables.
   c. Chest of drawers.
   d. Kitchen countertops.
8. List the four causes of common household accidents. Then describe ways they can be prevented.
9. (Falls/Fires) are the most common household accidents.
10. What are two ways that electricity can cause problems in the home?
11. List four ways to keep your home secure.
12. List three benefits of a clean home.
13. What cleaning tasks need to be done daily, weekly, and occasionally?
14. Tell how to make a cleaning schedule.

Vocabulary Quiz

Match the definitions in Column A with the terms in Column B.
Write your answers on a separate sheet of paper.

Column A

1. Anyone who manages or cares for a home.
2. Any place people live.
3. A path people follow as they move within a room.
4. A tool run by gas or electricity.
5. Poisonous.
6. An unexpected event causing loss or injury.
7. A freestanding, single-family dwelling.
8. A drawing that shows the size and shape of a room or home.
9. Deadly.

Column B

a. Home.
b. House.
c. Scale floor plan.
d. Hidden storage.
e. Accident.
f. Fatal.
g. Toxic.
h. Appliance.
i. Homemaker.
j. Traffic pattern.

Lesson 6-1
Your Environment

Objectives

After studying this lesson, you will be able to

→ *define* ecology, natural resources, pollution, recycling, *and* precycling.

→ *explain the relationship between ecology and environment.*

→ *give examples of how pollution affects everyone.*

→ *tell what you can do to protect natural resources.*

New Words

ecology: *the study of all living objects in relation to each other and the environment.*

natural resources: *conditions and substances that are supplied by nature and needed for survival.*

pollution: *the state of being unclean.*

precycling: *buying products that reduce waste.*

recycling: *taking a used product and turning it into a product that can be reused.*

New Ideas

→ *Ecology and the environment are closely related.*

→ *How people use their natural resources today affects everyone's future.*

→ *Pollution affects all people.*

→ *You can work to protect the environment by reusing products, reducing waste, and recycling.*

This lesson is about the environment. It is about the air you breathe and the water you drink. It is about your home, neighborhood, and school. It is about the energy you use in your home.

What happens to the environment affects all living objects. **Ecology** is the study of all living objects in relation to each other and the environment. Ecology helps people understand the environment better. It also teaches people what they need to do to protect it.

Use and Misuse of Natural Resources

Natural resources are a part of your environment. They are the conditions and substances that are supplied by nature and needed for survival. They include air, water, soil, sun, and fuel. All living beings need natural resources to live and grow.

Cars, trucks, trains, and airplanes use fuel made from petroleum. See 6-1. Many houses, office buildings, and schools are heated or cooled by petroleum products. Many items found in the home, such as plastics, are made from petroleum products.

Natural resources can be used up or damaged so that they are not useful. They can even become harmful to people. This can cause a crisis.

The energy crisis is a crisis related to a shortage of natural resources. Most energy comes from natural resources. For instance, coal and oil are natural resources. They are burned to provide energy needed to run machines and heat buildings. A crisis

6-1 The petroleum used to make gas is a limited natural resource.

6-2 Smoke from factories can create smog that is harmful to the environment.

occurs because these resources are limited. Also, the demand for energy is greater than the amount available.

Another type of crisis related to natural resources is pollution. **Pollution** is the state of being unclean. Smoke from factories and exhaust from cars, trucks, and airplanes cause the air to become dirty. See 6-2. *Polluted* air is harmful to breathe. It can cause health problems.

Water pollution has also resulted from people not protecting natural resources. Waste from boats and factories has been dumped into waterways. The polluted water has harmed fish and other animals that need the water to live. Millions of dollars are being spent to clean up rivers, harbors, and lakes to make them usable again.

Nuclear power is used in some areas of the country to produce electricity. The used fuel from this power produces nuclear waste. Companies must then find safe ways to dispose of this waste. It can pollute the air, water, and soil.

✔ Check What You Have Learned

1. Why do living objects need natural resources to live and grow?
2. What happens when natural resources are misused by people?

Protecting Natural Resources

Everyone in the world is affected by shortages and pollution. These problems will affect people in the future. People need to help prevent pollution and shortages. The cost for protecting resources is high but worthwhile.

Pollution is everyone's problem. If the air is dirty, you breathe dirty air. If the water is dirty, you use dirty water. Polluted air and water are not safe for plants, animals, or people. Pollution is not someone else's problem. Everyone needs to help prevent pollution.

Laws have been passed to protect the air, water, and other natural resources. For instance, cars must have features that cut down on air pollution. Factories cannot dump waste directly into rivers. Waste must be treated so that it is not harmful to the environment. See 6-3.

6-3   Water needs to be safe and clean for people to enjoy.

Many pollution problems have come from consumers who carelessly use and dispose of goods. It is important to dispose of waste responsibly. Consumers can protect natural resources by reusing products, reducing waste, and recycling products. Protecting natural resources shows respect for the environment.

Reusing products. Many people discard items they could reuse. They throw away items they could use in a different way. Consider these ways to reuse products.
- Carry a reusable tote bag to the store when shopping.
- Reuse wrapping paper, plastic bags, and boxes.
- Give outgrown clothes to others.
- Use the back sides of paper for notes.
- Cut up old sheets and towels for dust cloths or cleaning rags.
- Donate old books and magazines to hospitals, child care centers, or libraries.
- Make art projects out of discarded items.

Reducing waste. Start by analyzing what you throw away. What could you do to generate less waste? How can you reduce the amount of trash you generate? Consider these ways to reduce waste.
- Precycle. **Precycling** means buying products that reduce waste. Start by buying larger quantities with less packaging. For example, buying a large carton of juice instead of individual juice boxes reduces waste.
- Read labels. Avoid buying hazardous waste products. (Review Lesson 5-2.)
- Avoid buying disposable products, such as disposable razors and diapers. Use cloth hand towels instead of paper towels.
- Buy refills.
- Recycle products instead of throwing them away.

Recycle products. **Recycling** is a way to take a used product and turn it into a product that can be reused. It is one way to dispose of goods and get the most use from them. For example, paper products, bottles, and cans can be recycled to make new paper products, bottles, and cans. See 6-4. Scrap metal can be recycled to make other metal products. Consider these ways to recycle.

6-4   Look for this symbol on products you buy. It indicates that the product is recyclable.

- Place clean recyclables in a special container that is separate from your regular trash, then recycle them. If your neighborhood provides a recycling service, participate in it. If not, take used products to recycling centers.
- Buy from companies that use recyclable materials and practice recycling. As a consumer, you can influence how materials are made and disposed.
- Buy products that do not harm the environment by their packaging or production.
- Write to companies that generate a great deal of waste and ask about their recycling policies. For example, observe the waste generated at your favorite fast-food restaurant.

People need to respect and protect the environment. When you do, you are helping solve the problems of the environment.

✔ Check What You Have Learned

1. How have laws helped protect air, water, and other natural resources?
2. How can reusing products, reducing waste, and recycling products help protect natural resources? Give examples.
3. How can you precycle? Explain.

The Main Ideas

Natural resources are part of your environment. Living beings need natural resources to live. However, these resources are limited. Everyone should be responsible for protecting natural resources and the environment. You can protect natural resources by reusing products, reducing waste, and recycling. How you use your natural resources and care for the environment can help protect them for the future.

Apply What You Have Learned

1. Look through newspapers and magazines for an article about environmental problems. Share your article with the class. Discuss what this problem might do to the future of the earth. Also talk about how it could have been prevented.
2. Make a poster urging students in your school not to pollute. As a class, vote on the best posters to put on display in the school.
3. Visit a recycling center in your community. If your community does not have a recycling center, write for information from the nearest center. Find out what products they collect for recycling. Also find out where these products are sent and what you can do to help with recycling. Report your findings to the class.

Lesson 6-2
Conserving Energy

Objectives

After studying this lesson, you will be able to
- *define* conserve, solar energy, *and* insulation.
- *name sources of energy.*
- *give examples of how you can conserve energy.*

New Words

conserve: *to save.*
solar energy: *energy from the sun's rays.*
insulation: *material used to prevent the transfer of heat or cold.*

New Ideas

- *Most of the energy used in homes is for heating and cooling.*
- *It is important to learn ways to conserve energy.*

Families vary in the amount of energy they need. Your family's size and lifestyle affect how much energy is used. Climate, type of fuel, and type of heating and cooling systems also affect the amount used. You can learn to **conserve**, or save, energy. This will reduce the amount of energy your family uses.

Conserving Heat

Most central home heating systems use gas, oil, or electricity as energy sources. Some people use **solar energy,** which is energy from the sun's rays, to heat their homes. Using solar energy helps conserve more limited energy sources.

There are many ways you can conserve heat in your home. Do not turn the heat on until it is needed. Do not change the thermostat setting often. Keep it at 65°F to 68°F during the day and between 55°F and 60°F at night. See 6-5. Wear layered clothing instead of turning up the heat. When you

6-5 Setting the thermostat no higher than 68°F will help conserve heat in your home.

are away from home, lower the thermostat five to eight degrees.

To reduce heat loss, install weather-stripping around window and door frames. Tape clear plastic over windows. Storm windows and doors can also be used. Be sure to close draperies, shades, and windows during the night. Make sure your home has enough **insulation,** which is material used to prevent the transfer of heat or cold.

Energy is also needed to heat water. Most water heaters use gas or electricity. Solar energy can also be used to heat water. To save energy, turn the water heater off when you are away from home for several days. Do not overheat water. Most homes need water heated only to 120°F. Use hot water only when necessary. Use warm or cold water for normal laundry and cold water for the rinse. Take showers instead of baths, which use more water. Fix dripping faucets.

✔ Check What You Have Learned

1. What are three steps you can take to conserve heat in your home?
2. What household tasks require the use of hot water? How can you save hot water when doing these tasks?

Using Cooling Systems Wisely

Energy is needed to cool air in homes. You can save energy by using fans instead of air conditioners. Fans cool by causing air movement. Attic and window fans pull in cool air from outdoors. Ceiling fans move air within a room. They can also help conserve heat. Since heat rises, these fans can force the hot air down from the ceiling.

When the weather is hot, air conditioners may be needed to cool the air. Window or room air conditioners cool a room or just a small area of the house. Be sure to turn these units off when no one is in the room.

Central air conditioning cools the whole house or building. It uses a lot of energy. It should be carefully regulated. Set the thermostat at 78°F and keep it there. Turn the thermostat up or shut the system off when no one is home. Maintain your air conditioner. Check the filter monthly. Change the filter often for proper airflow across the coils.

You can help conserve the energy needed to cool your home. Keep heat outside by closing all windows and doors to the cooled space. Keep storm windows on. Pull shades or drapes across the windows during the day. Turn off the air conditioner and open the windows when it is cool outside. Avoid using appliances and lights during the hottest part of the day to prevent heat buildup. Schedule main meals, showers, laundry, and ironing in the morning or evening. See 6-6. Wear lightweight clothing as much as possible.

✔ Check What You Have Learned

1. What is the advantage of using a fan instead of an air conditioner to cool air?
2. How can you prevent energy waste when using an air conditioner?

6-6 Avoid cooking during the hottest part of the day to help conserve cooled air.

More Ways to Conserve Energy

To conserve energy, be sure to turn off appliances when you're not using them. Also keep your appliances in good repair. Buy appliances that use the least amount of energy. You can look at the EnergyGuide labels on appliances to compare energy costs.

Transportation uses a lot of energy. Walk or ride a bike instead of riding in a car whenever you can. Using public transportation also saves energy. See 6-7.

Programs to conserve energy have been started in this country and in others. Some of these programs are government programs. Others were started by citizen groups. These efforts have also helped to protect the environment. For instance, recycling programs have been started in many communities. Learn about programs in your area. Find out what you can do to take part.

6-7 Using public transportation cuts down on the need for gas.

✓ Check What You Have Learned

1. What kinds of appliances do you use at home? How can you save energy when using them?
2. What are some energy conservation programs that have been started in your community?

The Main Ideas

It is important to conserve energy to save money and to protect the future. The largest use of energy in the home is for heating and cooling. All appliances use energy to operate. There is much you can do to conserve energy. The future depends upon how people conserve now. Do your part to protect the future by conserving energy today.

Apply What You Have Learned

1. Conduct research on new sources of energy. You might choose solar or wind power as your topic. Write a two-page report based on your research.
2. Make a list of ways you can conserve heat energy in your home. Choose two and try them. Later, evaluate how well they worked. Make any needed changes and try them again. If they worked well, try some others.
3. Interview your parents about the increased costs of electricity, heating fuel, and gas. Ask them how much these cost when they were your age. Ask them how much costs have risen in your lifetime. Report back to the class.

Lesson 6-3
Technology in the Home

Objectives

After studying this lesson, you will be able to

➡ *define technology, computer, data, software, modem, and computer network.*

➡ *list uses of personal computers.*

➡ *describe how computers can be used to communicate with each other.*

➡ *explain how technology will affect your future home, work, and lifestyle.*

New Words

technology: *use of knowledge, tools, and systems to make life easier and better.*

computer: *an electronic machine capable of storing, processing, and controlling large amounts of data.*

data: *information.*

software: *a set of instructions that tells a computer what to do.*

modem: *a device that allows computers to communicate with each other over telephone lines.*

computer network: *a system where resources are shared among computer users.*

New Ideas

➡ *Computers are an important part of life in today's society.*

➡ *Technology affects you now and in the future.*

Technology is the use of knowledge, tools, and systems to make life easier and better. It affects your home. It shapes the future.

The Personal Computer

One of the biggest results of technology has been the computer. Almost everyone today has used a computer. A **computer** is a machine capable of storing, processing, and controlling large amounts of **data,** or information. Computers receive directions in the form of software. See 6-8. **Software** is a set of instructions that tells a computer what to do. Software most often comes as small disks that are inserted into the computer. If you have a CD-ROM drive, you can use software that is on CD-ROM discs. Computer CDs can store large amounts of data.

6-8   A variety of software is available for personal computers.

Personal computers may affect people's lives the most. There are many different types of personal computers on the market. They are used to help with many home tasks. They can be used to control appliances, lighting, and heating. Household budgets can be put on computers. Computers can also help families prepare tax forms and pay bills.

With the right software, a computer can be used as a word processor. A word processor allows you to type, edit, and print materials. You can write letters and do your homework. Some word processors will even correct your spelling and grammar.

Computers are good for storing lists and other information. For instance, you can make a list of your friends' birthdays and addresses.

Students can use computers to learn. Most schools have computer labs where students can learn to use computers. You should try to learn as much as possible about computers. In the future, most jobs will require some computer skills.

Learning with computers can be fun. A wide variety of software is available for learning. For instance, you can analyze the food you eat to see if you are eating right. You can draw and paint with computers. You can create music. Computers are limited only by the software you choose. See 6-9.

6-9 Music can be composed on a computer.

✔ **Check What You Have Learned**

1. What are three ways personal computers can be used in the home?
2. How could you use a word processor to help you do your homework?

Communicating Electronically

If your computer is hooked up to a modem, you can communicate with other computer users. A **modem** is a device that allows computers to directly communicate with each other over telephone lines. See 6-10.

With a modem, you can write to another computer through electronic mail. This is called *e-mail*. For example, Latisha lives in the United States and has a pen pal, Jacque, in France. Latisha writes to Jacque using e-mail. Jacque receives Latisha's letter almost instantly over his computer. This type of communication is much faster than regular mail service. It is also much less costly than a long-distance phone call.

Another option you have with a modem is to be connected to the Internet. The *Internet* links many computer networks around the world. Each **computer network** is a system that allows computer users to share information and other resources. Someone who is using the Internet is said to be "online."

To use the Internet, you need to sign up with an online provider. The provider may charge you a monthly fee. The phone company may also charge you for using the phone line. You need to investigate the costs of using online services before choosing a provider. Discuss these costs with your parents. They can help you choose a provider. They can also help set guidelines for using online services.

6-10 Computers can be linked to other computers with a modem.

A helpful tool on the Internet is the *World Wide Web*. Companies, organizations, and individuals create websites on the World Wide Web. Each *website* is a source of information. You can find websites on almost any topic. You can read reviews of movies. You can find out the weather forecast in other parts of the world. You can read college catalogs. You can even do research from library databases.

You may have noticed many companies using the World Wide Web to advertise products. The companies list website addresses in TV commercials. This encourages consumers to use their computers to gather more information about the companies' products.

When you are doing research, it is important to check the accuracy of a website. Just because you see something on the Web does not mean it is true. Websites created by government agencies or nationally known companies are likely to be most reliable.

The Internet allows you to do much more than conduct research. You can also use your computer to play games, bank, and shop. In fact, grocery stores in some large cities have online services. You can place an order through your computer and arrange to have your groceries delivered to your home. Services such as this often cost a small fee.

✓ Check What You Have Learned

1. What are the advantages of using e-mail?
2. What should you do before using an online service?
3. Why should you check the accuracy of a website?

Now and in the Future

Technology that is being explored now will affect your future. One area in which this will happen is communication. Computer communication already allows people to send e-mail instantly to other computer users anywhere in the world. You can also send mail instantly through facsimile transmission (fax) machines. New forms of communication will continue to speed the sharing of information in the future.

Technology also affects the way people work. Many people have office systems hooked up to their home computers. As this trend continues, more and more people will be working from home.

Your future home will be affected by increased technology. As the population grows, more multiple-family homes will be built. Computers are already being used to draw scale floor plans and arrange furniture. Homes of the future will be designed even better. They will be more energy efficient. Building materials and appliances will help conserve energy.

Technology will affect appliances. Tiny computer controls now allow you to program many appliances. In the future, you may be able to program appliances simply by talking to them.

Technology will affect leisure time in the future. Builders are already using more easy-care housing materials. Future homes may also have robots to help with the housework. This will probably make housework easier in the future, giving you more leisure time.

Today, cable TV gives you more choices than ever before about what to watch on TV. VCRs let you decide when you want to watch your favorite programs. In the future, satellite communication will further expand what you can see on TV. Advanced VCRs may allow you to customize your program schedule.

In the future, technology will give you more options from which to choose. Jobs and lifestyles will be more varied. You should learn how to control technology and not be controlled by it. Technology produces machines. Machines are designed to make people's lives easier. They are not designed to replace people. Machines can do only what you tell them to do. They do not have brains.

✓ Check What You Have Learned

1. How will technology affect your home and lifestyle in the future?
2. What kinds of tasks do machines help you perform?

The Main Ideas

The home of the future will be affected by increased technology. Personal computers can be used to help with many home tasks. Their use will increase in the future. You should learn as much as possible about technology now to prepare for the future.

Apply What You Have Learned

1. Write a journal for two days of your life in the year 2020. Describe your home, family, and work. Also, describe what kinds of technology will be available at that time.
2. If your school has a computer lab, visit it as a class. Ask to see what kind of software can be used in the home. Write a short report on what you find out.
3. Conduct a survey of five students at your school. Find out how often they use computers. Ask if they have computers in their homes. Ask how many of their parents use computers at work.
4. Research the costs and benefits of various online services available in your area.

Case Study

Read the story below and look at Lesson 6-1 again.
Then answer the questions below.

Protecting the Environment

Connie and Bob are members of the student council. They are also in family and consumer sciences class together. In class one day, their teacher, Ms. Rafferty, talked about the environment and what needs to be done to protect it.

At the student council meeting that day after school, the members discussed how to raise money for the spring dance. A few fundraisers were discussed and decided upon. However, the group still needed ways to raise more money.

Bob raised his hand and said, "How about if we recycle? We could collect used paper from the computer labs and aluminum cans from the juice machines. Then we could take the papers and cans to the recycling center and get money for them."

"That sounds great," Connie said. "We would be raising money and helping protect the environment."

Lita, president of the student council, said, "I think it sounds great, too. How would you two like to be in charge of this project?"

"I'd love to," said Bob.

"So would I," said Connie.

"Good. You two can get together and talk about how you want to start this recycling program. Then you can form a committee. You'll also need to have a teacher help you set up the program."

Connie said, "I'll ask Ms. Rafferty. I bet she'd be willing to help us."

To Discuss

1. What steps should Connie and Bob take to start setting up the recycling program?
2. How can they make other students in the school understand the importance of recycling?
3. What can they do to make it easy for the students and teachers to recycle?

Topic 6 Review

Topic Summary

Technology can make your life easier. Using computers, you can play games, makes lists, and keep track of budgets. Technology can also affect your future. It helps improve housing, communication, and jobs.

To be able to enjoy the future, you need to take care of what you have today. It is very important to protect the environment. If the environment isn't protected, the natural resources that all living beings need will be used up or damaged. Energy crises are the result of people using too many natural resources. Air and water pollution are caused by people abusing natural resources.

There are many ways for you and your family to help protect the environment. Laws are made to prevent pollution and protect natural resources. Glass, paper, aluminum, and other materials can be recycled and used again.

Another way to protect natural resources is to conserve energy. When you conserve energy, you are not using as much as before. There are many ways to conserve heating fuel. You can also learn to cool homes and use appliances more efficiently.

Technology can help you conserve energy. Computers can be used to turn lights off and on and control the thermostat. New, more efficient building materials, cars, and energy sources are always being developed.

To Review

Write your answers on a separate sheet of paper.

1. What is the relationship between ecology and the environment?
2. True or false. Ecology is the study of recycling.
3. Give two examples of natural resources in your environment.
4. True or false. Cars use fuel made from petroleum.
5. Which of the following is a cause of an energy crisis?
   a. Limited natural resources.
   b. Greater demand for energy than supply.
   c. Misused natural resources.
   d. All of the above.
6. How can you show respect for the environment?
7. What are three common sources of energy used in the home?
8. What are the advantages of using solar energy?
9. List four ways to conserve energy when heating your home.
10. List four ways to conserve energy when cooling your home.
11. True or false. Computers get instructions from software.
12. Data is another word for _____.
13. List three ways that computers can help people manage their homes.
14. How has technology affected communications?
15. What is the main difference between people and machines?

Vocabulary Quiz

Match the definitions in Column A with the terms in Column B.
Write your answers on a separate sheet of paper.

Column A

1. Use of knowledge, tools, and systems to make life better.
2. Reusing resources.
3. To save.
4. Material used to prevent the transfer of heat or cold.
5. An electronic machine capable of storing, processing, and controlling data.
6. Energy from the sun's rays.
7. The study of all living objects in relation to each other and the environment.
8. The state of being unclean.
9. A set of instructions that tells a computer what to do.
10. Conditions and substances that are supplied by nature.
11. A device that allows computers to communicate with each other over the telephone lines.
12. A system where resources are shared among computer users.
13. Buying products that reduce waste.

Column B

a. Technology.
b. Ecology.
c. Pollution.
d. Environment.
e. Conserve.
f. Gas energy.
g. Software.
h. Computer.
i. Recycling.
j. Solar energy.
k. Insulation.
l. Natural resources.
m. Precycling.
n. Modem.
o. Computer network.

Unit 3
You and Food

Learning to prepare food can help you meet guidelines for good health.

174

Topic 7 The Foods You Eat

Lesson 7-1
Food—Its Many Roles

Objectives

After studying this lesson, you will be able to
- *define traditions, culture, diet, Dietary Guidelines for Americans, saturated fat, and cholesterol.*
- *give examples of how food is related to family traditions.*
- *explain why food is often part of social events.*
- *describe how food is part of a country's culture.*
- *explain how your diet can affect you.*
- *list the Dietary Guidelines for Americans.*

New Words

traditions: *customs passed from one generation to another.*
culture: *the beliefs and customs of a certain racial, religious, or social group.*
diet: *the food and beverages consumed each day.*
Dietary Guidelines for Americans: *seven guidelines for a healthful diet.*
saturated fat: *a fat that is solid at room temperature.*
cholesterol: *a fatty substance found in foods from animal sources.*

New Ideas

- *Food is a part of many family traditions.*
- *Social events often include food.*
- *New foods are introduced to the United States from other cultures.*
- *Your diet affects your health, performance, fitness, and appearance.*
- *Following the Dietary Guidelines for Americans can help you have good health and avoid certain diseases.*

Food plays many different roles. It is often part of holidays and special events. See 7-1. Some people associate it with getting together with friends. Still others enjoy learning about the background of different foods and how to prepare them. Food is

7-1 Barbecued ribs, corn on the cob, deviled eggs, and baked beans are popular foods for a Fourth of July celebration.

also important to your health, performance, and wellness. When you eat the right foods, you will feel better about your appearance. Smart food choices help you enjoy a healthy lifestyle.

Food, Family, and Friends

Words such as *birthday, wedding, Fourth of July, New Year's Eve, Thanksgiving, Christmas,* and *Hanukkah* may make you think of different foods. The foods your family serves depends on traditions, likes, and dislikes.

Traditions are customs passed from one generation to the next. Food is part of many family traditions. Some foods may be served only at certain times of the year, such as holidays and other special events. These traditional foods may remind you of good times with family and friends.

Over time, families may adapt foods to meet the changing likes and dislikes of family members. However, the traditions often remain almost unchanged over the years.

Food and friends seem to go together. Your friends may offer you food when you are in their homes. You may serve your friends food when they come to visit in your home. You and your friends may also enjoy going to a fast-food restaurant together for a snack.

✓ Check What You Have Learned

1. What are some of the traditions in your family? How do foods become part of family traditions?
2. How do likes and dislikes affect family food choices?
3. Where do you go with your friends when you want to get something to eat?

Foods from Many Cultures

The foods you choose are related to your culture. **Culture** is the beliefs and customs of a certain racial, religious, or social group. See 7-2.

When people talk about their culture, they often describe special foods that are part of their background. Throughout the world, people enjoy foods that reflect their local cultures. In England, people dine on fish and chips. In Italy, pasta dishes are part of the culture. In the Middle East, people eat a dish called hummus, which is made from chickpeas. Borscht, a beet soup, is popular in Russian culture.

Today, a wide variety of foods is part of the culture in the United States. These foods were contributed by people from many different cultures. Native Americans were one of these cultural groups. Hundreds of years ago, Native Americans raised corn, beans, pumpkins, and squash. These foods are still part of the culture in the United States.

7-2   This 4-H leader shows how to wrap fish in leaves. Baking fish wrapped in leaves is sometimes done in Central American countries.

People from many different cultures settled in the United States. Each group of people brought its eating habits and food customs with it. For instance, people from China brought the cooking technique of stir-frying. People from Mexico brought foods like tacos and burritos.

Sometimes people could not find foods from their culture. Therefore, they adapted available foods to their ways of cooking. They also created new ways to prepare these foods. For instance, French people in Louisiana developed Cajun cooking.

As the United States grew, many people moved from one region to another. They again took their food customs with them. As a result, many cultural foods are now found throughout the United States.

Some of the foods your family eats may relate to your culture. They may be foods your relatives brought from another country. The region where you live is also part of your culture. Some of the foods you enjoy may be special to your region. Southern fried chicken and New England clam chowder are examples.

✓ **Check What You Have Learned**

1. Why are there so many food choices in the United States?
2. How have many new foods become part of the culture in the United States?

Food, Fitness, and Appearance

You need to be healthy to be physically fit and perform well. To be in good health, you need to form good health habits. That means getting enough exercise and sleep. It means getting good medical and dental care.

Eating the right foods while you are young will help you build a healthy body. See 7-3 and 7-4.

7-3   It is important to develop good eating habits when you are young.

7-4   When you eat the right foods, you will have more energy for activities.

A **diet** is the food and beverages consumed each day. Your diet affects how you perform in school, sports, and at social activities.

Learning is hard work. You need to eat good food to help you learn. Eating special foods, such as fish, will not make you smarter than people who don't eat fish. However, eating the right foods in the proper amounts will give you energy for learning.

Sports and social activities are fun. However, activities like dancing, running, skating, and swimming all require energy. Eating a balanced diet can give you the energy to enjoy these activities.

Most people care about their appearance. You probably care about how you look. You may notice how other people look. The food you eat can make a difference in your appearance. Eating the right foods will help you look and feel your best.

Your body size and shape are determined partly by traits you inherited from your parents. The colors of your eyes and hair are also inherited traits. You cannot change these traits. However, you can maintain the best weight for you by eating nutritious foods in the right amounts. Eating the right foods can also keep your hair shiny, your skin smooth, and your eyes bright.

✓ **Check What You Have Learned**

1. What are four good health habits you can form to help you stay in good health?
2. How can your diet affect your performance in school, sports, and at social activities?
3. How can eating the right food make a difference in how you look?

Dietary Guidelines for Americans

What foods should you choose each day to look and feel your best? Health experts recommend that you follow the **Dietary Guidelines for Americans.** See 7-5. These are seven guidelines for a healthful diet. They were developed by the U.S. Departments of Agriculture and Health and Human Services. Following them can help decrease your chances of getting certain diseases.

Eat a variety of foods. No single food provides every nutrient. That's why you should eat a number of different kinds of foods each day. This is the best way to make sure you are getting all the nutrients your body needs. Many foods are good sources of several nutrients. For example, vegetables and fruits provide vitamins A and C, folic acid, minerals, and fiber.

Balance the food you eat with physical activity. Maintain or improve your weight. Weighing too much or too little can increase the risk of developing certain health problems. Choosing nutritious foods that are not too high in calories will help you maintain or improve your weight. Regular exercise will help you control your weight, too. Long-term success in maintaining a healthy weight means making healthful eating and physical activity lifelong habits.

Choose a diet with plenty of grain products, vegetables, and fruits. These foods are good sources of vitamins, minerals, and carbohydrates. They also tend to be high in fiber and low in calories and fat. Health experts recommend that you eat at least three servings of vegetables and two servings of fruits daily. They also recommend eating at least six daily servings of grain products, such as breads, cereals, pasta, and rice.

Choose a diet low in fat, saturated fat, and cholesterol. Fat is an important nutrient in the diet. However, many people eat too much fat. Fat should not account for more than 30 percent of the calories you eat. **Saturated fat** is a fat that is solid at room temperature. No more than 10 percent of the calories in your diet should come from saturated fat. **Cholesterol** is a fatty substance found in foods from animal sources, like meat and eggs.

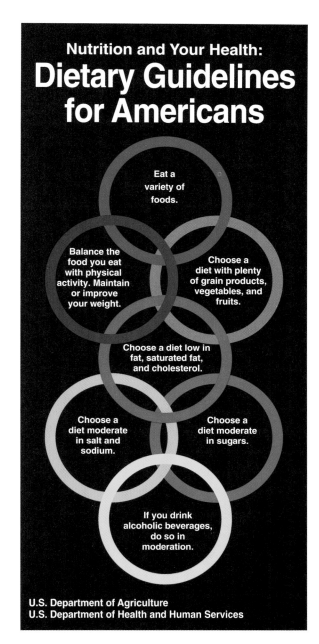

Nutrition and Your Health:

Dietary Guidelines for Americans

Eat a variety of foods.

Balance the food you eat with physical activity. Maintain or improve your weight.

Choose a diet with plenty of grain products, vegetables, and fruits.

Choose a diet low in fat, saturated fat, and cholesterol.

Choose a diet moderate in salt and sodium.

Choose a diet moderate in sugars.

If you drink alcoholic beverages, do so in moderation.

U.S. Department of Agriculture
U.S. Department of Health and Human Services

7-5 Following the Dietary Guidelines for Americans will help you make wise food choices for good health.

Diets containing too much fat, saturated fat, and cholesterol have been linked to heart disease and certain cancers.

Besides reducing your risk of disease, following this guideline can help you maintain a healthy weight. To limit fat in your diet, choose lean meats, fish, poultry without skin, and lowfat dairy products.

Choose a diet moderate in sugars. A diet with an excessive amount of sugar is likely to be high in calories. Sugar also contributes to tooth decay. Read food labels. Many high-sugar foods list sugar or a syrup as the first or second ingredient.

Choose a diet moderate in salt and sodium. Salt contains a large amount of sodium. Sodium has been linked to high blood pressure. Most people in the United States eat more salt and sodium than they need. Read labels to find out how much sodium is in foods. Choose foods lower in sodium most of the time. Use salt sparingly in cooking and at the table.

If you drink alcoholic beverages, do so in moderation. Aside from being illegal for young teens, drinking alcohol can lead to a number of health problems. Many accidents are related to the use of alcohol. Alcohol can also be addictive.

Following the Dietary Guidelines does not mean you have to give up favorite foods. You simply have to avoid overeating any one food. The goal is to make your *total diet* healthful. You can balance a meal that is high in fat and calories with another meal that is more nutritious. Suppose you eat a hamburger, French fries, and a milk shake for lunch. A salad with lowfat dressing and pasta with tomato sauce for dinner would help balance your daily diet.

✓ **Check What You Have Learned**

1. Why is it important to eat a variety of foods?
2. What is the goal in following the Dietary Guidelines for Americans?

The Main Ideas

Food plays many roles in your life. It is served at many special events and is part of family traditions. It is part of getting together with friends. Foods from many different cultures are available in the United States.

Besides the social and cultural roles food plays, it also affects you physically and emotionally. Eating the right foods helps you build a healthy body. It helps you to be fit and perform well in all areas of your life. It also helps you look and feel better. Following the Dietary Guidelines for Americans will help you enjoy good health.

Apply What You Have Learned

1. Make a list of holidays and events that are special to you. Then, interview members of your family. Ask them what foods they think of when you mention each holiday or event. Ask them what part they think food plays in these celebrations. Summarize your findings in a one-page report.
2. Look in cookbooks and magazines for recipes good for parties and get-togethers. Also, recall food you've had at parties you've given or attended. Put together a booklet of these recipes to use when entertaining. Share this with the class.
3. Have a "tasting party." Bring a special family food to class. Along with the food, include a half-page summary of the origin of the food and the recipe. Share this with your classmates.
4. Conduct research to find out what foods are good for athletes to eat when preparing for athletic events. Look up diets for different types of athletes. Depending upon which sports they play, athletes may need different diets. Put this information into chart form.
5. Make a poster illustrating the Dietary Guidelines for Americans. Display it in your kitchen at home to remind your family to practice healthy eating habits.

Lesson 7-2
Using the Food Guide Pyramid

Objectives

After studying this lesson, you will be able to

⟹ *define* nutrition, nutrients, Food Guide Pyramid, balanced diet, *and* enriched.

⟹ *give examples of the functions and sources of the six types of nutrients.*

⟹ *name the food groups in the Food Guide Pyramid.*

⟹ *describe how foods from each group help meet your body's needs.*

New Words

nutrition: *the study of how your body uses food.*

nutrients: *chemical substances from foods needed for the body to function.*

Food Guide Pyramid: *an outline of what to eat each day.*

balanced diet: *a diet that provides all the nutrients your body needs for good health.*

enriched: *to have nutrients added to a product to replace those removed during processing.*

New Ideas

⟹ *Nutrients in food help your body grow, develop, and be healthy.*

⟹ *Selecting the recommended daily servings from each group in the Food Guide Pyramid will help you eat a balanced diet.*

Nutrition is the study of how your body uses food and the effects food has on it. **Nutrients** are the chemical substances from foods needed for your body to function. Your body needs nutrients to grow, develop, and be healthy. Nutrients are used by your body to provide for growth and repair. They also furnish energy and heat and regulate body processes.

The Nutrients

Your diet provides the nutrients your body needs. There are six different types of nutrients. They are proteins, carbohydrates, fats, vitamins, minerals, and water. You can get the nutrients you need by eating many kinds of foods. Chart 7-6 shows the functions of the nutrients and their sources. You can refer to it as you read the rest of this lesson.

Proteins can be found in both meat and meat alternates. They give your body energy. They also help your body grow and repair body tissues, such as hair, skin, muscles, and nerves. Your heart, liver, lungs, and brain also need protein to function and stay in good shape. People of all ages need protein in their diets.

Carbohydrates and fats provide energy. Starch, sugar, and fiber are the three kinds of carbohydrates. They can be found in breads and cereals, fruits and vegetables, and products containing sugar. Fats add flavor to food and help satisfy your hunger. However, eating too much fat can lead to health problems. Heart disease, high blood pressure, and being overweight are linked to eating fat.

Vitamins are needed for the growth and repair of your body. Fat-soluble vitamins are stored in

The Nutrients

Functions	Sources
Proteins	
★ Needed for growth and repair of body tissues. ★ Help body organs function and stay in good condition. ★ Supply energy.	Meat, eggs, poultry, fish, legumes, peanuts, nuts, seeds, milk, cheese, and yogurt.
Carbohydrates	
★ Supply energy. ★ Provide fiber to aid in digestion and getting rid of body wastes.	Breads, cereals, rice, pasta, fruits, vegetables, legumes, and sugar and other sweets.
Fats	
★ Provide energy. ★ Insulate the body. ★ Cushion body organs. ★ Help promote growth and healthy skin.	Oil, butter, margarine, salad dressing, meat, poultry, eggs, cheese, nuts, and peanut butter.
Vitamins	
Vitamin A	
★ Helps with normal vision. ★ Helps keep body tissues healthy. ★ Helps with growth.	Dark green vegetables, deep yellow or orange vegetables and fruits, and eggs.
B Vitamins (thiamin, riboflavin, niacin)	
★ Help your body use other nutrients in food for energy. ★ Help keep skin, hair, muscles, and nerves healthy. ★ Help keep appetite and digestion normal. ★ Help your body use oxygen more efficiently.	Meat, poultry, fish, eggs, whole grain and enriched breads and cereals, milk, cheese, yogurt, and ice cream.
Vitamin C	
★ Helps keep gums healthy. ★ Helps cuts and bruises heal. ★ Helps you body fight infections. ★ Helps with growth.	Oranges, grapefruit, lemons, limes, tangerines, berries, papaya, melons, broccoli, spinach, peppers, kale, collards, mustard greens, turnip greens, potatoes, tomatoes, and cabbage.
Minerals	
Calcium	
★ Helps build strong, healthy bones and teeth. ★ Helps the heart beat properly. ★ Helps muscles move.	Milk, cheese, yogurt, ice cream, leafy green vegetables, and fish with tiny bones.
Iron	
★ Helps blood carry oxygen. ★ Helps cells use oxygen.	Meat, eggs, liver, legumes, and whole grain and enriched breads and cereals.
Water	
★ Carries nutrients to the cells and wastes away from cells. ★ Helps regulate body processes such as digestion. ★ Helps maintain normal body temperature. ★ Helps cells operate.	Milk, juices, soups, drinking water, juicy fruits and vegetables, and some solid foods.

7-6 Knowing the functions and sources of nutrients can help you eat nutritiously.

your body. You can eat foods rich in these every other day and still get the amount you need. Water-soluble vitamins are not stored in your body. You need to eat foods rich in these every day.

Minerals help regulate body processes. Two important minerals are calcium and iron. Calcium is needed to build strong bones and teeth. Iron helps blood cells function.

Water is a very important nutrient. Your body can survive only a few days without water. It carries nutrients to every cell in your body and then carries waste away.

✔ Check What You Have Learned

1. What are the three kinds of carbohydrates? In what foods are carbohydrates found?
2. Why is water such an important nutrient? What does it do in your body?

The Food Guide Pyramid

Health experts recommend using the **Food Guide Pyramid** as an outline of what to eat each day. It is based on the Dietary Guidelines for Americans. It helps you select the right foods for a balanced diet. A **balanced diet** is one that provides all the nutrients your body needs for good health.

The Food Guide Pyramid divides commonly eaten foods into groups. See 7-7. The foods in each of these groups have certain nutrients in common.

The Food Guide Pyramid can be used by people of all ages. When planning meals, use it to select the suggested amounts of food from each group. Then you can adjust the amounts needed by family members who have other nutritional needs. Children, teens, pregnant women, and older people have other needs. By following the Food Guide Pyramid, your entire family's nutritional needs can be met.

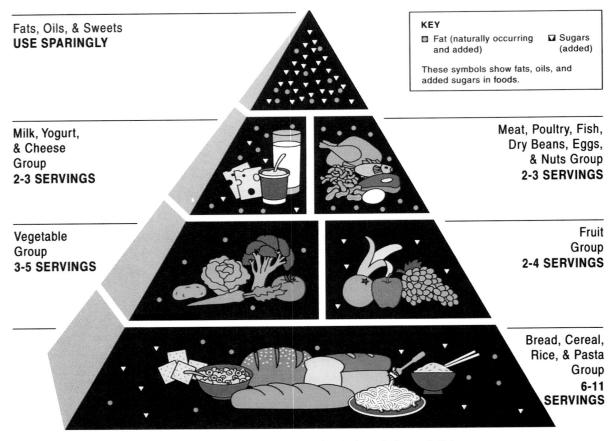

KEY

☐ Fat (naturally occurring and added) ☑ Sugars (added)

These symbols show fats, oils, and added sugars in foods.

Fats, Oils, & Sweets
USE SPARINGLY

Milk, Yogurt, & Cheese Group
2-3 SERVINGS

Meat, Poultry, Fish, Dry Beans, Eggs, & Nuts Group
2-3 SERVINGS

Vegetable Group
3-5 SERVINGS

Fruit Group
2-4 SERVINGS

Bread, Cereal, Rice, & Pasta Group
6-11 SERVINGS

7-7 The Food Guide Pyramid will help you select the right foods for a balanced diet.

✓ **Check What You Have Learned**

1. What do the foods in each food group in the Food Guide Pyramid have in common?
2. How can you make sure the nutritional needs of each family member are met?

The Bread, Cereal, Rice, and Pasta Group

The bottom of the Pyramid represents the *bread, cereal, rice, and pasta group.* See 7-8. Foods in this group are made from grains, such as wheat, oats, corn, rice, and barley. These foods are good sources of carbohydrates and the B vitamins. Protein and iron can also be found in many grain products.

Read labels on breads and cereals to look for those that are whole grain or enriched. *Whole grain*

products provide fiber that aids in digestion and getting rid of body wastes. **Enriched** products have nutrients added to them to replace those removed during processing.

This is the largest section of the Pyramid to remind you that you need the most daily servings from this group. A serving equals one slice of bread, one ounce of ready-to-eat cereal, or one-half cup of cooked cereal, rice, or pasta. Teenage girls need 9 servings from this group each day. Most teenage boys need 11 servings daily.

Bread, Cereal, Rice, & Pasta Group
6-11 SERVINGS

7-8   Breads, cereals, rice, and pasta make up the largest group in the Pyramid.

✓ **Check What You Have Learned**

1. Which nutrients are found in foods from the bread, cereal, rice, and pasta group?
2. Why are whole grain and enriched bread and cereal products good for you?

The Vegetable Group and the Fruit Group

The next level of the Pyramid is made up of two groups of plant foods. See 7-9. The *vegetable group* includes raw and cooked vegetables and vegetable juices. A cup of raw leafy vegetables counts as a serving. One-half cup of cooked vegetables or three-fourths cup of juice is also a serving. Teenage girls need four servings from this group daily. Teenage boys should eat five daily servings.

Beside the vegetable group is the *fruit group*. Foods in this group include fresh, canned, frozen, and dried fruits and fruit juices. Three servings per day should meet the needs of most teenage girls. Four servings per day are recommended for teenage boys. A serving is a medium-sized piece of fresh fruit. One-half cup of cooked or canned fruit or three-fourths cup of juice also counts as a serving.

Fruits and vegetables are good sources of vitamins, minerals, and carbohydrates. Two important vitamins provided by fruits and vegetables are vitamins A and C. It is easy to remember which vegetables contain vitamin A by their color. Both dark green and deep yellow or orange vegetables are rich in vitamin A. Deep yellow or orange fruits contain vitamin A. Spinach, winter squash, and apricots are good sources of vitamin A. The fruits richest in vitamin C are the citrus fruits, such as oranges and grapefruit. Strawberries, cabbage, and tomatoes also contain vitamin C.

Vegetable Group
3-5 SERVINGS

Fruit Group
2-4 SERVINGS

7-9   You need to eat a variety of fruits and vegetables daily.

The Milk, Yogurt, and Cheese Group

The two food groups on the next level of the Food Guide Pyramid come mostly from animal sources. See 7-10. The *milk, yogurt, and cheese group* includes foods that are good sources of vitamins and protein. These foods are also rich in minerals, especially calcium.

These foods are extra important when your body is growing. When children do not get enough calcium in their diets, their bones may be weak or misshapen. Older people who didn't get enough calcium when they were young may also have problems. Their bones may break easily and mend slowly.

Teenagers, both boys and girls, need three servings from this group daily. A serving is one cup of milk or yogurt. One and one-half ounces of natural cheese or two ounces of process cheese also equals one serving.

Milk, Yogurt,
& Cheese
Group
2-3 SERVINGS

Meat, Poultry, Fish,
Dry Beans, Eggs,
& Nuts Group
2-3 SERVINGS

7-10 Foods from these two groups provide rich sources of protein, vitamins, and minerals.

The Meat, Poultry, Fish, Dry Beans, Eggs, and Nuts Group

The *meat, poultry, fish, dry beans, eggs, and nuts group* contains a variety of protein-rich foods. Look again at 7-10. These foods also provide B vitamins and iron. Teens need two to three daily servings from this group. Together, these servings should equal six ounces of cooked lean meat for girls and seven ounces for boys. One-half cup of cooked dry beans, one egg, or two tablespoons of peanut butter equals one ounce of cooked meat.

Protein foods are divided into two main groups. Animal sources of protein are called *complete proteins.* Most plant sources of protein, such as nuts and dry beans, are called *incomplete proteins.* They need to be combined with certain other foods to make complete proteins. A balance of complete and incomplete proteins will provide your body with the nutrients it needs.

Many foods in this group are also rich sources of iron. Iron is an important part of blood. It helps your blood carry oxygen to all the cells in your body. If you don't eat foods that supply iron, your body will not get enough oxygen.

✓ Check What You Have Learned

1. What nutrients are provided by meat, poultry, fish, dry beans, eggs, and nuts?
2. Why is getting enough iron from the foods you eat important?

Fats, Oils, and Sweets

At the tip of the Pyramid, you will find *fats, oils, and sweets.* Such foods include butter, margarine, salad dressing, candies, syrups, soft drinks, and sweet desserts, 7-11. These foods provide little more than calories in the diet. The small size of this area in the Pyramid should remind you to use these foods sparingly.

Note that foods in all parts of the Pyramid can contain fat and added sugars. For instance, two pancakes from the bread group contain three grams of fat. Flavored yogurt from the milk group may contain about eight teaspoons of added sugar. One ounce of peanuts from the meat group contains 14 grams of fat. You need to carefully choose foods from each group to limit fat and sugar in your diet.

When planning meals, choose foods from the five main groups first. If you need more calories in your diet, select extra servings from these groups.

7-11 Limit fats, oils, and sweets from the tip of the Pyramid.

✓ Check What You Have Learned

1. Why should you avoid eating too many fats, oils, and sweets?
2. Which foods should you add to your diet if you need more calories?

Meals to Meet Your Needs

When counting servings, think about portion sizes. A large portion counts as more than one serving. For instance, a dinner portion of spaghetti may count as three servings of pasta. Suppose you eat two slices of bread with your spaghetti. This would equal nearly half your bread and cereal servings in a single meal.

Remember that snacks can also help meet your daily serving requirements. Save chips and cookies for a special treat. Choose nutritious snack foods most of the time. Fruit, carrot sticks, yogurt, and peanut butter sandwiches are all healthful snack choices. See 7-12.

Daily Menu			
Breakfast	cereal with milk 2 pieces toast orange juice	**Snack**	peanut butter sandwich
Snack	carrot sticks yogurt	**Dinner**	baked chicken breast rice green beans tossed salad 2 dinner rolls spiced peaches milk
Lunch	ham sandwich baked beans coleslaw apple milk	**Snack**	banana popcorn

7-12 This menu includes the recommended number of daily servings from the Food Guide Pyramid for a teenage boy.

✔ Check What You Have Learned

1. Why should you think about portion sizes when counting servings?
2. What are three nutritious foods you could eat as snacks?

The Main Ideas

You need food to grow, develop, and be healthy. Your diet can provide your body with the nutrients it needs to function well. The Food Guide Pyramid is based on the Dietary Guidelines for Americans. It can help you choose foods you need each day for a balanced diet. It divides foods into groups that have certain nutrients in common. They are bread, cereal, rice, and pasta; vegetables; fruits; milk, yogurt, and cheese; meat, poultry, fish, dry beans, eggs, and nuts; and fats, oils, and sweets.

Apply What You Have Learned

1. Clip food and nutrition articles from newspapers and magazines. Place them in a nutrition notebook. Add articles throughout your school years. Reread them from time to time. Compare what they say with your study of nutrition.
2. List all the foods you ate yesterday for breakfast, lunch, dinner, and snacks. Note how much of each food you ate. Then check the Food Guide Pyramid to see if your diet included the recommended number of servings from each group.

Lesson 7-3
Managing Your Weight

Objectives

After studying this lesson, you will be able to

➡ *define* energy, calories, appetite, anorexia nervosa, *and* bulimia.

➡ *explain why your body needs calories.*

➡ *describe how calories, body weight, and exercise are related.*

➡ *give examples of good ways to manage your weight.*

New Words

energy: *the capacity for doing work.*

calories: *units of energy provided by proteins, carbohydrates, and fats.*

appetite: *the desire to eat.*

anorexia nervosa: *an eating disorder in which people starve themselves.*

bulimia: *an eating disorder in which people eat large amounts of food and then purge themselves of the food.*

New Ideas

➡ *Your body needs calories to work, play, grow, and be healthy.*

➡ *The amount of calories you take in and your body weight are related.*

➡ *A good way to manage your weight is to exercise and eat the proper amounts of nutritious foods.*

Most teens want to look and feel their best. When you look at yourself in the mirror, you may be concerned about your size and shape. You may think that you should gain or lose a few pounds. You may want to stay the way you are. This can be done if you learn to manage your weight.

Calories

Energy is the capacity for doing work. The energy you get from food helps you stay alive, work, play, grow, and be healthy. **Calories** are units of energy provided by proteins, carbohydrates, and fats. For instance, an orange has around 60 calories. This means it will supply your body with this much energy. You need to eat a certain number of calories each day. They provide your body with the energy it needs to function. Your body also needs energy to walk, sit, exercise, and perform other tasks.

You need to learn about calories. You should find out how many calories you need. This amount depends on your age, sex, body size, and level of activity. See 7-13. Level of activity refers to how much exercise you get. Exercise helps you use calories.

You should also find out how many calories are in the foods you eat. Some cookbooks and nutrition books have calorie charts. Ask your teacher or librarian to help you find this information.

7-13 Your body needs more calories to play stickball than it does to watch TV.

✓ **Check What You Have Learned**

1. Why might you and your friends have different calorie needs?
2. How can you find out how many calories are in your favorite foods?

Calories and Weight

Your diet provides your body with the calories it needs. If you eat a balanced diet and do not have a weight problem, you are probably eating the right number of calories. This means you use all the calories you take in from the foods you eat.

When your body uses fewer calories than you take in, you gain weight. The extra calories are turned into fat and stored by your body. When you take in fewer calories than your body needs, you lose weight. Your body uses the stored fat for energy.

To lose weight, you have to reduce the calories you take in. A good rule to follow is "cut down, not out." You can still eat many of the foods you like, but in smaller amounts. It's the total number of calories you eat each day that affects your weight.

Foods in the fats, oils, and sweets group contain very few nutrients. Choose foods from the other five groups when selecting what you eat.

Your **appetite**, or desire to eat, may be a good guide to how much food you need. However, it may not guide you to the kinds of food you need. If you have been eating second helpings, eat only one instead. Choose healthful snacks between meals. Fruit and skim milk are good choices.

To gain weight, you need to take in more calories than your body uses. Once again, use the food groups as a guide. Try eating more foods from each of these groups. Sometimes, it may be hard to eat a lot at one meal. Instead, try eating several small meals throughout the day. Also, be sure to get plenty of rest.

If you want to lose or gain weight, talk to a dietitian, doctor, or school nurse. Follow the advice you are given. You may be told to change your diet and eating habits. You might have to learn how to count calories. See 7-14.

Do not try crash or fad diets. (These are the kind that tell you that you will lose a lot of weight fast.) They usually do not include enough of the right kinds of food. They can be harmful to your health. Instead, when planning a diet, remember to

- Choose foods from the five main groups in the Food Guide Pyramid.
- Eat regular meals.
- Eat a variety of foods.
- Choose lower calorie foods and eat smaller amounts to lose weight.
- Choose nutritious higher calorie foods and eat larger amounts to gain weight.
- Avoid fats, oils, and sweets.

Some teens, mostly girls, have abnormal eating patterns known as *eating disorders*. People with one common eating disorder, **anorexia nervosa,** starve themselves. These people have a strong fear of being overweight. They also have a warped body image. They may see themselves as fat when they are really skin and bones.

Another eating disorder, **bulimia,** involves bingeing and purging. *Bingeing* means eating large amounts of food in a short time. *Purging* means getting rid of the unwanted food by vomiting or taking laxatives. People with bulimia often are suffering from emotional stress.

Anorexia nervosa and bulimia are grave health conditions. Early treatment helps improve chances of getting better. A physician, a psychiatrist, and a dietitian may work together to provide care. They treat the emotional and physical sides of the disorders.

7-14 A calorie guide can help you find out how many calories are in the foods you choose.

✔ Check What You Have Learned

1. How does the statement "cut down, not out" apply to losing weight?
2. Why shouldn't you go on a crash or fad diet to try to lose weight?
3. What helps improve chances of recovering from an eating disorder?

Calories and Exercise

One way to manage your weight is to exercise daily. Exercise can help you lose weight by increasing the calories you use. Walking, bicycling, jogging, and swimming are all good forms of exercise. Nutritionists, doctors, or school nurses can help you plan a diet and exercise program.

If you exercise regularly, your body will use up extra calories. Exercise can also keep your muscles in good shape. See 7-15. This helps you look good and feel energetic.

If you want to gain weight, exercise can also play a part. It can help you build well-toned muscles. Exercise may help increase your appetite and improve how you feel.

When you start a new exercise program, take it easy. Work up to more exercise slowly. If you are not careful, you may damage your muscles. If you have health problems, check with your doctor before you start exercising.

7-15 Aerobics can tone your muscles and help you manage your weight.

✔ Check What You Have Learned

1. How can exercising regularly help you manage your weight?
2. Why should you start slowly when you begin a new exercise program?

💡 The Main Ideas

Calories are units of energy in food. You should learn about calories because they can make a difference in your weight and health. If you take in more calories than your body needs, you gain weight. If you take in fewer calories than your body needs, you lose weight. Nutritionists, doctors, or school nurses can help you plan diet and exercise programs to manage your weight.

⫸ Apply What You Have Learned

1. Keep a record of all the foods you eat in one day. Use a calorie chart to find out how many calories were in each food. Then ask your teacher to help you figure out how many calories you should have each day. Compare this number with the number of calories you actually take in. This can tell you if you need to eat more or less to manage your weight.
2. Look at the six points to remember when planning a diet. In small groups, choose one that looks like it may be hard to follow. Then brainstorm ideas for making it easier to follow. You may want to also brainstorm ideas for other points that look hard to follow.

Case Study

Read the story below and look at Lesson 7-3 again.
Then answer the questions below.

Eating Healthy

Simeon and Maurice are cochairs of the planning committee for the youth center spring picnic. They are having a meeting with their committee members, Nadine and Lanita. The group is discussing what kinds of foods it wants to serve at the picnic.

"It seems like a lot of people these days want to eat healthier foods," said Simeon. "They don't want to eat a lot of high-calorie foods like potato chips and cookies."

"I think that's true, too," said Maurice. "Let's try to serve foods from the five main food groups. We should try to stay away from foods in the fats, oils, and sweets group."

"I'll bring a vegetable tray," said Nadine. "I have a really good recipe for yogurt dip, too. It has less calories than dip made with sour cream."

"Instead of hot dogs and hamburgers, we should serve chicken as the meat," said Simeon.

Lanita said, "That's a good idea. I'll bring whole wheat rolls and buns."

"For dessert, we can have frozen yogurt," said Nadine. "It'll be better for us than ice cream. We can also serve watermelon and other fresh fruits."

"We can also serve fruit juices to drink," said Maurice.

To Discuss

1. How do the foods the committee chose to serve meet the need for healthier foods?
2. How do you think the students at the youth center will react to the healthy foods served at the picnic? What can be done to make this a positive change?
3. Besides serving nutritious foods, how else can the committee promote good health at the picnic?
4. How many of the food groups from the Food Guide Pyramid are represented in their menu plans?

Topic 7 Review

Topic Summary

Food plays many different roles in your life. Special events usually include food. Families often eat traditional foods on holidays. You may enjoy having something to eat when you are with your friends. In the United States, the foods you choose to eat can come from many different cultures.

Following the Dietary Guidelines for Americans can help you make healthy food choices and decrease your chances of getting certain diseases. The foods and beverages you consume each day provide your body with the nutrients it needs to function. The Food Guide Pyramid divides foods into five main groups. They are bread, cereal, rice, and pasta; vegetables; fruits; milk, yogurt, and cheese; and meat, poultry, fish, dry beans, eggs, and nuts. Your daily meals and snacks should include the recommended number of servings from these groups. At the tip of the Pyramid are fats, oils, and sweets, which you should use sparingly.

Knowing how many calories are in food can help you manage your weight. To lose weight, you need to take in fewer calories than your body needs. To gain weight, you need to take in more calories than your body needs. Be aware of eating disorders, which can seriously harm your health.

Exercise can help you manage your weight. Choose a type of exercise you enjoy and will do often. Nutritionists, doctors, or school nurses can help you plan diet and exercise programs.

To Review

Write your answers on a separate sheet of paper.

1. Give an example of how food can be a part of family traditions.
2. Give the name of a food you associate with the following events:
   a. Birthday party.
   b. Wedding reception.
   c. Prom.
   d. Thanksgiving.
3. Give three examples of cultural foods that can be found in the United States.
4. A(n) _____ is the food and beverages you consume each day.
5. True or false. Eating the right foods can give you the energy you need for learning.
6. List the seven Dietary Guidelines for Americans.
7. Name the six types of nutrients and list five food sources for each.

8. A diet that provides all the nutrients your body needs for good health is a(n) _____ diet.
9. List the six food groups in the Food Guide Pyramid and the suggested number of servings for teens from each group.
10. (Enriched/Whole grain) breads have nutrients added to replace those removed during processing.
11. True or false. Butter and margarine are in the milk and milk products group.
12. True or false. Snacks can help meet daily serving requirements from the Food Guide Pyramid.
13. How can you determine the number of calories you need each day?
14. True or false. All teens need the same number of calories each day.
15. Give examples of how a person can lose weight.
16. How can a person gain weight?

Vocabulary Quiz

Match the definitions in Column A with the terms in Column B.
Write your answers on a separate sheet of paper.

Column A

1. The study of how your body uses food.
2. Seven guidelines for a healthful diet.
3. The capacity for doing work.
4. The desire to eat.
5. A nutrition guide that helps you choose foods that provide you with needed nutrients.
6. Customs passed from one generation to another.
7. An eating disorder in which people starve themselves.
8. A fatty substance found in foods from animal sources.
9. Units of energy provided by proteins, carbohydrates, and fats.
10. The beliefs and customs of a certain racial, religious, or social group.
11. Chemical substances from foods needed for the body to function.
12. A fat that is solid at room temperature.

Column B

a. Nutrition.
b. Cholesterol.
c. Nutrients.
d. Calories.
e. Anorexia nervosa.
f. Food Guide Pyramid.
g. Energy.
h. Traditions.
i. Saturated.
j. Culture.
k. Bulimia.
l. Appetite.
m. Dietary Guidelines for Americans.

Planning menus before shopping can help you make wise selections at the grocery store.

Lesson 8-1
Planning Menus

Objectives

After studying this lesson, you will be able to

⟹ *define menu, meal patterns, course, and appetizer.*

⟹ *give examples of meal patterns.*

⟹ *plan menus that include foods your family will like.*

⟹ *plan menus that are nutritious and attractive.*

New Words

menu: *a list of foods to be prepared and served.*

meal patterns: *guides for planning menus.*

course: *all the foods served as one part of a meal.*

appetizer: *small, light food served before a meal.*

New Ideas

⟹ *Meal patterns can help you achieve nutrition goals.*

⟹ *You should think about your family's likes and dislikes when planning menus.*

⟹ *Nutrition and the appearance and taste of food should be considered when planning menus.*

People like different foods. There are many reasons for this. They include taste, variety, convenience, cost, and nutrition. When planning menus, these factors should be considered. A **menu** is a list of foods to be prepared and served. When planning menus for your family, you need to keep your culture and family customs in mind.

Daily Meal Patterns

Meal patterns are guides for planning menus. Choose meal patterns that meet your family's nutritional needs. See 8-1. Choose nutrient-rich foods from the Food Guide Pyramid. The size of

Daily Meal Patterns	
Breakfast:	Fruit
	Cereal or bread
	Beverage
Lunch or supper:	Soup or salad
	Sandwich or casserole
	Fruit or dessert
	Beverage
Dinner:	Main course
	Salad and/or vegetables
	Bread
	Dessert
	Beverage

8-1 Using meal patterns can make menu planning easier.

your servings depends upon your calorie needs. Three common meal patterns are discussed here. You can use these as a guide for planning other menus.

Breakfast provides nutrients and energy to start the day. You should take in about one-fourth to one-third of the nutrients and calories you need for the day. A common breakfast pattern is fruit, cereal or bread, and beverage.

Lunch is eaten at midday. Supper is eaten in the evening. Lunch and supper follow the same meal pattern. These meals provide about one-fourth to one-third of the food you need each day. A common lunch or supper pattern is soup or salad, sandwich or casserole, fruit or dessert, and beverage.

Dinner is a heavy meal eaten at noon or in the evening. It is the meal that people most often share with their family and friends. Dinner may be plain or fancy. Special events often call for special dinners.

Healthy dinners include foods from the Food Guide Pyramid. Dinner should provide about one-third of the calories for the day. The normal dinner pattern is a main course, salad, bread, dessert, and beverage.

In all meal patterns, especially dinner, food may be served in courses. A **course** is all the foods served as one part of a meal. For instance, the main course includes the meat or meat alternate dish. A vegetable and rice or pasta might also be part of the main course. Sometimes a light food, such as soup or juice, is served before the meal. This food is supposed to stimulate the appetite. This first course is called an **appetizer.**

✓ Check What You Have Learned

1. What is the difference between supper and dinner? What kinds of foods do you eat at these meals?
2. What dishes may be included in the main course of a dinner?

Planning Pointers

Keeping certain points in mind can help you plan any meal. These points include your family's food likes and dislikes, variety, and nutrition.

The foods you serve will be based on your family's likes and dislikes. Their likes may be affected by your culture and family customs. Taste, convenience, and cost may also affect which foods they enjoy. See 8-2.

Serving new foods can add variety to meals. You can help your family try new foods along with old family favorites. You might want them to try new foods you've had at a friend's home or when eating out. Some of these new foods may soon join the list of favorites.

8-2 A waffle with fruit and milk may be a favorite family breakfast.

You also need to keep nutrition in mind when planning meals. The kinds and amounts of food people need depend on their age, health, work, and activities. Babies need foods to help them grow. Sick people need food to get well. Active people need more food than those who are less active. If you plan carefully, menus can meet the whole family's nutritional needs.

Family members need food energy throughout the day. This means they should eat balanced meals at set times during the day. Follow the Food Guide Pyramid when you plan menus. It tells you what foods need to be included each day. Skipping an important meal, such as breakfast, can make it harder for family members to function at their best.

✓ **Check What You Have Learned**

1. What factors can affect the foods your family chooses?
2. Why do you need to keep nutrition in mind when planning meals?

Appearance and Taste

The appearance and taste of food often affects whether or not it is eaten. When you plan menus that look and taste good, your family will eat them.

When planning a menu, ask yourself if the foods look good together. Foods that are all the same color are not appealing. See 8-3. They should have a variety of colors to be interesting.

The shape of food also makes a difference. Think about how it looks on a plate. A variety of shapes can make a meal more appealing.

Think about the flavors of foods when planning menus. There are many foods that taste better when eaten with other foods. Often, highly seasoned, strong-tasting foods should be eaten with mild-tasting foods. This makes each food taste more enjoyable. For instance, spicy chili may be served with mild cornbread.

You also need to think about the textures and temperatures of foods. Avoid serving too many soft or crisp foods in the same meal. A grilled cheese sandwich mixes both soft and crisp textures. Serve

hot and cold foods at the same meal for variety and interest. Soup with a green salad is a good example. See 8-4.

8-3 Meals with many colors are more attractive than those with similar colors.

8-4 This breakfast includes foods that add variety in color, temperature, and texture.

The Main Ideas

Meal patterns are guides to use when planning menus. Menus should be planned according to family food choices and nutritional needs. When you plan menus, be sure to follow the Dietary Guidelines for Americans and the Food Guide Pyramid.

Apply What You Have Learned

1. Make a list of your family's favorite foods. Compare this list with others in the class. Discuss how you and your family can learn to like new foods.
2. Get a copy of a lunch menu from your school cafeteria and one from a fast-food restaurant. Compare the foods they include. Think about the nutrient content of the foods. Think about how they are alike and how they are different. Then decide which menu is the most nutritious.
3. Plan nutritious, appealing meals for three days. Be sure to follow the Dietary Guidelines for Americans. Also, follow the Food Guide Pyramid for the suggested number of servings each day. Make drawings showing how you will use color and shape when planning these meals.

Lesson 8-2
You—A Food Shopper

Objectives

After studying this lesson, you will be able to

- *define shortage, label, universal product code, nutrition label, and Daily Value.*
- *explain what affects the cost of food.*
- *give examples of how to be a skillful shopper.*
- *describe three types of food stores.*
- *discuss how information on food labels can be used by shoppers.*

New Words

shortage: *a condition in which there's not enough to go around.*

label: *a small piece of paper, fabric, or plastic attached to a product that gives information about the product.*

universal product code: *a group of bars and numbers found on packages. This code provides pricing and other product information to a computer scanner.*

nutrition label: *a panel on a food product package with information about the nutrients the food contains.*

Daily Value: *reference figures on food labels that help consumers see how food products fit into a total diet.*

New Ideas

- *You can learn skills to become a better food shopper.*
- *There are many factors that affect food costs.*

- *Different types of stores offer different services that may affect food prices.*
- *Food labels include information that can help consumers make wise food purchases.*

As a food shopper, you have power. When you shop, you can decide how much you want to spend for food. You can also choose where and when you will shop. You can use package labels to help you make wise food choices.

You need to be aware of outside pressures that affect your food buying decisions. Your peers may introduce you to food products they enjoy. Advertisements on TV and radio and in magazines and newspapers might persuade you to try new products. Developing the shopping skills discussed in this lesson will help you avoid these pressures. You can learn to use peers and advertisements as sources of information. However, you will resist the urge to buy foods that are not right for you and your family.

The Shopping Game

Shopping can be like a game. You play to win. There are three stages in this game. The first stage is to decide how much to spend and what to buy. Your food budget will be based on your income and what your other expenses are. Your shopping list will be based on your menu plans. Your menu plans should include only foods you can afford to buy.

The second stage is to decide where to shop. Your choice of stores will be based on several factors. Perhaps you'll choose a store that is close to you. You may choose a store that has low prices. You might select a store that offers a wide range of products.

The third stage is to decide when to shop. You might pick a time when the stores aren't crowded. You might want to shop when you don't have much extra time. You should also shop at a time when you are not hungry. These last two hints will help you avoid browsing and picking up extra items.

The more you play a game, the more skilled you become. You begin to win more often. Shopping for food often helps you learn to make better choices. There are many skills you can learn to become better at the food shopping game. This lesson will teach you some of them.

✔ **Check What You Have Learned**

1. What are the three stages in the food shopping game? How can they help you be a better shopper?
2. Why should you shop at a time when you are not hungry?

Food Costs

The cost of food affects how much you buy with the money you decide to spend. A number of factors affect food costs. Being aware of these factors can help you get the most from your food dollar.

The amount of food available affects food costs. When food is plentiful, there is enough or more than enough to go around. It costs less than when there is a shortage. See 8-5. A **shortage** means there is not enough to go around. When there are shortages, food prices go up.

The season of the year can affect food costs. In some parts of the country, fresh fruits and vegetables can be grown only part of the year. Some fruits and vegetables can't be grown at all. This means they must be shipped in from other parts of the country and from other countries. Shipping adds to the cost of food.

How foods are sold and who makes them are factors in the cost. Fresh, frozen, and canned foods have different prices. Larger packages may be better values than small packages. Store brands may be better buys than name brands. Comparing prices of food items will help you get the best brands.

8-5 The price of fresh fruits and vegetables depends on the season.

You should learn to get the most nutritious food for your money. Foods can be high in nutrients, and yet low in cost. For instance, spinach, liver, canned tuna, lowfat milk, eggs, and carrots are good nutritional buys.

✓ Check What You Have Learned

1. What are three factors that affect food prices? How do shortages affect food prices?
2. Why do fruits and vegetables need to be shipped to certain parts of the country?

Making a Shopping List

Having a shopping list can help you control food costs. When making a list, include only the items you need. Then buy only what is on the list. If you follow the list, you will not have to make extra shopping trips. When you make fewer trips to the store, you spend less money. Shopping lists also help prevent impulse buying.

Making a shopping list can also save you time. If you only shop in one store, you can list the foods in the order they are found in the store. This helps you avoid retracing your steps.

It is easy to make a shopping list at the same time you plan menus. When you plan menus several days in advance, include in your shopping list the foods you need for those menus. You can develop a routine for planning and making a shopping list. The steps in this routine are the following:

1. Write menus for several days at a time.
2. Check the foods you already have.
3. Write down what you need to buy.
4. Take your shopping list with you to the store.

✓ Check What You Have Learned

1. How can making a shopping list help you spend less money?
2. What are the steps in the routine for planning and making a shopping list?

Deciding Where to Shop

Supermarkets, specialty food stores, and convenience stores are three types of food stores. You can also find food for sale at outdoor markets and food co-ops. See 8-6. Compare the prices, quality, and variety of foods in each type of store.

Where you shop can affect the price of food. If you have shopped in different stores, you may have noticed that foods are not always priced the same. Prices vary because stores pay different prices for the food they buy. The services they offer also affect prices.

Supermarkets are large stores that offer a wide variety of foods. They are often part of a chain that lets them buy food in large amounts. This means they pay lower prices for food. The price they pay affects what you pay.

8-6 Some farmers sell fruit, such as strawberries, to customers who pick their own.

Specialty food stores offer one type of food such as baked goods, meats, or imported products. The prices are often high. However, many shoppers think that the freshness and high quality of the food is worth the cost.

Convenience stores are often small and stay open longer hours than other stores. They offer less variety, and their prices are often high. When stores buy in small amounts, they pay higher prices. If they are part of a chain, their prices may be lower.

Each type of store has different services to offer. For instance, some may carry the groceries to your car. Others deliver them to your home. Some have bakeries or delis. See 8-7. Some offer lower prices for buying large amounts. Some stay open later than others. A store may offer all of these services. However, stores often specialize in a few services. Each service has costs that are passed along to you through food prices.

You may have certain reasons for choosing one store over another. Your decision about where to shop should depend on prices, services offered, and the location of the store. Wherever you shop, get to know the store. The list below tells you what to look for in a good store.

- Fresh, clean fruits, vegetables, and meats.
- Well-packaged foods with prices clearly marked.
- Clean, airy surroundings with good lighting.
- Clean, polite clerks who handle food carefully.
- Well-organized display counters.
- State- or city-inspected and approved store conditions.

8-7 Special departments, such as this sausage kitchen, attract customers to some stores.

✔ Check What You Have Learned

1. How can the type of store you shop at affect the price of the food?
2. What are the qualities of a good food store? What other qualities do you look for?

Nutrition Labeling

Be sure to read the labels on packages. A **label** is a small piece of paper, fabric, or plastic attached to a product that gives information about the product. Labels must include the name and form of the food. The manufacturer's name and address and the weight must also be included, as well as a list of ingredients. See 8-8.

A **nutrition label** is a panel on a food product package with information about the nutrients the food contains. See 8-9. It can help you see how a certain food fits into your total daily diet.

Nutrition labels are required to appear on nearly all food packages. They are also required to include certain kinds of information. Information is listed under the heading "Nutrition Facts." The first item found under the heading is the *serving size*. This is the amount that a person would normally eat. Similar products have the same serving size. This allows you to easily compare products. Serving sizes are given in both household and metric measurements.

Following the serving size is *servings per container*. This is the number of portions that are in the food package.

Calorie information appears next. The number of calories in one serving of the food is stated. The number of those calories that come from fat is also given. This can help you limit fat to no more than 30 percent of your total calories.

The next type of information is a list of *dietary components*. This is a list of nutrients found in each serving of the food product. The list includes total fat, saturated fat, cholesterol, sodium, total carbohydrate, dietary fiber, sugars, and protein. Vitamin A, vitamin C, calcium, and iron are also listed. Some food products may list other nutrients as well.

Beside the dietary components, *percent Daily Values* are given. **Daily Values** are reference figures on food labels that help consumers see how food products fit into a total diet. At the bottom of the nutrition label is a *reference of Daily Values*. This information is the same on every nutrition label. It shows the greatest amount of fat, saturated

8-8 Be sure to read the information on packages to help you learn about a product before you purchase it.

fat, cholesterol, and sodium most people should consume each day. It also shows the smallest amount of total carbohydrate and dietary fiber people should consume. Daily Values are given for two calorie levels: 2,000 and 2,500.

The percent Daily Values on nutrition labels are based on a 2,000-calorie diet. Most teens need more than 2,000 calories per day. Therefore, their Daily Values are higher. The percent of their Daily Values met by a food product is lower than figures shown on the label. For instance, the Daily Value for total fat for a 2,000-calorie diet is 65 grams. If you need 2,800 calories per day, you can consume up to 93 grams of total fat. Suppose a food contains 13 grams of fat per serving. It will show 20 percent of the Daily Value for fat on the label. However, this food would provide only 14 percent of *your* Daily Value for fat.

At the bottom of the label is a *conversion guide*. This can help you figure how many calories in a food come from carbohydrate and protein.

Some food products may carry a simpler version of the nutrition label. All manufacturers must follow labeling guidelines set by the Food and Drug Administration. Make it a habit to read labels as you shop.

Nutrition Label

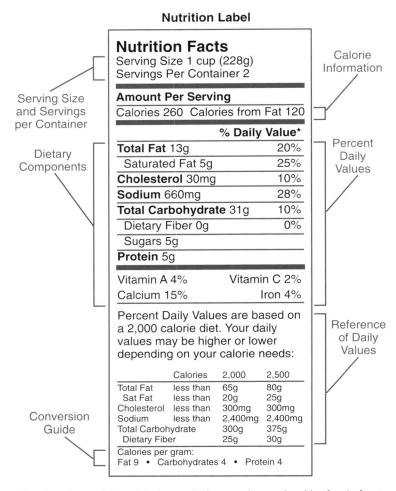

Serving Size and Servings per Container

Dietary Components

Conversion Guide

Calorie Information

Percent Daily Values

Reference of Daily Values

Nutrition Facts
Serving Size 1 cup (228g)
Servings Per Container 2

Amount Per Serving

Calories 260   Calories from Fat 120

% Daily Value*

Total Fat 13g	20%
Saturated Fat 5g	25%
Cholesterol 30mg	10%
Sodium 660mg	28%
Total Carbohydrate 31g	10%
Dietary Fiber 0g	0%
Sugars 5g	
Protein 5g	

Vitamin A 4%	Vitamin C 2%
Calcium 15%	Iron 4%

Percent Daily Values are based on a 2,000 calorie diet. Your daily values may be higher or lower depending on your calorie needs:

		Calories	2,000	2,500
Total Fat	less than		65g	80g
Sat Fat	less than		20g	25g
Cholesterol	less than		300mg	300mg
Sodium	less than		2,400mg	2,400mg
Total Carbohydrate			300g	375g
Dietary Fiber			25g	30g

Calories per gram:
Fat 9 • Carbohydrates 4 • Protein 4

8-9   Reading nutrition labels can help you choose healthy foods for a balanced diet.

Many food packages have a group of bars and numbers on them. This is the **universal product code (UPC).** It provides pricing and other product information to a computer scanner. Each product has its very own code. Some stores have computerized checkout equipment that reads the code and rings up the sale. This also tells the store manager how much of that item is on hand. The manager knows how fast items are being sold and when and how much to order.

The Main Ideas

Learning about food pricing and packaging can help you be a more skillful shopper. Several factors determine the cost of food. They include how plentiful food is, how it is packaged, and where it is purchased. You should make shopping lists at the same time you plan menus. This saves time and money. Labels give you information about the foods you are buying. Using the information on nutrition labels will help you eat a balanced diet.

⫸ Apply What You Have Learned

1. Look at food ads in magazines and newspapers and on TV. Identify which ones attract your attention and which ones don't. In small groups discuss how these ads were able to attract your attention.
2. Plan two menus for your family. Check the foods you have on hand. Then make a shopping list for the menus, showing which foods you need to buy.
3. Observe five people shopping for food. See if they use a shopping list, comparison shop, or read labels. Put this information in chart form. Then compare to see who is the best shopper. Discuss this with the class.
4. Compare the nutrition labels on two similar food products. Write a brief summary stating which product you would choose based on the label information. Be sure to give reasons for your choice.

Topic 8 Planning Meals

Lesson 8-3
Buying and Storing Food

Objectives

After studying this lesson, you will be able to

➡ *define* produce, ripe, pasteurization, *and* homogenization.

➡ *tell what to look for when buying various types of foods.*

➡ *describe how to properly store foods to preserve their goodness.*

New Words

produce: *fresh fruits and vegetables.*

ripe: *fully grown and developed.*

pasteurization: *a process where milk and milk products are heated to destroy harmful bacteria.*

homogenization: *a process where milk fat is broken into tiny pieces and spread throughout the milk.*

New Ideas

➡ *You can learn how to buy good quality foods.*

➡ *Storing foods carefully protects quality, nutrients, flavor, and freshness.*

You need to shop carefully for good quality foods. Once you buy food, you need to store it as well as possible. This helps protect its nutrients, quality, flavor, and freshness. When shopping for quality, you need to look at different factors for different foods. The type of food also makes a difference in how it is stored.

Buying and Storing Fruits and Vegetables

Fresh fruits and vegetables are called **produce.** Buy produce from a store or market where many fresh fruits and vegetables are sold. They are more likely to be fresh. Try to buy produce "in season" whenever possible. That is the time of year when a new crop is being harvested. Produce is freshest at this time. Handle produce carefully when choosing it. If you squeeze or pinch produce, it can bruise easily.

Choose produce that looks tasty. How ripe produce is makes a difference in its taste. **Ripe** means fully grown or developed. A fully ripened tomato tastes better than an unripe one. The signs of ripe produce are good color and a firm texture that yields slightly to gently pressure. If you buy unripe produce, keep it at room temperature until it ripens. Then store it in the refrigerator. See 8-10.

Wash produce carefully before storing it. Use cold water and a vegetable brush to get rid of dirt.

To keep produce fresh and crisp, drain and store it in plastic bags or covered containers in the refrigerator. If you store it in water, it will lose nutrients. Do not wash berries until you are ready to eat them. Store them loosely covered in the refrigerator. Some vegetables, such as potatoes and onions, keep best in a cool, dry place.

When fresh items are not in season, you might choose canned or frozen fruits and vegetables instead. Look for cans that are not bulging, dented, or leaking. Store them on shelves in clean, dry cupboards. Look for frozen packages that are frozen solid. Store them in the freezer until you are ready to use them.

8-10 Like other fruits, bananas should be stored at room temperature until they ripen.

✓ **Check What You Have Learned**

1. How can you tell if produce is ripe? What should you do if you buy produce that is not ripe?
2. How can you store most produce to keep it fresh and crisp?

Buying and Storing Breads and Cereals

When buying bread, cereal, rice, or pasta, choose enriched or whole grain products. These items are more nutritious. Packages for these foods should be clean and tightly sealed. Bread should be fresh and free from mold.

Rice, pasta, and most flours should be stored in sealed containers in cool, dry places. Whole wheat flour needs to be stored in the refrigerator to maintain freshness. Bread should be wrapped tightly to keep it fresh. Open cereal packages should be closed tightly when not in use. This helps the cereal stay crisp and fresh.

✓ **Check What You Have Learned**

1. Why should you buy enriched or whole grain bread or cereal products?
2. Where should whole wheat flour be stored to maintain freshness?

Buying and Storing Milk and Milk Products

Milk and milk products sold in stores are pasteurized. **Pasteurization** is a process where milk and milk products are heated to destroy harmful bacteria. Whole milk is usually homogenized. **Homogenization** is a process where milkfat is broken into tiny pieces and spread throughout the milk. There are many different types of milk available. See 8-11.

Types of Milk

★ **Whole milk:** milk containing 3 to 4 percent butterfat.

★ **Lowfat milk:** milk with some of the fat removed.

★ **Fat free milk:** milk with all the fat removed.

★ **Nonfat dry milk:** fat free milk with all the water removed.

★ **Evaporated milk:** whole or fat free milk with about half the water removed. It is sealed in cans.

★ **Buttermilk:** made by special processes from whole or fat free milk.

8-11 There are many types of milk from which to choose.

The two main types of cheese are natural and process. The difference between natural and process cheese is how they are made. *Natural cheese* is made from milk. Natural cheese may be either hard or soft. *Process cheese* is made by melting and blending natural cheeses. Process cheese melts well and has a mild flavor.

Cheese comes in many forms. You can buy it in chunks or sliced, cubed, shredded, or grated. Aside from packages, cheese comes in jars and pressurized cans. These are convenient, but often cost more.

When buying milk and cheese products, choose the types that meet your needs. Choose fat free and lowfat products to fit into a healthful diet. Check the freshness date stamped on cartons and packages. See 8-12. Be sure you will be able to use these products within a few days after this date.

Store fresh milk in the refrigerator or it will spoil. Store nonfat dry milk in an airtight container in a cool place. After it is mixed with water, store it in the refrigerator. Unopened cans of evaporated milk can be stored on a shelf. After cans are opened, unused portions of evaporated milk should be refrigerated.

Cheese should be stored in the refrigerator to preserve nutrients and to prevent spoilage. Soft cheeses do not keep as long as hard cheeses. Store soft cheeses, such as cottage cheese, in tightly covered containers. Wrap hard cheeses, such as Swiss and Cheddar, tightly to prevent drying.

8-12 The date printed on a food package tells you when the food will no longer be good to eat.

✓ **Check What You Have Learned**

1. What does pasteurization do to milk? What does homogenization do?
2. What are the differences between the two types of cheese?

Buying and Storing Meat and Meat Alternates

A large part of the money spent on food often goes toward protein-rich foods. Smart shopping can help you get your money's worth.

Choose meat, poultry, and fish carefully. Look for lean meat cuts that have fresh coloring. Choose poultry that is meaty and free from blemishes and pinfeathers. Select fish that has firm flesh and no strong odor. Look on fresh meat packages for information about how to handle products safely at home.

Meat, poultry, and fish can also be purchased canned or frozen. Choose these products with the same care you use when buying other canned and frozen foods. Cans should not be dented or bulging. Frozen packages should be frozen solid and should be free from ice crystals.

Eggs come in many sizes. You should make sure they have smooth shells and regular shapes. Do not buy them if the shells are cracked.

Beans can be bought in both dry and ready-to-use canned forms. There are many kinds of dry beans and peas you can use to prepare tasty meals.

Fresh meat, poultry, and fish spoil quickly if not stored promptly. For short-term storage, loosely wrap meat and poultry and tightly wrap fish. Store these foods in the coldest part of the refrigerator or in the meat drawer. For long-term storage, store fresh and frozen foods in the freezer. Eggs should be stored large end up in the carton in the refrigerator. Dry beans should be stored in tightly covered containers. Colored glass or plastic containers preserve the nutrients. See 8-13.

Product	Refrigerator (40°F)	Freezer (0°F)	Product	Refrigerator (40°F)	Freezer (0°F)
Eggs			**Bacon & sausage**		
Fresh, in shell	3 weeks	Don't freeze	Bacon	7 days	1 month
Hardcooked	1 week	Don't freeze well	Sausage, raw from pork,		
Egg substitutes, opened	3 days	Don't freeze	beef, turkey	1-2 days	1-2 months
unopened	10 days	1 year	Precooked smoked		
TV dinners, frozen casseroles			breakfast links, patties	7 days	1-2 months
Keep frozen until ready to serve		3-4 months	**Ham**		
Deli & vacuum-packed products			Ham, canned shelf stable	Shelf-2 years at room temperature	
Store-prepared (or	3-5 days	This product	Label says keep		
homemade) salads		doesn't freeze well.	refrigerated	6-9 months	Don't freeze
			Ham, fully cooked–whole	7 days	1-2 months
			Ham, fully cooked–		
Mayonnaise, commercial			half, and slices	3-5 days	1-2 months
Refrigerate after opening	2 months	Don't freeze	**Fresh meat**		
			Beef, steaks, roasts	3-5 days	6-12 months
			Pork, chops, roasts	3-5 days	4-6 months
Ground meats			Lamb, chops, roasts	3-5 days	6-9 months
Ground beef, turkey, chicken, pork	1-2 days	3-4 months	Veal, roast	3-5 days	4-6 months
			Meat leftovers		
Hot dogs & lunch meats			Cooked meat and meat		
Hot dogs, opened package	1 week		dishes, soups & stews	3-4 days	2-3 months
unopened package	2 weeks	In freezer wrap,	Gravy and meat broth	1-2 days	2-3 months
Lunch meats, opened	3-5 days	1-2 months	**Fresh poultry**		
unopened*	2 weeks		Chicken or turkey, whole	1-2 days	1 year
			Chicken or turkey, pieces	1-2 days	9 months
			Cooked poultry, leftover		
			Fried chicken	3-4 days	4 months
*But not more than one week after the sell-by date			Cooked poultry	3-4 days	4-6 months

8-13 Use this chart as a guide to help you store food safely in your refrigerator and freezer.

1. What should you look for when buying fresh meat, poultry, and fish?
2. In what part of the refrigerator should fresh meat, poultry, and fish be stored?

The Main Ideas

There are different guidelines for buying and storing different types of food. Learning these guidelines will help you buy foods that give you the best quality for your money. They will also help you store foods safely to protect nutrients, flavor, and freshness.

Apply What You Have Learned

1. Look for meat, poultry, and fish at a grocery store. See what forms are available in the frozen food and the fresh food areas. See how each type is packaged. Look on the package for safe handling instructions. Report your findings to the class.
2. In your family's kitchen, look at the space available for food storage. Make sketches of the cabinet, pantry, refrigerator, and freezer shelves. Then fill in which foods you would store in each of these spaces. Use the information you learned in this lesson to help you.
3. Take a notebook and pencil to the grocery store. Look at the labels of 10 different foods. Try to include foods from all food groups. Read the labels to see how these foods should be stored. Write down this information. Then make a poster showing how different foods should be stored. Display this in your classroom.

Lesson 8-4
Serving Meals

Objectives

After studying this lesson, you will be able to
- *define* tableware, flatware, centerpiece, cover, family service, buffet service, *and* plate service.
- *tell what is in a table setting.*
- *show how to set a table correctly.*
- *describe different ways to serve meals.*

New Words

tableware: *dishes, flatware, and glassware.*

flatware: *forks, knives, and spoons used for serving and eating.*

centerpiece: *a decorative object placed in the middle of the table.*

cover: *the table space in front of a person's seat.*

family service: *a style of meal service where people serve themselves as dishes are passed around the table.*

buffet service: *a style of meal service where people help themselves to food set out on a serving table.*

plate service: *a style of meal service where plates are filled in the kitchen. Then they are carried to the table and served to each person.*

New Ideas

- *You can learn to set attractive tables.*
- *There are different styles of meal service.*

There are as many ways to set a table as there are different kinds of meals to serve. For instance, you may set the table one way when serving a sandwich and a bowl of soup. However, you may set it another way for a special dinner.

Meals can be casual or formal depending on the event. Meals are often more formal for special events and may need more complex table settings. Family customs often affect how the table is set and the meal is served.

Table Trimmings

The items needed to set a table include tableware, table covers, and centerpieces. **Tableware** is dishes, flatware, and glassware. Dishes include plates, bowls, mugs, cups, and saucers. They can be made from glass, pottery, wood, plastic, china, metal, or paper. Dishes come in many colors, shapes, and patterns. Forks, knives, and spoons are called **flatware.** They are often made from metal or plastic. Glassware includes all types of drinking glasses. They are available in glass, metal, plastic, or paper in many different sizes, styles, and colors.

Tablecloths or place mats are used to protect the table from food spills. They also reduce the noise of dishes and other items being placed on the table. Special pads or old sheets can be placed under tablecloths to protect the table from hot dishes.

A **centerpiece** is a decorative object placed on the table. See 8-14. Centerpieces are often made from flowers. However, they can be made out of many different materials. The centerpiece should go with the type of meal you serve. For instance, a basket of noisemakers and black and white balloons would be a great centerpiece for a New Year's Eve dinner. Choose centerpieces that are low enough for people to see over.

8-14 Centerpieces add color and make tables look attractive.

✔ Check What You Have Learned

1. What are table covers? Why should you use them?
2. How can centerpieces make your table more attractive?

Setting the Table

The first part of setting a table is learning to set a cover. See 8-15. The **cover** is the table space in front of a person's seat. It is large enough to hold a person's dishes, flatware, and glassware. Meals can be made more enjoyable if the cover is arranged in a pleasing manner.

Whether your table is large or small, round or square, it can be attractively set. Wipe or wash off the table before and after each meal. Make sure the tableware is clean. Choose the correct dishes, glassware, and flatware for the food you are serving. Choose colors that go together.

No matter how fancy or simple your meal is, the basics for setting a cover are the same. More tableware is often added as meals become fancier. Begin setting the table by putting down the table cover. Center tablecloths evenly over pads or sheets. If you are using place mats, be sure to line them up evenly with the edge of the table.

8-15 Practicing setting a cover in class is good experience.

The dishes for the main course should be put on the table first. Place plates in the center of each person's cover. Place the knife on the right side of the plate with the blade facing the plate. Place the spoon to the right of the knife. Place the fork on the left side of the plate. (If extra flatware is used, place the flatware to be used first farthest away from the plate.) Line flatware up with the bottom of the plate. Glassware should be placed at the point of the knife. Salad plates should be placed above the fork. See 8-16.

Use only the dishes, flatware, and glassware you need. This saves you the extra work of setting and cleaning extra tableware. People also feel more comfortable when there isn't excess tableware on the table.

Birthday parties or family holidays are good times to use creative table settings. You can use creative centerpieces and table covers. When you eat out, you may notice that tables are set

8-16 Other cover settings are based on this basic cover.

differently from the way they are at home. Pay attention to the type of meal service used in restaurants. This can make you feel more at ease when you eat at nice restaurants.

✔ Check What You Have Learned

1. Why are plates the first dishes to be placed on the table?
2. Where should glassware be placed when setting a table?
3. Why should you use only the dishes, flatware, and glassware you need?

Serving the Meal

There are many ways to serve a meal. The type of service you choose depends upon the event and the food served. Family customs and the number of people to be served also affect meal service. When you eat out, you may find that restaurants have their own style of meal service. See 8-17.

Family service is a style of meal service where people serve themselves as dishes are passed around the table. This is how meals are often served at home.

Buffet service is a style of meal service where people help themselves to food set out on a serving table. They may eat while standing or holding plates in their laps. Desserts and beverages may be

8-17 Restaurants can offer informal service.

served at a different time. Buffet service is a good way to serve large groups of people.

Plate service is a style of meal service where plates are filled in the kitchen. Then they are carried to the table and served to each person at the table. This kind of service is used in hotel dining rooms, restaurants, and banquet halls. The guests are seated first and then the food is placed on the table. This type of service needs more planning and effort. However, it makes certain events seem more special.

Some people want to eat smaller servings at social events and family celebrations. If you are entertaining, you may want to choose a type of meal service that will allow others to eat less food. Family service and buffet service allow you to take a smaller serving.

Plate service means you will need to ask for smaller servings. You may have to ask to omit the gravy. You might ask for other changes in the food service. You might ask to have salad dressing served on the side so you can add as much as you want. If you are served more food than you want, you do not have to eat it. Leave rich sauces and gravies on your plate if you do not want them.

✔ **Check What You Have Learned**

1. What are three factors that affect how you serve a meal?
2. What are the differences among the three types of meal service?
3. Which meal service would be best to allow guests to control serving sizes?

💡 **The Main Ideas**

Tableware should be clean and neatly arranged on the table. Choose a cover and style of meal service that best fits the needs of the people eating. Also think about family customs, the menu, event, and number of people eating.

Apply What You Have Learned

1. Think about your favorite meal. Make a list of the tableware needed to set a cover for this meal. Then draw a picture of how you would set the cover.
2. Demonstrate how to set a basic table cover. Discuss with your classmates when you may need to set the cover differently.
3. Make a chart showing what style of meal service you would use for each of the following events:
   a. A lunch for your friends.
   b. A family dinner for a relative from out of town.
   c. A church banquet.
   d. A wedding reception.

Lesson 8-5
Caring About Behavior

Objectives

After studying this lesson, you will be able to

➡ *define* etiquette, manners *and* a la carte.

➡ *list reasons why it is important to use good manners every day.*

➡ *tell why having good table manners can help you feel confident.*

➡ *explain how you can help guests feel welcome.*

New Words

etiquette: *proper behavior in social settings.*

manners: *guidelines for behavior.*

a la carte: *a menu term meaning each food or course is listed and priced separately.*

New Ideas

➡ *Good manners should be used every day.*

➡ *Knowing how to behave when eating out helps you feel confident.*

➡ *You can help guests feel welcome and comfortable.*

When you care about your behavior, you make meals more enjoyable for yourself and others. **Etiquette** is proper behavior in social settings. Etiquette is guided by **manners.** Try to use good manners every day. Proper behavior will soon become a habit that is easy to use when you entertain or eat away from home.

Using Table Manners

You should use good table manners at home as well as when you eat out. See 8-18. If you practice good manners at home, they will become a habit. They will help you feel at ease in any situation. You will not have to think about how to behave when you are with others.

8-18 Your classmates will enjoy eating with you if you use good table manners in the school cafeteria.

Table manners can vary. Family and religious customs can affect table manners. What people do in one city or country may be different from what you do. It is easy to adjust to most situations when you use basic good manners.

Table manners are based on care and respect for others. When you eat, follow the guidelines in 8-19. They can help make meals more pleasant for everyone.

Part of having good table manners is knowing how to use tableware properly. You should practice using different types of tableware until you feel comfortable. See 8-20.

Accidents will happen at the table. They may include dropping a piece of food or spilling a drink. If you are involved in an accident, apologize. You should also offer your help. Then you should forget about the matter. Do not keep talking about the accident. This only makes others feel uncomfortable.

Guidelines for Good Table Manners

★ Wait in line quietly in a cafeteria or restaurant.

★ Arrive on time for meals. Wait until everyone is seated before you start to eat.

★ Pass food to others carefully. Ask politely for food to be passed to you.

★ Use good posture. Sit as quietly as possible. Relax and enjoy the meal.

★ Eat slowly and quietly, taking small bites. Chew with your mouth closed. Do not talk when your mouth is full.

★ Keep you plate neat. Do not stir your food. Be careful not to spill food on the table.

★ If you do not like a certain food, leave it on your plate. Do not make rude comments about it. Give others a chance to enjoy their food.

★ Remain seated at the table when you finish eating. It is polite to wait for everyone to finish. If you must leave the table early, ask to be excused.

★ When eating in a cafeteria, carry your tray and tableware to the proper place as you leave the table.

★ Help keep the conversation pleasant and interesting when eating with others. At restaurants, keep your voice low so you do not bother other guests.

8-19 Good table manners are important for everyone to use.

Using Tableware Properly

★ Place your napkin in your lap during a meal. Take the napkin from your lap to wipe your mouth. Wipe your fingers without taking the napkin away from your lap. At the end of the meal, place the napkin to the left of your plate.

★ Use a fork to carry food to your mouth. Use a spoon if food is soft or liquid. Do not point or gesture with your flatware.

★ Cut tender meats and salads with the side of a fork. Use a knife to cut food that cannot be cut easily with a fork.

★ Spread butter or jam on bread with a knife.

★ When you finish using a knife, place it across the rim of the plate. Do not put it on the table or tablecloth. It may be greasy or sticky.

★ Dip a soup spoon away from you. Then move it from the back of the bowl to your mouth. Eat from the side of the spoon. Do not bend over the bowl, lift the bowl to your chin, or make any noise while eating soup.

★ You can eat some foods with your fingers. They are often crisp or dry. Some finger foods are vegetable sticks, most fresh fruits, and snack chips. Fried chicken or barbecued ribs may be eaten with the fingers at informal events. Sandwiches are eaten with the fingers.

★ After use, spoons should be placed on the saucers under cups and bowls.

★ Place flatware across the center of the plate when you finish eating. This makes it easier to clear the table, and flatware will not fall off the plate.

8-20 Following these guidelines will help you feel comfortable using tableware.

Eating Away from Home

When eating out, good table manners include being able to properly order your food. Understanding how to read a menu can help you do this with ease. Menu forms vary from place to place. However, menus often list foods and prices in standard ways.

Some restaurant menus list food as complete meals. One price includes all the courses for a meal. For instance, the price for a full dinner might include the appetizer, main course, bread or rolls, and dessert. A beverage may not be included in the price. However, milk or soda is usually available at an extra cost.

On some menus, you may see the words **a la carte.** This means that each food or course is listed and priced separately. Appetizers, soups, salads, main dishes, desserts, and beverages are all individually priced. It often costs less to buy a complete meal than it does to buy the same foods a la carte.

Menus may be different in restaurants that feature cultural or ethnic foods. For instance, Chinese, Indian, Turkish, or Mexican restaurants may have their own ways of listing foods and prices.

Besides understanding how foods are priced, you need to understand how they are prepared. Restaurant menus sometimes include terms that may not be familiar to you. Some of these are listed in 8-21.

Some menus carry nutritional information about the food offerings. Read the menu carefully to select the foods that are best for your nutritional needs. To reduce fat, saturated fat, and cholesterol, choose tasty fresh vegetable or fruit salads.

Menu Terms

a la mode. Served with ice cream.
au gratin. Served with cheese.
au jus. Served with natural juices.
basted. Prepared by spooning juices over the food to keep it moist and add flavor.
braised. Cooked in a small amount of liquid.
browned. Cooked to give the surface of the food a brown color.
deep-fried. Cooked in a large amount of hot fat.
du jour. Of the day, such as soup du jour, which means soup of the day.
garnished. Decorated with small pieces of food, such as parsley sprigs or lemon twists, to add color.
grilled. Cooked over hot coals.
julienned. Cut into thin strips.
marinated. Soaked in a flavorful liquid.
poached. Cooked in simmering liquid.
pureed. Blended to turn a solid food, such as fruit, into a thick liquid, such as a fruit sauce.
roasted. Cooked in an oven.
sautéed. Cooked in a small amount of hot fat.
steamed. Cooked in steam.
stir-fried. Cooked quickly in a small amount of fat until the food has a crisp-tender texture.

8-21 Being familiar with these menu terms will help you know how restaurant foods are prepared.

See if lowfat dressing is available or ask to have dressing served on the side. Avoid foods served with gravies, cheese, or cream sauces. Check the preparation method for meat, poultry, and fish. Avoid fried dishes. Instead, select main dishes that are baked, roasted, broiled, grilled, poached, or steamed.

Once you have decided what you want, give your order to the server. Be sure to speak clearly. Your server may ask you some questions about how you would like your food to be prepared. For instance, the server might ask how you would like your eggs to be cooked. You can also ask the server questions if you are uncertain about something on the menu.

If you are with a group, you will need to tell the server how to make out the bill. Maybe each group member plans to pay for his or her food. If so, one member of the group should collect the money and pay the bill. It is easier for the server to write one bill. However, if everyone is ordering different food items, you might want to ask for individual bills or "separate checks."

Tipping is done to show a server that you appreciate good service. Menu prices generally do not include the tip. You must decide how much to leave for a tip. A rule of thumb is to leave 15 percent of the price of the meal for good service.

Using good table manners is especially important when you are eating in a restaurant. Talk quietly with the people at your table so you do not disturb other diners. If you have a problem with your food, quietly call it to your server's attention. If your server is unable to help you, ask to speak to the manager. Avoid making a loud scene.

✔ Check What You Have Learned

1. Why would ordering a complete meal cost less than ordering a meal a la carte?
2. How can you reduce fat, saturated fat, and cholesterol when ordering from a restaurant menu? Give examples.
3. What should you do if you have a problem with your food in a restaurant?

Entertaining at Home

You may like to entertain at home. If so, you need to plan and prepare for the event. You also need to have good manners. You need to be ready when your guests arrive. You will want your guests to have a good time and feel welcome.

When you have guests, you need to introduce people to one another. You may feel uncomfortable when you first make introductions. Take your time and try to feel relaxed. To make an introduction, state the names of your guests as clearly as you can.

If you forget a person's name, ask him or her to remind you. It is better to ask a person's name again than to hide the fact that you don't remember it.

You should also try to help start conversations. When you make introductions, say something interesting about each person. This may help your guests think of something to say to one another.

When you have guests, you set the mood. This means you need to plan activities and entertainment. You also need to show respect for your family and neighbors. Your guests will follow your example.

The Main Ideas

You can show care and respect for others by using good table manners. People will enjoy eating with you more when you use good table manners. You will also feel more comfortable when eating out and when entertaining if you practice manners daily.

Apply What You Have Learned

1. Work with a classmate to study the table manners of a group of students in your school. List their good manners and manners that could be improved. Write suggestions for ways you might praise their manners or suggest improvement.
2. Role-play a situation in which you are eating at a restaurant with friends. First show a situation where you use bad table manners. Then show a situation using good table manners. Have the class discuss which meal they would have wanted to share with you and why.
3. Ask about the nutritional value of foods at your favorite fast-food restaurant. If this information is not available at the restaurant, ask for an address where you can write for it. Find out the calorie, total fat, saturated fat, cholesterol, and sodium content of menu items. Decide which foods you could choose for a meal that would limit calories, total fat, saturated fat, cholesterol, and sodium.
4. Write a guest list for a small birthday party for a family member. Write something interesting you could say about each person when making introductions.

Case Study

Read the story below and look at Lesson 8-2 again.
Then answer the questions below.

Playing the Shopping Game

Olivia and Peter Carlson are twins. Their 11th birthday is on Saturday. On Friday afternoon, they are going shopping with their mother to buy food for their birthday party.

"Can we go to the new supermarket?" Peter asked as they were driving to the supermarket near their home. "It's the one with all the flags and balloons outside. Mark said that last Saturday clowns were handing out bubble gum in the store."

Mrs. Carlson said, "Maybe another time. I haven't shopped there yet. It would take me a while to find where all the foods are located. Also, we can't spend a lot of time shopping today. We still have to make some of the food for the party after we get home."

When they got to the supermarket, Mrs. Carlson handed each of the twins a shopping list. "I want you to look for the items I have written on the list," she said. "I wrote down the brand name and the size I want you to find. You can look for those items while I look for the foods on my list."

"Hey, Mom," said Olivia after looking at her list. "Can we get taco-flavored potato chips instead of the plain ones on the list? I like them better."

"No, Olivia," said Mrs. Carlson. "We need to follow the shopping list. I have budgeted only enough money for the foods on the list. If we buy anything different, we will not have enough money."

To Discuss

→ 1. How have the Carlsons followed the three stages of the shopping game?
→ 2. What other factors should the Carlsons consider before they decide whether or not to shop at the new supermarket?
→ 3. How is Mrs. Carlson teaching the twins the importance of following a shopping list?

Topic 8 Review

Topic Summary

When you are planning a meal, there are several factors that you need to consider. They include planning the menu, shopping for the food, and buying and storing the food.

By planning carefully, you can make a meal that is nutritious, attractive, and tasty. You can make this process easier by following meal patterns.

When you buy food, you need to shop skillfully. This will help you get the best quality food for your money. When you bring food home, you need to store it properly. Otherwise, it may spoil. Then it will have to be thrown away.

After the meal has been planned, you need to decide how you are going to serve it. You can choose from many different types of meal service. You also need to set the table properly and use good table manners. This will give you more confidence when you eat out.

To Review

Write your answers on a separate sheet of paper.

1. What is the difference between supper and dinner?
2. Write menus for the following meals:
   a. Breakfast.
   b. Lunch.
   c. Dinner.
3. List hints for planning meals that your family will like.
4. What are the five points you should keep in mind when planning attractive and pleasing menus?
5. True or false. Shop when you have extra time.
6. What happens to the price of food when there is a shortage?
7. List three advantages of writing a shopping list.
8. Name three different types of food stores.
9. How can a nutrition label help you?
10. What information must be on a nutrition label?
11. List three hints for buying and storing foods from the Food Guide Pyramid.
12. How can you tell when fruits and vegetables are ripe?
13. What is the difference between natural and process cheese?
14. Give an example of centerpieces that could be used for the following events:
    a. Thanksgiving dinner.
    b. Super Bowl party.
    c. Fourth of July picnic.
15. True or false. When setting the table, use only the tableware you need.
16. True or false. Forks are placed to the right of the plate.
17. Sasha is having a party. She plans to place the food on the table along with the plates and flatware. Her guests will serve themselves. Which type of meal service is she using?
    a. Family.
    b. Buffet.
    c. Plate.
18. What are three advantages of practicing good table manners at home?
19. List three ways to make your guests feel welcome in your home.

223

Vocabulary Quiz

Match the definitions in Column A with the terms in Column B.
Write your answers on a separate sheet of paper.

Column A

1. Guidelines for behavior.
2. Guides for planning menus.
3. The table space in front of a person's seat.
4. Not enough to go around.
5. A panel on a food product package with information about the nutrients the food contains.
6. A list of foods to be prepared and served.
7. All the foods served as one part of a meal.
8. Fresh fruits and vegetables.
9. Forks, knives, and spoons used for serving and eating.
10. Dishes, flatware, and glassware.
11. A decorative object placed in the middle of the table.
12. Small, light food served before a meal.
13. A process where milkfat is broken into tiny pieces and spread throughout the milk.
14. A menu term meaning each food or course is listed and priced separately.
15. The process where milk and milk products are heated to destroy harmful bacteria.
16. Reference figures on food labels that help consumers see how food products fit into a total diet.
17. Proper behavior in social settings.

Column B

a. Meal patterns.
b. Course.
c. Shortage.
d. Homogenization.
e. Centerpiece.
f. Tableware.
g. Flatware.
h. Cover.
i. Glassware.
j. Manners.
k. Etiquette.
l. Menu.
m. A la carte.
n. Produce.
o. Nutrition label.
p. Appetizer.
q. Pasteurization.
r. Daily Value.

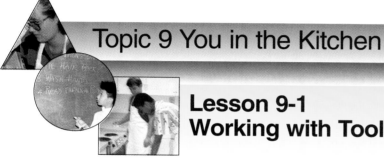

Topic 9 You in the Kitchen

Lesson 9-1
Working with Tools

Objectives

After studying this lesson, you will be able to

➡ *define* utensil, use and care manual, cookware, *and* bakeware.

➡ *identify appliances and utensils used in the kitchen.*

➡ *explain why you should use and care for kitchen tools properly.*

New Words

utensil: *handheld, hand-powered tool used to prepare food.*

use and care manual: *a booklet of instructions for a tool.*

cookware: *pots and pans used on the range.*

bakeware: *pots and pans used in the oven.*

New Ideas

➡ *Appliances and utensils make preparing food easier.*

➡ *You should properly use and care for kitchen tools.*

Appliances and utensils are important kitchen tools. A **utensil** is a handheld, hand-powered tool used to prepare food. Appliances and utensils are the backbone of your kitchen. They help you prepare food as well as save time and energy. As you become skilled at using kitchen tools, preparing food will become easier.

Kitchen Tools

To prepare food, you need to use different kinds of kitchen tools. Kitchen tools include large and small appliances, pots and pans, and utensils. Large appliances are often costly and use a lot of energy. Small appliances are less costly and use less energy. Tools such as pots, pans, and utensils are also needed. Their costs vary and they use human energy.

The tools you choose will depend on many factors. They include the type of cooking you do and how much storage space you have in the kitchen.

Manufacturers provide use and care manuals with their tools. A **use and care manual** is a booklet of instructions for a tool. It tells you how to safely operate the tool and ways it may be used. You should keep all use and care manuals handy.

Tools will last longer and work better if you use and care for them properly. You will avoid wasting energy. You may also reduce the cost of operating appliances.

Large Appliances

Large appliances include refrigerators, freezers, ranges, ovens, microwave ovens, and automatic dishwashers. See 9-1. They are used to cook and store food.

Large Appliances

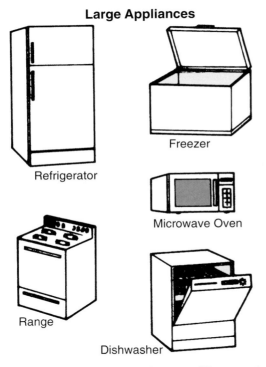

Refrigerator

Freezer

Microwave Oven

Range

Dishwasher

9-1 Large appliances come in many different styles. These are a few basic ones.

Certain foods should be stored in the refrigerator to keep from spoiling. Refrigerator temperatures should be between 35°F and 40°F. Higher temperatures will cause foods to spoil. Lower temperatures will cause foods to freeze. Some refrigerators have special sections for storing various foods such as milk products, meats, and vegetables. The temperature of each section is best for the type of food being stored there.

A freezer can be a part of the refrigerator or it can be a separate appliance. Freezers are used to keep foods frozen. Freezer temperatures should be 0°F or below to maintain food quality.

Ranges are used for cooking and heating foods. They are available in many sizes. Ranges may have three to six surface cooking units on top of the oven. These units are called *burners* if they use gas and *elements* if they use electricity. Surface units may be separate from the oven and built into a countertop. The oven may be built into a nearby wall or cabinet area.

Microwave ovens are often used in addition to ranges. They heat food quickly and evenly, saving you both time and energy. Microwave ovens may be placed on countertops, special carts, or be built into the wall.

Automatic dishwashers save you the time and energy it takes to wash dishes by hand. This time can be spent on other tasks. Dishwashers can be portable or built in under a countertop.

Small Appliances

Small appliances help you perform tasks that would be much harder to perform by hand. See 9-2. Some common small appliances are electric skillets, toasters, electric mixers, blenders, slow cookers, and popcorn poppers.

Small appliances can help conserve energy when preparing food. If you cook food in an electric skillet instead of on a range, you will save energy.

You need to be careful when using small appliances. The outside finish can be easily damaged. Glass or plastic parts can be broken if you're careless. Follow the directions in the use and care manuals that come with appliances. The manuals tell you how to use appliances without damaging them.

Small Appliances

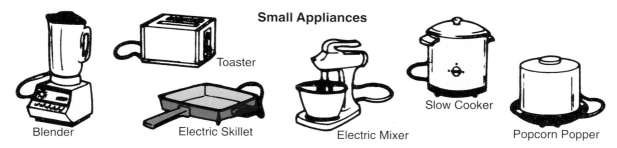

9-2   Each of these small appliances has its own use in preparing food.

✓ Check What You Have Learned

1. How can small appliances help you conserve energy?
2. Why should you be careful when using small appliances?

Pots and Pans

The pots and pans you use on top of the range are called **cookware.** Examples of cookware are saucepans, pots, and skillets. See 9-3. The items used in the oven are called **bakeware.** They include cake, pie, muffin, and pizza pans; cookie sheets; and roasting pans and racks. See 9-4. Items for the microwave oven are called *microwave cookware.*

The materials used to make pots and pans differ. They include aluminum, cast iron, copper, stainless steel, enamel, glass, and pottery. Each material is used for a certain reason. For instance, aluminum conducts heat evenly. Glass can be used in microwave ovens.

Cookware

9-3   Saucepans, pots, and skillets are the basic tools for cooking on top of the range.

Bakeware

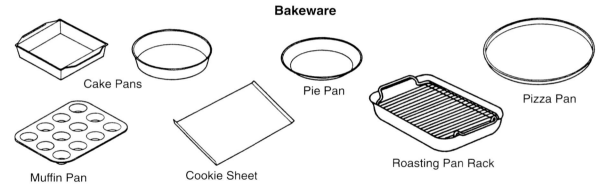

Cake Pans

Pie Pan

Pizza Pan

Muffin Pan

Cookie Sheet

Roasting Pan Rack

9-4   These are just a few of the many pots and pans that can be used in the oven.

✓ **Check What You Have Learned**

1. What are the differences among cookware, bakeware, and microwave cookware?
2. What are some materials that are used to make pots and pans?

Utensils

Utensils make preparing food easier. You can use them to measure, cut, mix, and cook foods. They can also be used to perform a variety of other tasks around the kitchen. Basic kitchen utensils include measuring spoons and cups, knives, cutting boards, mixing bowls, wooden spoons, rubber scrapers, spatulas, and colanders. See 9-5.

There are a wide variety of utensils you can use to prepare food. When you begin cooking, you should start with a basic set of utensils. As you begin to cook more, you may find that you need other utensils such as ladles and kitchen shears. Before buying any utensils, think about how you will use them.

Basic Kitchen Utensils

Knives

Cutting Board

Spatula

Wooden Spoon

Rubber Scraper

Mixing Bowls

Measuring Spoons

Colander

Dry Measuring Cups

Liquid Measuring Cup

9-5   These are some of the basic utensils used for food preparation.

✓ **Check What You Have Learned**

1. How can utensils be used to make preparing food easier?
2. Why should you start with a basic set of utensils?

The Main Ideas

Kitchen tools consist of large and small appliances, pots and pans, and utensils. Each tool has its own purpose and use. Tools should be used according to their use and care manuals. This helps prevent them from wasting energy and being damaged.

Apply What You Have Learned

1. At home or at school, make a file of the use and care manuals for all the kitchen tools. Place this file in an easy-to-reach place in the kitchen. When you need to find out how to operate or care for a tool, the manual will be available.
2. With a partner, demonstrate a small appliance to the class. Show how to care for it so it does not get damaged. Also show how it is used to make food by preparing an easy-to-make food product.
3. Look at all the kitchen utensils available at a local store. Note which ones you have not seen before or don't know how to use. Write these down and bring the list to class. In small groups, research what these tools are and how they are used.

Topic 9 You in the Kitchen

Lesson 9-2
Safety and Sanitation

Objectives

After studying this lesson, you will be able to

➡ *define* sanitation *and* food-borne illnesses.

➡ *explain how to work safely in the kitchen.*

➡ *tell how using proper sanitation can prevent food-borne illnesses.*

➡ *describe how to clean a kitchen to prevent the spread of germs.*

➡ *explain how to keep food safe when taking it to places away from home.*

New Words

sanitation: *the process of making conditions clean and healthy.*

food-borne illnesses: *illnesses caused by bacteria or toxins produced by bacteria in food.*

New Ideas

➡ *Kitchen accidents can be prevented.*

➡ *You can prevent food-borne illness from occurring.*

➡ *It is important to keep your kitchen clean.*

When you work in the kitchen, you may be busy preparing food. However, you need to pay attention to safety and sanitation no matter how busy you are. **Sanitation** is the process of making conditions clean and healthy. Otherwise, the health and safety of everyone who uses the kitchen may be in danger.

Safety

Burns, fires, falls, cuts, and poisonings are the most common types of kitchen accidents. They can be prevented by following these guidelines.

Burns and fires. It is important not to become careless when cooking food. Below are tips for preventing burns and fires in the kitchen.

- Turn pan, pot, and skillet handles toward the center of the range.
- Use dry, clean potholders to handle hot kitchen tools. See 9-6.
- Lift pot and pan lids away from you.
- Do not reach over open flames, hot burners, or steaming pans.
- When lighting a gas oven, strike the match before turning on the gas.
- Never leave food cooking on the range unattended.
- Use appliances according to the use and care manual.
- Use low to medium heat when cooking. This prevents boilovers, burnt food, and fires.
- If a grease fire starts, turn off the burner and cover the pan with a lid. You may also smother the fire with baking soda.

9-6   Oven mitts can protect you when you are removing hot pans from the oven.

Cuts. To prevent yourself from getting cut while in the kitchen, follow the guidelines below.

- Wash sharp knives one at a time.
- Keep knives sharp. Dull knives are not as safe as sharp knives.
- Always cut away from yourself.
- Use a cutting board for cutting and slicing.
- Store knives away from other utensils. See 9-7.
- Keep fingers away from blender and food processor blades.
- Don't put hands in the food waste disposer to try to dislodge food.
- Sweep broken glass onto a piece of paper or cardboard to throw away. Use a damp paper towel to wipe up tiny slivers.

Poisonings. Poisonings can be fatal. The following are a few tips for preventing poisonings in the kitchen.

- Keep all medicines, cleaning supplies, and other household chemicals away from food storage areas.
- Keep food out of the way when spraying chemicals. Clean all work surfaces when you are finished spraying.

- Do not try to put out a grease fire with water. Water will cause the grease and fire to spread.

Falls. Falls are the most common accident to occur in the home. To help prevent them from happening in the kitchen, follow the hints below.

- Wipe up spills right away.
- Use a sturdy step stool when reaching for objects from high shelves or cabinets.
- Make sure rugs have nonskid backings.
- Keep kitchen traffic areas free from objects that may block them.

9-7   A knife block is a safe place to store knives.

✓ Check What You Have Learned

1. Why shouldn't you put out grease fires with water? How should they be put out?
2. Why should you wash sharp knives one at a time?

Sanitation

Having a sanitary kitchen is important. Your food stays wholesome and food-borne illnesses are prevented from occurring. **Food-borne illnesses** are caused by bacteria or toxins produced by bacteria in food. To help keep your kitchen sanitary, follow the steps below.

- Wash your hands before handling food. See 9-8.
- If you handle unsanitary items, wash your hands again before touching food.
- Wash your hands after coughing, sneezing, blowing your nose, or going to the bathroom.

9-8 Use lots of soap and hot water to get your hands clean.

- Wear rubber gloves if you have an open cut or sore on your hand.
- Keep your hands away from your face and hair.
- If your hair is long, keep it pulled back.
- Use only clean kitchen tools, containers, and work surfaces.
- Use one spoon for tasting and another for stirring.

- Wash cutting boards after each use to prevent the spread of germs from raw foods to cooked foods.
- Thoroughly wash fresh foods with cool water.
- Thaw meat and poultry in the refrigerator.
- Keep hot foods hot and cold foods cold.
- Cook all foods thoroughly.
- Use separate towels for drying dishes and drying hands.

✓ Check What You Have Learned

1. Why do you need to make sure that your hands are kept clean?
2. Why should hot foods be kept hot and cold foods kept cold?

Cleaning Up

After a meal is over, you need to clean up. By following these guidelines, you can keep your tools, dishes, and kitchen clean and prevent the spread of germs.

- Repackage any unused food that does not need refrigeration.
- Store leftovers in tightly covered containers in the refrigerator right away. Otherwise the food may spoil.
- If you do not have an automatic dishwasher, wash dishes with dish detergent and water as hot as your hands can stand.
- Wash dishes in the following order: glasses, flatware, cups, plates, bowls, serving dishes, pots, and pans.
- Rinse dishes well to remove all germs and traces of detergent.
- Scald washed dishes with boiling water to kill any germs left on the dishes.
- Air dry dishes instead of towel drying them. Towel drying can spread germs.
- Place garbage in food waste disposer or covered garbage container.
- Clean the sink and areas around the faucets, drains, and under the sink to get rid of grease and pieces of food that can cause odors and germs. See 9-9.

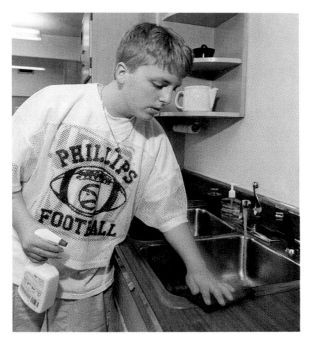

9-9 Clean the sink daily with a good cleanser. Avoid harsh cleansers that may scratch the surface of the sink.

- After washing the dishes, wipe off the table, countertops, and range.
- Sweep the floor daily and mop it on a regular basis.

✔ Check What You Have Learned

1. In what order should you wash your dishes? Why?
2. How can you prevent the spread of germs? Give examples.

Safe Food to Go

For bag lunches, picnics, or celebrations away from home, food must be kept safe for eating. This is necessary to prevent food-borne illnesses. First, you must handle and cook food safely at home. Then you must keep food cold while transporting and serving it. Keep foods refrigerated until it is time to leave home. Then use a cooler to transport foods that must be kept cold.

If taking food on a picnic, try to plan just the right amount of perishable foods to take. You won't have to worry about the storage or safety of leftovers. Make sure you have a cooler that is large enough for the foods that need refrigeration.

Some items do not require refrigeration. These include fruits, vegetables, canned meats or fish, chips, and breads. Crackers, peanut butter, jelly, mustard, and pickles also do not need refrigeration. You do not need to pack these items in a cooler.

Some people like to keep uncooked hamburger patties frozen. At the picnic, be sure to grill each burger until the center is no longer pink. It is perfectly safe to store uncooked hamburger patties in the refrigerator for a day or so until you are ready to pack the cooler.

If you plan to purchase take-out foods for the picnic, eat them within two hours of pick up. This applies to foods such as fried chicken or barbecued meat. Otherwise, buy cooked foods ahead of time to chill before packing them into the cooler.

✔ Check What You Have Learned

1. What is important to remember when preparing food at home to take to a picnic?
2. Name five food items that would need refrigeration to take to a picnic.

The Main Ideas

A safe and sanitary kitchen protects everyone who uses it from accidents and illness. Burns, fires, falls, cuts, and poisonings can be prevented. When you correctly prepare food and clean the kitchen, germs that can cause food-borne illnesses can be prevented from spreading. For bag lunches, picnics, or celebrations away from home, plan ahead to keep food safe.

Apply What You Have Learned

1. Observe the safety rules your family practices in the kitchen at home. Make a list of other kitchen safety rules you think your family should follow. Then make a poster with both the old and new rules to post on your refrigerator at home.
2. Prepare a demonstration on how to properly wash dishes by hand. Include the information given in this lesson. Then give your demonstration in front of the class or to members of your family.

Topic 9 You in the Kitchen

Lesson 9-3
Using Recipes

Objectives

After studying this lesson, you will be able to
⟶ *define* recipe, ingredient, *and* abbreviation.
⟶ *list the information that should be included in recipes.*
⟶ *identify abbreviations used in recipes.*
⟶ *explain why you should follow recipes carefully.*

New Words

recipe: *a set of directions used to pre-pare a food product.*
ingredient: *a food item needed to pre-pare a food product.*
abbreviation: *shortened form of a word.*

New Ideas

⟶ *Recipes should include the informa-tion needed to create a food product.*
⟶ *Abbreviations are often used in recipes.*
⟶ *You should follow recipes carefully to get good results.*

Knowing how to prepare food is a good skill to have. You can use this skill throughout your life. Recipes are an important part of preparing food. A **recipe** is a set of directions used to prepare a food product. Before you begin cooking, you need to know how to read and follow recipes. This will make cooking much easier.

Reading Recipes

Most recipes in cookbooks and magazines have been tested and are based on scientific princi-ples. As you read recipes, you will note that they include the following information:

- the kind of food being prepared
- the ingredients needed
- the amount of each ingredient
- the mixing directions
- the cooking directions
- the cooking time
- the number of servings

Besides the above information, some recipes include nutritional information for each serving. This helps you make healthy choices when decid-ing which recipes to prepare.

When you first learn to prepare food, use recipes that are easy to read and understand. As you become better at preparing food, you may want to try harder recipes.

Recipes are broken down into two parts. See 9-10. First you will find a list of the ingredients used and the amounts needed. An **ingredient** is a food item needed to prepare a food product. Ingre-dients are often listed in the order they are used.

Raisin Nut Oatmeal Cookies

(Makes about 4 dozen medium-sized cookies)

2 eggs	1 t. cinnamon
1 c. brown sugar	1/2 t. each of ginger, cloves,
1 c. vegetable oil	and nutmeg
1/3 c. molasses	1/2 c. raisins (softened in water
3 T. milk	and drained)
2 c. sifted flour	1/2 c. chopped nuts
1/2 t. salt	2 1/4 c. quick rolled oats
1 t. baking soda	

1. Preheat oven to 325°F.
2. Beat eggs well in a large mixing bowl.
3. Add brown sugar and beat until well blended.
4. Slowly pour in vegetable oil. Mix well.
5. Add molasses and milk. Blend well.
6. Sift together flour, salt, baking soda, and spices.
7. Add to mixture along with raisins and nuts. Mix just to blend.
8. Add oats and stir lightly.
9. Drop from a teaspoon on ungreased baking sheet.
10. Bake 20 minutes or until light brown.

Per cookie: 105 calories (51% from fat), 1 g protein, 12 g carbohydrate, 6 g fat, 11 mg cholesterol, 41 mg sodium.

9-10 Recipes should include both the ingredients and directions you need to prepare a food product.

The next part is the directions for mixing and cooking. They are written in the order that the ingredients need to be mixed. You need to follow this order to get good results.

To get good results, you also need to have certain skills. For instance, you need to be able to measure, cut, mix, and cook ingredients. (These skills will be discussed in Lesson 9-4, "Measuring and Cutting Ingredients" and Lesson 9-5, "Mixing and Cooking Ingredients.")

You also need to know how to read abbreviations. See 9-11. An **abbreviation** is a shortened form of a word. Look at the list of ingredients in 9-10. Abbreviations are used instead of words. For instance, the letters *c, t,* and *T,* are used in place of the words *cup, teaspoon,* and *tablespoon.* In food preparation, abbreviations stand for units of measure.

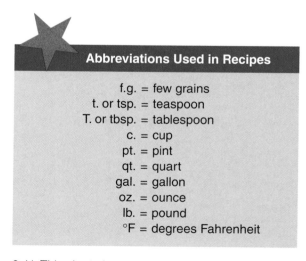

Abbreviations Used in Recipes

f.g. = few grains
t. or tsp. = teaspoon
T. or tbsp. = tablespoon
c. = cup
pt. = pint
qt. = quart
gal. = gallon
oz. = ounce
lb. = pound
°F = degrees Fahrenheit

9-11 This chart shows common abbreviations used in recipes and on measuring tools. Understanding these abbreviations can help you follow recipes.

Following Recipes

Recipes tell you what ingredients to use and in what amounts. To get the best results, use the right amounts of ingredients. Changing the amounts used can affect how food products turn out.

If you copy a recipe from a cookbook or magazine, check carefully to make sure you have copied it right. See 9-12. If you leave out an ingredient, your product might not turn out right. Also, be careful not to change the letters in abbreviations or the numbers. For instance, two teaspoons (t.) of salt in whole wheat bread make it taste good. However, two tablespoons (T.) of salt would make it taste so salty that you could not eat it.

Sometimes recipes call for costly or special ingredients that you may not have at home. Buying these ingredients can place demands on your food budget. Think about the cost of all the ingredients when you choose recipes. You may decide to use recipes that do not call for these special ingredients.

Before you begin cooking, make sure you will have all the ingredients and tools you need. Be sure to use the type and size cookware and bakeware called for in the recipe. Make sure you understand the recipe. Following the steps below will help ensure that your food product turns out right.

1. Read the recipe all the way through. (If you are using a packaged mix, read the directions on the package.)
2. Collect the ingredients.
3. Collect the tools.
4. Complete preparation tasks, such as boiling, chilling, chopping, squeezing, greasing, cubing, melting, and preheating.
5. Measure the dry ingredients.
6. Measure the liquid ingredients.
7. Cook the ingredients according to the directions in the recipe. See 9-13.

9-12 Pay careful attention as you copy recipes.

9-13 Preparing and cooking the ingredients for these tacos as the recipe directs will ensure that they turn out right.

The Main Ideas

Recipes guide you in making food products. They include a list of ingredients needed and directions for mixing and cooking. To get good results when using recipes, you must understand the directions and follow them carefully.

Apply What You Have Learned

1. Choose and read a recipe from a cookbook or magazine. Make a list of the information that you do not understand. Ask your teacher to help you find out what this information means.
2. Make a set of flash cards for the abbreviations used in recipes. Write the abbreviations on the front of 3-by-5-inch index cards and what they stand for on the back. Make flash cards for each abbreviation in this lesson and any others you may want to learn. With a classmate, use the flash cards to drill each other on the meanings of the abbreviations. See who can guess the most abbreviations correctly.

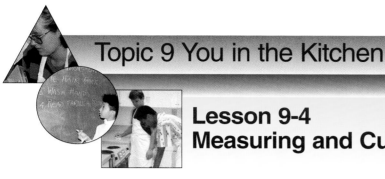

Topic 9 You in the Kitchen

Lesson 9-4
Measuring and Cutting Ingredients

Objectives

After studying this lesson, you will be able to

➧ *define* measure, cut, *and* standard measuring tools.

➧ *measure liquid, dry, and solid ingredients correctly.*

➧ *demonstrate how to cut foods according to recipe directions.*

New Words

measure: *to determine the amount of an item.*

cut: *to divide foods into small pieces.*

standard measuring tools: *specially marked cups and spoons used to measure ingredients.*

New Ideas

➧ *You need to measure ingredients accurately when following recipes.*

➧ *Knowing which tools to use to cut food correctly is important.*

Recipes often include ingredients that need to be measured or cut. **Measure** is to determine the amount of an item. **Cut** is to divide food into small pieces with a sharp knife or kitchen shears. Some other tools are also used to cut foods. These tools include vegetable peelers, graters, and choppers. This lesson will teach you how to perform these skills.

Measuring Ingredients

Specially marked cups and spoons are used to measure ingredients. They are called **standard measuring tools.** See 9-14. They are marked to show exact amounts. Use standard measuring tools every time you prepare food. They will help make your recipes turn out just right.

Measuring Tools

Measuring Spoons

Dry Measuring Cups

Liquid Measuring Cups

9-14 Standard measuring tools come in different sizes to help you measure ingredients accurately.

There are three different types of standard measuring tools. The first type is *liquid measuring cups.* They are used to measure liquid ingredients, such as milk and oil. They are made of clear glass or plastic with pouring spouts. They come in 1-cup, 2-cup, and 4-cup sizes. Lines on the sides of these cups measure fractions of a cup.

The second type of standard measuring tools is *dry measuring cups.* They are used to measure ingredients like flour and sugar. They often come in 1-cup, 1/2-cup, 1/3-cup, and 1/4-cup sizes. They may come in other sizes too.

The last type of standard measuring tools is *measuring spoons.* Measuring spoons are used to measure both liquid and dry ingredients. They are used when the recipe calls for less than 1/4 cup of any ingredient. They come in 1-tablespoon, 1-teaspoon, 1/2-teaspoon, and 1/4-teaspoon sizes. They may also come in other sizes.

There are many ways to measure ingredients used in recipes. Different methods are used to measure different ingredients. Ingredients like brown sugar and peanut butter require special measuring methods. See 9-15.

Sometimes you may decide to cut a recipe in half or double it. You will need to figure out what amounts of ingredients are needed. Using equivalent measures is helpful. It tells you how many of one measure equals another. See 9-16.

Measuring Methods

★ To measure liquid ingredients, such as milk, water, juice, oil, and melted fat, follow these steps:
 1. Place a liquid measuring cup on a level surface.
 2. Pour the liquid into the cup to the correct line.
 3. Check the measure at eye level to be sure you have measured the right amount.

★ To measure dry ingredients, such as flour, granulated sugar, salt, baking powder, cocoa, spices, and confectioners' sugar, follow these steps:
 1. Use a dry measuring cup or spoon.
 2. Use a spoon to fill the measuring cup or spoon to overflowing. Do not pack or shake down the ingredient into the cup or spoon unless the recipe tells you to do so.
 3. Level the measuring cup or spoon with a straight-edged spatula.
 4. If needed, sift the ingredients before measuring. If the recipe calls for 2 cups sifted flour, sift the flour before measuring. If the recipe calls for 2 cups flour and then tells you to sift it, sift it after measuring. Confectioners' sugar should be sifted before measuring. Granulated sugar should be sifted if it has lumps in it.

★ To measure brown sugar, follow these steps:
 1. Use a dry measuring cup or measuring spoon.
 2. Lightly pack the brown sugar into the cup or spoon.
 3. Level the cup or spoon by packing the brown sugar, so that it is even with the top of the cup or spoon. You can also level the cup or spoon with a straight-edged spatula.
 4. If it is measured correctly, the brown sugar will stay the shape of the cup or spoon when it is emptied.

★ To measure shortening and foods like peanut butter and mayonnaise, follow these steps:
 1. Use a dry measuring cup or measuring spoon.
 2. Pack the food into the cup or spoon so there are no air spaces.
 3. Level with a rubber scraper.
 4. Use the rubber scraper to scrape all the food from the cup or spoon.

9-15 Using the proper methods is important when measuring ingredients.

Equivalent Measures

★ **Dry and Liquid Measures**
   3 teaspoons = 1 tablespoon
   4 tablespoons = $1/4$ cup
   8 tablespoons = $1/2$ cup
   12 tablespoons = $3/4$ cup
   16 tablespoons = 1 cup
 few grains, dash, or pinch = less than $1/8$
                                       teaspoon

★ **Liquid Measures**
   2 tablespoons = 1 fluid ounce
   1 cup = 8 fluid ounces
   2 cups = 16 fluid ounces = 1 pint
   4 cups = 32 fluid ounces = 1 quart
   2 pints = 1 quart
   4 quarts = 1 gallon

★ **Dry Measures**
   16 ounces = 1 pound
   8 quarts = 1 peck
   4 pecks = 1 bushel

9-16 Understanding how equivalent measures are
 used helps when doubling or halving recipes.

 Check What You Have Learned

1. When should you use a measuring spoon instead of a measuring cup?
2. When do you need to refer to an equivalent measures chart?

Cutting Ingredients

Recipes often refer to cutting in different ways. For instance, cheese can be cubed, grated, or sliced. When following recipes, you need to know how to cut ingredients correctly. Otherwise your food product will not turn out right. You need to know which tools to use. Using the right tools will help you work safely. See 9-17.

How to Cut Ingredients

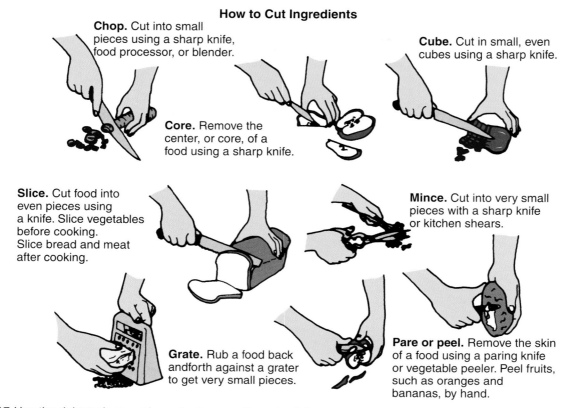

Chop. Cut into small pieces using a sharp knife, food processor, or blender.

Cube. Cut in small, even cubes using a sharp knife.

Core. Remove the center, or core, of a food using a sharp knife.

Slice. Cut food into even pieces using a knife. Slice vegetables before cooking. Slice bread and meat after cooking.

Mince. Cut into very small pieces with a sharp knife or kitchen shears.

Grate. Rub a food back andforth against a grater to get very small pieces.

Pare or peel. Remove the skin of a food using a paring knife or vegetable peeler. Peel fruits, such as oranges and bananas, by hand.

9-17 Use the right tools to cut ingredients correctly and safely.

✓ **Check What You Have Learned**

1. Why do you need to know how to cut foods correctly when following recipes?
2. What are some different tools that can be used for cutting?

The Main Ideas

Ingredients must be measured and cut correctly and carefully. Be sure to use the correct standard measuring tools for measuring dry and liquid ingredients. If the recipe calls for ingredients to be cut a certain way, this must also be done correctly to get good results.

Apply What You Have Learned

1. In the school foods lab or at home, practice measuring 1 cup and 1 tablespoon of each of the following ingredients: milk, flour, brown sugar, and shortening. Be sure to follow the directions given in this lesson.
2. Divide a sheet of paper into two columns. In the first column, list the following food items: onion, pear, cheese, lemon peel, garlic, potato, meat loaf. In the second column, write down how you would cut each food item. Compare your answers with the class and discuss.

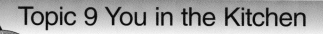

Topic 9 You in the Kitchen

Lesson 9-5
Mixing and Cooking Ingredients

Objectives

After studying this lesson, you will be able to
→ *define* mix, cook, *and* microwaves.
→ *demonstrate how to mix ingredients according to recipes.*
→ *identify cooking terms used in recipes.*

New Words

mix: *to combine ingredients.*
cook: *to prepare food for eating using heat.*
microwaves: *high-frequency energy waves often used to cook food.*

New Ideas

→ *Mixing ingredients correctly is important.*
→ *Following the cooking directions in recipes is important.*

To follow the directions in a recipe, you need to understand the mixing and cooking terms used. You also need to learn which tools to use. Following mixing and cooking directions can result in your food turning out right.

Mixing Ingredients

Mix means to combine ingredients. Recipes use mixing terms to tell you exactly how to combine ingredients. See 9-18. They also tell you which tools to use. When you mix ingredients properly, you will get good results.

Recipes also give you mixing directions. Sometimes ingredients need to be mixed quickly. Other times, they need to be mixed slowly. Ingredients can also be mixed for short or long periods of time. Recipes may tell you to mix all the ingredients together at once or only a few ingredients at a time. Be sure to follow these directions. Otherwise, your food may not turn out right.

Mixing Methods

Blend. Mix slowly using a spoon or an electric mixer on low speed.

Beat. Mix fast bringing the contents to the top of the bowl and then back down again. Spoons, rotary beaters, or electric mixers are used for beating.

Combine. Mix two or more ingredients together using a spoon.

Fold. Mix a light, airy substance with a more solid substance by folding the two together with a rubber scraper. An example is mixing whipped cream with chocolate syrup. Use a very slow, careful over and over motion.

Cream. Beat a mixture until it is light and fluffy using a spoon or electric mixer. This method is often used to mix sugar and shortening.

Stir. Mix in a circular motion using a spoon.

Cut in. Mix solid shortening into a flour mixture using two knives or a pastry blender to cut through the shortening.

Whip. Beat quickly using a wire whisk or rotary beater to add air to one or more ingredients.

9-18 These are a few common ways to mix ingredients.

✓ Check What You Have Learned

1. Why is it important to know what mixing terms mean?
2. What are some different tools used for mixing?

Cooking Ingredients

Cook means to prepare food for eating using heat. The source of heat may be a range, oven, grill, small electric appliance, or microwave oven. (Microwave ovens use **microwaves,** which are high-frequency energy waves, to cook foods.) Recipes will tell you which heat source to use. Recipes are often developed to use only certain heat sources. However, sometimes more than one source can be used. See 9-19. Microwave ovens can often be used in place of ranges and ovens.

Recipes will also tell you the proper temperature for cooking foods. Read the directions carefully.

Sometimes you may need to use two different temperatures for one recipe. For instance, cream puffs are cooked at 425°F for 20 minutes. Then, the heat is lowered to 350°F for 10 to 15 minutes. Cooking foods at the wrong temperature can burn the food or change the traits of the ingredients. The foods may not turn out as you expected.

Another way to help your food turn out right is to understand the cooking terms used in recipes. These terms describe the different ways food can be cooked. See 9-20. Be sure you carefully follow the directions for these terms. Otherwise, the food may be overcooked or undercooked.

Meat Loaf

(Serves 6 to 8)

2 pounds lean ground beef	2 eggs, well-beaten
1 cup fresh bread crumbs	2 teaspoons salt
$1/2$ cup minced onion	$1/4$ teaspoon freshly ground pepper
$1/2$ cup milk	1 teaspoon oregano
$1/4$ cup ketchup	

• Microwave:
1. Combine ground beef, bread crumbs, onion, milk, ketchup, eggs, salt, pepper, and oregano. Mix well
2. Spoon into a12-by-8-inch glass baking dish.
3. Shape into an 8-by-5-inch loaf, making ends square.
4. Cover tightly with plastic film cover, turning back edge to vent.
5. Microwave at 70 percent power 28 to 30 minutes.
6. Let stand 5 minutes
7. Lift out of baking dish and place on warm platter.

• Conventional:
1. Preheat oven to 350 °F.
2. Combine ground beef, bread crumbs, onion, milk, ketchup, eggs, salt, pepper, and oregano. Mix well.
3. Spoon into a 12-by-8-inch baking pan or glass baking dish.
4. Shape into an 8-by-5-inch loaf, making ends square.
5. Bake 1 hour.
6. Lift out of baking pan or dish and place on a warm platter.

9-19 This recipe lets you choose between microwave or conventional cooking methods.

Bake. Cook in an oven in an uncovered container.

Boil. Heat a liquid on a range at a high temperature. Bubbles should constantly rise and break the surface

Broil. Cook by direct heat under the broiling unit in an oven or on a barbecue grill.

Fry. Cook in fat or oil in a pan.

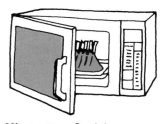

Microwave. Cook in a microwave oven.

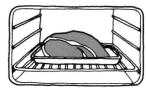

Roast. Cook uncovered in an oven without liquid.

Saute. Cook small pieces of food in a small amount of fat, stirring often.

Simmer. Cook in a liquid at just below the boiling point. Bubbles form only along the edges of the pan and do not break the surface.

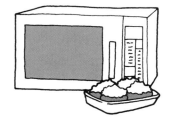

Standing Time. Allow food to finish cooking by internal heat after being removed from a microwave oven. This is sometimes also used in conventional cooking.

9-20 These are just a few of the many cooking terms that you will find in recipes.

✓ Check What You Have Learned

1. Why should you only use the heat sources called for in the recipe?
2. What can happen to food if you cook it at the wrong temperature?

The Main Ideas

Recipes use special terms to tell you how to mix and cook ingredients. When you mix ingredients, you need to use the correct tools. You need to know what cooking terms mean in order to follow recipes correctly. When you understand mixing and cooking terms, your food will turn out right.

Apply What You Have Learned

1. Choose a mixing or cooking term and demonstrate it to the class. As you demonstrate, show the proper way to perform this task. Make sure you use the right tools.
2. Create a word game to help you learn the different mixing and cooking terms in this lesson. Be creative. Play this game with your classmates.

Lesson 9-6
Preparing Foods

Objectives

After studying this lesson, you will be able to
- ➡ *define* leavening agent, curdling, scum, moist heat cooking methods, *and* dry heat cooking methods.
- ➡ *discuss how to prepare fruits and vegetables to be eaten raw or cooked.*
- ➡ *explain how to prepare bread and cereal products.*
- ➡ *demonstrate how to prepare milk and milk products correctly.*
- ➡ *describe the cooking methods used to prepare meats and meat alternates.*
- ➡ *give tips for preparing desserts.*

New Words

leavening agent: *an ingredient that causes foods to rise during baking.*
curdling: *lumping of milk proteins caused by cooking with high heat.*
scum: *film that forms on the surface of heated milk.*
moist heat cooking methods: *water or other liquids are added when cooking protein foods.*
dry heat cooking methods: *water and other liquids are not added when cooking protein foods.*

New Ideas

- ➡ *Using proper cooking methods makes foods taste better.*
- ➡ *Cooking foods correctly helps them retain their nutritive value.*

Now that you know how to measure, cut, mix, and cook ingredients, the next step is to prepare the food. There are some simple rules for preparing food. If you follow these guidelines, your foods will not only look and taste good, but they will be nutritious.

Fruits and Vegetables

Fruits and vegetables can be served raw or cooked. Fruit can be served as an appetizer, snack, or part of a dessert or side dish. See 9-21. Fresh fruits should be washed before eating. To prevent fresh fruits such as apples, peaches, and bananas from turning brown after you slice them, dip the slices in lemon or orange juice.

9-21 Fresh fruits can be served as a light dessert.

Frozen fruit should be thawed slightly before serving. If fruit is fully thawed, it will be too soft. Canned fruit can be served chilled or at room temperature. Dried fruit can be eaten as is or used in baked products.

Fruit can be simmered, baked, or broiled. Cooking changes the flavor and texture of fruit. To get the best flavor, simmer peeled, cored fruits in small amounts of water. Sugar may be added for flavor. To help fruit hold its shape, cook it for a short amount of time and add sugar. Dried fruits should be soaked in hot water for an hour before simmering. Canned fruits can be heated in their juices.

Fruits may also be cooked in the microwave oven. Little or no water is needed for this method. If the skin is still on the fruits, be sure to pierce it with a fork before microwaving.

Fresh vegetables are crisp and flavorful. They add color to salads and appetizers. Some good vegetables to eat uncooked are carrots, celery, cucumbers, lettuce, bean sprouts, mushrooms, and broccoli. To make fresh vegetables more attractive, you can cut them into different shapes and sizes before serving. See 9-22.

Cooked vegetables are often served as side dishes. They are also used in casseroles, stews, and soups. Vegetables can be simmered, steamed, microwaved, or stir-fried. Cook vegetables until they are tender but crisp. Use only a small amount of water when cooking vegetables. This helps them retain their color, flavor, and nutrients.

Frozen vegetables should be cooked while they are still frozen. Canned vegetables should be heated before serving. Dried beans should be soaked in cold water overnight or for an hour in boiling water before cooking. Dried vegetables need to be cooked for a longer amount of time than other vegetables.

9-22 Fresh vegetables can be colorful and fun to eat.

✔ Check What You Have Learned

1. How can you help fruit keep its shape when cooking?
2. Why should fruits and vegetables only be cooked in small amounts of water?

Breads and Cereals

Breads and cereals are served at almost every meal. There are many kinds of bread, but just two basic types, quick breads and yeast breads. Their ingredients are similar, but they are made differently. *Dough* is thick and needs to be shaped before baking. *Batter* is thin and can be poured into a cooking pan. However, both include a **leavening agent** that causes the dough or batter to rise during baking.

Muffins, biscuits, nut breads, and pancakes are examples of quick breads. They can be prepared in a short amount of time. Baking soda and baking powder are the leavening agents added to flour, liquid, salt, and fat. They cause air bubbles to form during baking. This is what makes quick breads light and airy.

Rolls and loaves of bread are examples of yeast breads. Yeast is the leavening agent added to sugar, flour, liquid, fat, and salt. Yeast breads take longer to make than quick breads. To prepare yeast bread, first mix the ingredients and let the dough rise for about an hour. Then shape the dough into rolls or loaves and let it rise again. See 9-23. Finally, bake the dough.

Most cereal products need to be cooked. The time and temperature for each type differ. Cereals, such as pasta and rice, expand when cooked. Therefore, a large amount of water is needed for cooking. When pasta is done cooking, it should be a little chewy but not crunchy. Rice should be ten-

9-23 This whole grain yeast bread was shaped into a round loaf before baking.

der and fluffy. Do not wash rice before or after cooking. Otherwise, most of its nutrients will be washed away.

Breakfast cereals, such as oatmeal and farina, should be cooked until they are done. If the temperature is too high, the cereal can become tough or lumpy. If the temperature is too low, the cereal will not swell properly. Cereals need to be added to liquid according to the recipe. Otherwise they will not cook right.

Pasta, rice, and breakfast cereals can also be prepared in the microwave. Follow the package directions. Always allow room for the pasta and rice to expand.

✔ Check What You Have Learned

1. What is the difference between quick breads and yeast breads?
2. Why do pasta and rice need to be cooked in large amounts of water?

Milk and Milk Products

Recipes often call for milk and milk products. Dairy products add a rich flavor and creamy texture to many soups, casseroles, sauces, and desserts.

Be sure to use fresh milk in cooked foods. Also use low cooking temperatures. The proteins in milk burn when they get too hot. This produces a bitter taste and a brown color. High temperatures can cause milk proteins to form small lumps, too. This is called **curdling.** Curdling can also occur when milk is mixed with hot foods or acid foods, such as oranges or tomatoes. You should add these foods to milk slowly to help prevent curdling.

When heating milk, remove any film that forms on the surface. This is called **scum.** Scum will not dissolve. It can leave small particles in the milk that can affect the texture of the food product. Covering the pan or stirring milk gently during cooking can help keep scum from forming.

You need to be careful when cooking with cheese. Otherwise it may overcook. Overcooking cheese makes it tough and rubbery. When cooking, cut cheese into small pieces and add toward the end of cooking. See 9-24. The cheese will be less likely to overcook and it will melt faster.

Milk and milk products are often used to make desserts. When making desserts that need to be cooked, such as pudding or custard, use low cooking temperatures. Some people use ice cream freezers to make ice cream, frozen yogurt, and sherbet.

9-24 You should add cheese to a dish when it is almost finished cooking.

✓ Check What You Have Learned

1. What are two reasons that milk might curdle?
2. How can you prevent cheese from overcooking?

Meat, Poultry, Fish, and Eggs

When cooking meat, poultry, fish, and eggs, choose the best method for bringing out the flavor and tenderness. The two main cooking methods are moist heat cooking and dry heat cooking.

Water or other liquids are added when cooking protein foods using **moist heat cooking methods**. These cooking methods include braising, poaching, and steaming. They are best for less tender protein foods. They help make foods more tender and juicy.

No water or other liquid is added when using **dry heat cooking methods** to cook protein foods. These methods include roasting, baking, broiling, grilling, and frying. See 9-25. They are best for tender meat, poultry, and fish.

The cut of meat affects which cooking method you use. Tender beef steaks, lamb chops, or pork chops can be broiled. Tender chicken and fish can be fried. Stewing chickens should be cooked in liquid to make the meat tender. Beef stew meat should be cooked in liquid to bring out flavor and

9-25 Dry heat was used to cook this herbed rib roast.

9-26 Poached eggs must be cooked carefully to prevent overcooking.

tenderness. Some seafood, such as oysters and clams, needs to be cooked in liquid.

You want to be sure protein foods are thoroughly cooked. However, you do not want them to be overdone. No matter which cooking method you use, you need to carefully control cooking time and temperature. Meat, poultry, and fish can become dry and tough if they are cooked too long. Meat cooked at too high a temperature can lose juices and shrink. Fish cooks quickly, so you need to watch it carefully. Controlling cooking time and temperature will help meat, poultry, and fish to be tender, moist, and flavorful.

Many people enjoy eating eggs for breakfast. However, eggs are also used as ingredients in many foods. These foods include mayonnaise, meat loaf, baked goods, ice cream, and puddings and custards.

Frying, scrambling, and cooking in the shell are common ways to prepare eggs. Eggs cook fast. If they are overcooked, they become tough and rubbery. See 9-26. It's important to remember that eggs should always be cooked before they are eaten. Food poisoning could occur otherwise.

✔ Check What You Have Learned

1. Which cooking methods are best for less tender protein foods? Which cooking methods are best for tender protein foods?
2. Why is it important to cook eggs before you eat them?

Desserts

Cakes, cookies, pastries, and doughnuts are just a few types of food served as dessert. You probably like desserts. Their rich flavor often comes from fat and sugar. However, desserts should not be the main part of your diet. They are high in calories.

Each type of dessert is prepared differently from the others. Therefore, you need to follow the recipe carefully when making a dessert. Make sure you combine the ingredients properly. Use the right size pan. Cook at the correct temperature. Follow directions for storing and serving desserts. See 9-27. By doing so, you will prepare a tasty dessert.

9-27 Frozen desserts must be served quickly to prevent melting.

✓ Check What You Have Learned

1. Why shouldn't desserts be a large part of your diet?
2. Why do you need to follow recipes carefully when preparing desserts?

The Main Ideas

Fruits and vegetables can be eaten raw or cooked. The two types of bread are quick breads and yeast breads. Cereals should be cooked in the right amount of water at the right temperature. Milk and milk products should be cooked with low heat to prevent curdling. Moist heat and dry heat methods are used to cook meat, poultry, and seafood, depending on their tenderness. Desserts should always be prepared according to the recipe.

Apply What You Have Learned

1. Find a recipe that calls for heated milk. Demonstrate to the class how to heat the milk without burning it or making it curdle.
2. Write a creative skit about what 12 eggs want to become when they leave the carton. For instance, one wants to become a scrambled egg; another wants to become part of a cake. Have the characters tell why they want to become different egg products.

Lesson 9-7
Making Meal Preparation Easy

Objectives

After studying this lesson, you will be able to

⟹ *define* time schedule, dovetail, *and* work center.

⟹ *describe how to use a time schedule to make meal preparation easier.*

⟹ *tell how to organize your kitchen.*

New Words

time schedule: *a written plan for a person that lists when tasks should be started and completed.*

dovetail: *to do more than one task at a time.*

work center: *an area of a kitchen that has been designed around a specific activity or activities.*

New Ideas

⟹ *Using a time schedule can make meal preparation easier.*

⟹ *It is important to plan your kitchen so meal preparation is easy.*

You may have heard the saying, "If you want to get something done, give it to a busy person." People who plan and organize their work often get a lot done. Planning and organizing are important in meal preparation. They will save you both time and energy. This lesson will help you plan your meal preparation and organize your kitchen.

Planning Meal Preparation

Planning meal preparation takes both time and energy. However, to have successful meals, you need to take the time to plan. You may already help plan and prepare meals at home. You need to do the same at school. Because class time is limited, a **time schedule** will help. A time schedule is a written plan for a person that lists when tasks should be started and completed. This helps prevent a last-minute rush.

When making a time schedule, first read all the recipes. Decide how long it will take to prepare, cook, and serve each food. Then make a chart showing when you will start and finish each of these tasks. See 9-28. The goal of having a time schedule is to be able to serve all the foods at the same time. Be sure to include time to set up and clean up in your schedule.

While following your time schedule, you can plan to perform more than one task at a time. This is called **dovetailing** your work. For instance, you can prepare a tossed salad while the main dish is cooking.

Breakfast Time Schedule

7:00 Set table (include butter and syrup).
       Get out tools and ingredients for pancakes.
       Place sausage in skillet.
       Set hot chocolate mugs on counter; add hot chocolate mix.

7:15 Prepare pancake batter.
       Pour batter onto griddle; cook pancakes and place on plate.
       (This task can be dovetailed with other tasks.)

7:30 Begin cooking sausage over moderate heat, turning occasionally.

7:35 Put eggs in water; place on range burner and bring quickly to a boil.

7:40 Remove eggs from heat; cover and set timer.
       Put water on to boil for hot chocolate.
       Pour juice; place on table.
       Place plate of pancakes in microwave oven and heat.

7:45 Serve eggs, sausage, and pancakes onto plates.
       Add water to hot chocolate and serve.

9-28 A meal like this breakfast can be prepared quickly when you follow a time schedule.

There are many other ways you can make meal preparation easier. Here are some ideas to think about before you begin to work in the kitchen.

- Make sure you have all the ingredients you need. If not, make a shopping list and buy them.
- Plan meals according to other activities. On busy days, plan meals that are easy to prepare and serve. This leaves you free to do other tasks.
- Prepare food for more than one meal when you can. The extra food may be served the next day or frozen for later use.
- Store extra food in containers that can be used in both the refrigerator and the range or microwave. This prevents unnecessary dishwashing.
- Rinse and stack tools as you finish using them. This makes dishwashing easier.
- Peel fruits and vegetables over a large piece of paper to help keep your work area clean.

✔ Check What You Have Learned

1. How can making and following a time schedule help you when preparing meals at school?
2. How can dovetailing help you manage your time better?

Organizing Your Kitchen

Part of being a good cook is organizing your kitchen so that meal preparation is easy and enjoyable. You should begin planning your kitchen by arranging your tools. See 9-29.

9-29 Kitchens can be planned to be both functional and attractive. In this kitchen, tools are placed at the correct work centers and help give the room a pleasing look.

Tools should be stored at the correct work center. A **work center** is an area of a kitchen that has been designed around a specific activity or activities. These activities include preparing and serving food, storing food, and cleaning up.

Storing tools near where they are used can make working in the kitchen much easier. If you always have to stop and look for the tools you need, you'll waste time and energy. See 9-30.

Tools that are often used together, such as mixing bowls and rubber scrapers, can be stored in the same place. You can also store the same type of tools in two different places. For instance, you may

Storing Ingredients and Kitchen Tools

★ In the preparation and serving area of your kitchen, you should store
  cooking tools
  cookware and bakeware
  standard measuring tools
  pot holders
  serving dishes

★ In the food storage area of your kitchen, you should store
  food storage containers
  foods that do not need to be refrigerated
  foil and plastic wrap
  tools for serving refrigerated and frozen foods

★ In the cleanup area of your kitchen, you should store
  knives
  cutting board
  tableware
  flatware
  cleaning supplies
  wastebasket

9-30 Tools and ingredients are easy to find when they are stored in the correct work center.

store mixing spoons at the range and where you mix foods.

You should also store tools that you use often in easy-to-reach places. Tools that you use less often should be stored in the backs of drawers and cabinets. For instance, can openers should be stored in the front of a drawer in the food preparation area. Holiday cookie cutters can be stored in the back of a cabinet.

✓ Check What You Have Learned

1. What are the three types of activities that make up work centers?
2. Why is it helpful to store tools that are used together in the same place?

The Main Ideas

There are many ways to make meal preparation easy. Making a time schedule is one. This will save you time and energy before you begin preparing food. Organizing your kitchen is important. You will save time and energy when your tools are stored in easy-to-find places.

Apply What You Have Learned

1. Plan to make a meal for your family. Choose the foods you want to prepare. Then make a time schedule to follow when preparing the meal. After you have prepared your meal, write a short report. Tell whether or not you were able to follow your schedule. Also report whether or not all the foods were served at the right time.

2. On a piece of paper, make a diagram of the work centers in your kitchen at home. Show how you would arrange the tools needed for each work center. Compare your plan with how your kitchen is arranged now. Share your plans with your family.

Lesson 9-8
Working with Others

Objectives

After studying this lesson, you will be able to

⇒ *define work plan.*

⇒ *demonstrate how to work with others in the kitchen.*

⇒ *explain how to make and follow a work plan.*

New Word

work plan: *a list of tasks to be done, who is to perform them, and the tools and ingredients needed.*

New Ideas

⇒ *You can learn to work well with others in the kitchen at home or in the school foods lab.*

⇒ *A work plan can help you work with others to complete food preparation tasks.*

⇒ *Food preparation and cleanup tasks are shared at home or in the school foods lab.*

You may prepare certain foods or an entire meal by yourself. However, preparing meals often involves more than one person. Others may help you by setting the table and cleaning up after the meal. Someone may also help you prepare the food.

Sharing in food preparation and cleanup tasks is important both at home and in the school foods lab. Knowing how to work well with others can make this work more enjoyable.

Ready for Class

In your foods lab, you need to use class time wisely. You should begin working right away to make good use of your time. See 9-31. You should

9-31 In the foods lab, you can start work by putting on an apron.

not waste time standing around talking with your friends. This isn't fair to the other people in your lab group.

You should also come to class prepared. Be sure to bring the supplies you need. This will let you start working right away. For some classes, you may need only pencil and paper. For other classes, you may need your textbook, an apron, or other supplies.

✔ **Check What You Have Learned**

1. Why is wasting time in the foods lab unfair to your lab partners?
2. How can being prepared help you in class? Give examples.

The Work Plan

Preparing meals in a foods class may seem harder than at home. There are several reasons for this. There are usually fewer people working in the kitchen at home. Working with family members can be less confusing because you know one another's habits. You also have more time to prepare meals at home. Because class time is limited, you need to schedule time more carefully.

Making plans is an important part of cooking. You need to make plans when you cook alone and in a group. When you work alone, you should use a time schedule. When working in a group, you should use a **work plan**. A work plan is a list of tasks to be done, who is to perform them, and the tools and ingredients needed.

Work plans can help you work well with others in a group. They let you know what is expected of you as a part of the group. They also let you know whether you are completing your assigned tasks. If you are not happy with how tasks are assigned, you should take time to discuss your concerns and feelings with your group.

When writing a work plan, be sure to include all the tasks that need to be performed. First you must decide what foods you are going to prepare. This will be done by your teacher or by you and your lab partners. Then you need to make a time schedule. Include what tasks need to be done and in what order. Finally you need to decide who will perform each task. See 9-32. Write your work plan two or three days before you plan to cook. This will give you time to get your supplies together.

At home, you may want to make a work plan if several family members are helping in the kitchen. This work plan doesn't need to be as detailed as the one at school. It can list the tasks to be done and whose turn it is to do each task.

9-32 Each student should be assigned a different food preparation task.

✓ **Check What You Have Learned**

1. How can a work plan help you when you are working in the school foods lab?
2. When you are cooking with other people, why is it important to plan the tasks each person will perform?

Preparing Food

When tasks are divided, only one or two people in the group are responsible for the actual food preparation. The other members of the group are assigned serving and hosting tasks. See 9-33. Each task is needed to create a successful meal. The experience you gain from performing each of these tasks will help you prepare meals in the future.

Group tasks should be rotated each time a new work plan is written. This gives you a chance to practice all the tasks involved in food preparation. In a *rotation work plan,* you are assigned a task to perform for a day or a week. Then, you are assigned another task the next day or week.

Cleanup tasks should be included in your work plan. These tasks are needed to put a room or work area in order. It is easier to work in a clean and orderly foods lab than a messy one. You should know what your assigned cleanup task is and do it well. The next people using the kitchen or work area will appreciate it.

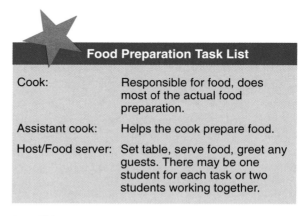

Food Preparation Task List	
Cook:	Responsible for food, does most of the actual food preparation.
Assistant cook:	Helps the cook prepare food.
Host/Food server:	Set table, serve food, greet any guests. There may be one student for each task or two students working together.

9-33 This chart shows one way to divide food preparation tasks.

✓ **Check What You Have Learned**

1. How does a rotation work plan help you learn all the tasks involved in food preparation?
2. Why should you leave your school foods lab clean and orderly?

260

The Main Ideas

Working well with others is important whether you are working in your kitchen at home or in the school foods lab. You should learn to use your time wisely. A work plan can help you complete all the tasks that need to be done. It is important to do all the tasks you are assigned. When working with others in the kitchen, food preparation and cleanup tasks are often rotated.

Apply What You Have Learned

1. Some students may not come to class prepared. As a class, think of ways to solve this problem. Make posters using your ideas for encouraging students to come to class prepared and ready to work. Hang these posters in your classroom or foods lab.
2. In your group, make a work plan for a meal you are going to prepare. Follow the work plan as you prepare the meal. Afterwards, discuss any problems that may have occurred. Brainstorm ideas for how to solve these problems in the future.
3. Prepare a work plan that you might use at home. Include the menu and list each person's task.

Case Study

Read the story below and look at Lesson 9-8 again.
Then answer the questions below.

Making a Work Plan

Hannah, Ron, Jenny, and Connor are getting ready for their foods lab tomorrow. They will be making a fruit salad. Today, they need to make a work plan. They will have 45 minutes to prepare the salad, eat it, and clean up.

"We first need to decide what jobs need to be done," said Hannah.

"This recipe says that the fruit needs to be washed and cut into bite-size pieces," said Jenny. "Then it needs to be put in a bowl and tossed gently."

Connor said, "We'll probably need a cook and an assistant cook. The assistant can wash and peel the fruit, while the cook can cut and toss it."

"We'll also need someone to clean up and someone to set the table and serve the food,"
said Ron. "How are we going to decide who does which job?"

"I don't know," said Jenny. "But I do know that I don't want to do the same job every week. I may not like it and may get bored."

"How about if we do the jobs in alphabetical order?" said Hannah. "Then next week we can rotate jobs and do something new."

"That sounds like a great idea, Hannah," said Connor. "This week, I'll be cook, and you'll be my assistant."

"Ron can clean up, and I'll serve the food," said Jenny.

"This will be fun," said Ron. "This way we can all learn how to do different jobs. Even if we don't like a job, we get to do something else next week."

To Discuss

→ 1. How are these students learning to work together as a group?
→ 2. What other steps does the group need to take to complete their work plan?
→ 3. How will using a rotation work plan help group members learn each of the food preparation skills?

Topic 9 Review

There is more involved in making food than just preparing it. There are several guidelines you need to follow to make sure the food turns out right.

You first need to use the correct kitchen tools. Before you begin preparing food, you need to find out what the different kinds of tools are and how to use them. You also need to follow the safety and sanitation guidelines. Otherwise, accidents and illnesses may occur.

Correctly reading and following recipes is also important. Part of following recipes is knowing how to correctly measure, cut, mix, and cook foods. You need to use the correct tools and follow the correct methods when preparing the food.

To prepare food, there are simple rules to follow. They are different for each type of food. Follow these guidelines carefully to prepare food that is nutritious, attractive, and tasty.

Meal preparation can be made easier by making a time schedule and organizing your kitchen. This will help you save time and energy. These same guidelines apply when you are working with others. You need to make a work plan and follow it. Work plans help you organize the work to be done and decide who will do each task.

To Review

Write your answers on a separate sheet of paper.

1. List three reasons you should use and care for kitchen tools properly.
2. What are two benefits of using a microwave oven?
3. Give two examples of bakeware and two examples of cookware.
4. List three common kitchen accidents. Give two hints for preventing each accident listed.
5. What are five ways to prevent food-borne illnesses?
6. List four pieces of information that should be included in recipes.
7. List the steps for measuring dry ingredients.
8. Fill in the blanks.
   a. _____ teaspoons = 1 tablespoon.
   b. _____ tablespoons = 1 cup.
   c. _____ ounces = 1 pound.
   d. _____ quarts = 1 gallon.
9. Why is it important to understand the measuring, cutting, mixing, and cooking terms used in recipes?
10. Why do you need to cook food at the correct temperature?
11. What is the difference between moist heat cooking methods and dry heat cooking methods?
12. List hints for cooking foods from each food group.
13. What should you do to prevent a banana from turning brown after it has been sliced?
14. What is the first step in making a time schedule?
15. Perry is making dinner tonight. While the potatoes bake, he is preparing the salad and making the main course. Which term best describes what he is doing?
    a. Dovetailing.
    b. Scheduling.
    c. Organizing.
    d. Arranging.
16. True or false. You need to organize your kitchen according to work centers.
17. True or false. Work plans are used when cooking by yourself.

263

Vocabulary Quiz

Match the definitions in Column A with the terms in Column B.
Write your answers on a separate sheet of paper.

Column A

1. A set of directions used to prepare a food product.
2. The process of making conditions clean and healthy.
3. Pots and pans used on the range.
4. Pots and pans used in the oven.
5. A food item needed to prepare a food product.
6. A shortened form of a word.
7. To determine the amount of an item.
8. A handheld, hand-powered tool used to prepare food.
9. An ingredient that causes dough or batter to rise during baking.
10. To divide food into small pieces.
11. Illnesses caused by bacteria or toxins produced by bacteria in food.
12. To prepare food for eating using heat.
13. Specially marked cups and spoons used to measure ingredients.
14. High-frequency energy waves often used to cook food.
15. A booklet of instructions for a tool.

Column B

a. Dovetail.
b. Cookware.
c. Bakeware.
d. Sanitation.
e. Leavening agent.
f. Utensil.
g. Use and care manual.
h. Recipe.
i. Cut.
j. Cook.
k. Microwaves.
l. Abbreviation.
m. Ingredient.
n. Measure.
o. Standard measuring tools.
p. Food-borne illnesses.
q. Mix.

Learning to work with others in the kitchen can make food preparation tasks easier and more fun.

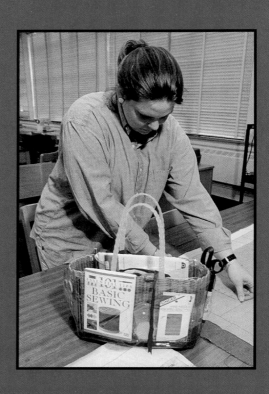

Unit 4
You and Your Clothes

People who have sewing skills can build and maintain their wardrobes by making and repairing many of their clothes.

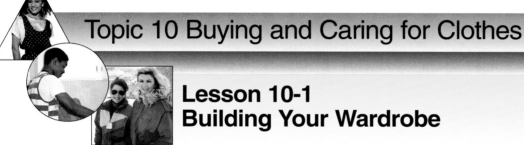

Topic 10 Buying and Caring for Clothes

Lesson 10-1
Building Your Wardrobe

Objectives

After studying this lesson, you will be able to
- → *define* wardrobe, style, fashion, classic, fad, accessories, *and* inventory.
- → *give examples of factors that affect clothing needs.*
- → *explain the importance of taking a wardrobe inventory.*

New Words

wardrobe: *all the clothes and accessories you have to wear.*
style: *the design of a garment.*
fashion: *a style that is popular at the current time.*
classic: *a style that stays in fashion for a long time.*
fad: *a style that is popular for only a short time.*
accessories: *items worn to accent clothing.*
inventory: *a list of items on hand.*

New Ideas

- → *Clothing needs are affected by your climate, standards of dress, and activities.*
- → *Knowing the different fashion terms can help you plan your clothing purchases.*
- → *Taking a wardrobe inventory lets you know exactly what clothes you have.*

You probably spend a lot of time thinking about your clothes. It is natural to be interested in clothes. They can express your personality. They can make you feel good about yourself.

However, you often are not able to buy all the clothes you want. This lesson will help you learn how to build your wardrobe without spending a lot of money. A **wardrobe** is all the clothes and accessories you have to wear.

Clothing Needs

As you build your wardrobe, you need to think about your clothing needs. Your needs may be very much like those of your friends and other people in your community. If you move to another city or state, your clothing needs may change. There are three factors that affect clothing needs. They are standards of dress, activities, and climate. See 10-1.

Your *standards of dress* are the clothes that are acceptable in your community. Your school is a community. Students at your school probably dress in a similar fashion. In some schools, students tend to wear casual clothing. In other schools, this is not true. Students may wear uniforms or dress up.

It is also important to think about the activities you are in when choosing your clothing. If you play sports, you need clothes that let you be active. You may own a lot of swimsuits if you live near a beach.

10-1 Clothing needs differ according to standards of dress, activities, and climate.

Perhaps you live in a part of the country that has definite seasons—winter, spring, summer, and fall. Your clothing needs would not be the same as those of a person who lives where it is warm or cold all year long. He or she would mainly need clothes for only warm or cold weather. On the other hand, you would need clothing for all types of weather.

✓ Check What You Have Learned

1. How do your friends and community affect your clothing needs?
2. How do activities affect your clothing needs? Give examples.

Planning Your Wardrobe

To build a wardrobe, you need to first make a plan. However, before you plan your wardrobe, you need to know the fashion terms. These terms help you understand the different types of clothing you can buy. A **style** is the design of a garment. For instance, slacks and blue jeans are two different styles of pants. A **fashion** is a style that is popular at the current time. The legs of your blue jeans may have been wide last year, while this year they are narrower.

There are two types of fashions. One is a classic. A **classic** is a style that stays in fashion for a long time. Blue jeans are a good example of a classic. A **fad** is a style that is popular for only a short time. See 10-2. Stonewashed blue jeans were a fad.

Because fads go out of style very quickly, it is smart to spend most of your clothing money on fashions and classics. To keep your wardrobe up to date, you can buy **accessories,** such as jewelry, ties, belts, hats, and scarves, to accent your clothing. This is one way to wear the latest fads without spending a lot of money.

You can increase the size of your wardrobe by buying clothes that match those you already have. You will be able to mix and match your clothes to create more outfits. You can also increase the size of your wardrobe by sharing clothes, such as

10-2 Use care in selecting styles.

sweaters or jackets, with your brothers or sisters. Always ask permission before borrowing another person's clothes. Some people have large wardrobes because they make and repair their own clothes.

✓ Check What You Have Learned

1. How can knowing the different fashion terms help you plan your wardrobe?
2. How can you increase your wardrobe? Give examples.

A Wardrobe Inventory

When you plan your wardrobe, you first must know what clothes you have. This can be done by taking an **inventory**, which means making a list of the clothing items you have on hand. First, remove all your clothing from dresser drawers and closets. Put it on your bed. (This will give you room to

work.) Then divide your clothing into groups such as jeans, sweaters, and shirts. This makes it easier for you to check and list each item.

Inspect each item of clothing. Set aside all the clothes you no longer wear. Think about why you no longer wear them. If the clothes are damaged or the wrong size, you can mend or alter them. You may also decide to give away the clothes that do not fit. Someone else may be able to get some use from them.

Then take an inventory of the clothing and accessories you still wear or plan to keep. See 10-3. List all the items you have under different headings. If an item of clothing needs to be repaired or altered, note this on your list. This will remind you to make these repairs.

Based on your inventory, decide what clothes and accessories you need to buy to complete your wardrobe. Have your parents help you decide how you will buy these clothes. You may have to buy some of these clothes yourself.

Wardrobe Inventory			
List of My Clothes	**Description/Color**	**Condition**	**Notes**
Shirts			
Sweaters			
Suits/Dresses			
Pants			
Shorts			
Undergarments			
Socks			
Coats			
Accessories			
Shoes			

10-3 Using a wardrobe inventory chart can help you decide what clothes and accessories you need.

✓ Check What You Have Learned

1. Why is it important to know exactly what clothes you own?
2. How does taking a wardrobe inventory help you plan your wardrobe?

The Main Ideas

Planning your wardrobe is important. When you plan ahead, you can build a large wardrobe without spending a lot of money. Planning includes understanding your clothing needs, knowing the fashion terms, and taking a wardrobe inventory.

Apply What You Have Learned

1. Make a list of your clothing needs in terms of your climate, standards of dress, and activities. Discuss your list with your classmates. Compare how their needs are different from yours.
2. Interview three adults about fads that were popular when they were your age. Ask them if any of these fads have become popular again. Summarize your findings in a one-page report.
3. Take an inventory of your clothing and accessories. Discuss this list with one of your parents. Have him or her help you decide what clothes you need to buy to complete your wardrobe.

Topic 10 Buying and Caring for Clothes

Lesson 10-2
Shopping for Clothes

Objectives

After studying this lesson, you will be able to
- ⟹ *define* layaway plan *and* credit.
- ⟹ *explain how to decide where to shop.*
- ⟹ *list the different ways to pay for clothes.*
- ⟹ *give examples of how to save money when shopping for clothes.*
- ⟹ *tell how to behave when shopping.*

New Words

layaway plan: *placing a small deposit on an item so the store will hold it for you.*
credit: *a way to pay that lets you buy now and pay later.*

New Ideas

- ⟹ *Variety, quality, price, service, and location should all be considered when deciding where to shop.*
- ⟹ *Cash, checks, and credit are three ways to pay for clothes.*
- ⟹ *There are many ways to save money when shopping for clothing.*
- ⟹ *Using good manners can make shopping more pleasant for everyone.*

After you have decided what clothes you need to complete your wardrobe, you need to make a buying plan. Your plan should include where you are going to shop and how you are going to pay for your clothes. When you make a plan and follow it, you will be more organized and will have more time to shop. This will give you a chance to find the best buys possible.

Deciding Where to Shop

The first part of the plan is knowing where you are going to shop. There are many types of clothing stores. Each type offers different variety, quality, price, and service. Some examples of services offered by stores are free delivery, parking, fashion advisers, credit plans, alterations, restaurants, and mail order.

Department stores. These stores have a wide variety of clothing. The quality and prices are often high. Some department stores offer special services.

Discount stores. These stores have a wide variety of clothing. The quality of the clothes can range from high to low. The prices are often lower than department stores. Discount stores have fewer salesclerks and offer fewer customer services.

Factory outlet stores. These stores sell surplus clothing from the factory and clothing that may not be perfect or did not pass the first quality inspection at the factory. These products are sold at a reduced price. Services at these stores are often limited.

Mail-order catalogs. These catalogs let you buy a wide variety of clothing through the mail or over the telephone. See 10-4. Pictures and descriptions of the clothing are given. However, you are not able to try on the clothing to check for fit before ordering. Prices vary and a delivery charge is often added.

10-4 Ordering clothes from catalogs lets you shop without leaving your home.

Specialty stores. These stores sell a limited type of goods, such as shoes. There is often a wide variety available and quality can vary. Prices can range from high to low. The services offered depend on the price of the merchandise.

Variety stores. These stores sell a wide variety of goods. You may find accessories and a limited amount of clothing. The quality varies. Prices are often low. Fewer customer services are offered.

Thrift shops, secondhand stores, and yard sales. These places sell used clothing. The variety and quality vary. Prices can be low. Services are limited.

Store location is another factor to think about when you are deciding where to shop. Convenience, variety, and price should be considered when choosing between stores located in malls, your neighborhood, or downtown areas. Shop around to find the location that best meets your needs.

✓ Check What You Have Learned

1. What are the advantages and disadvantages of mail-order shopping?
2. Why is the store location important to consider when deciding where to shop?

Paying for Clothes

You can pay for clothes using cash, checks, or credit. You can also use a layaway plan. When you go shopping, decide in advance how you are going to pay. This will save you time when you get to the cash register.

Using cash is an easy way to pay for clothes. When you use cash, you know exactly how much money you have to spend. As you pay, count out the bills and change carefully. Be sure to count the change you get back. Before you pay, make sure you have enough cash with you.

If you do not have enough cash, you may want to use the store's **layaway plan.** See 10-5. A layaway plan is placing a small deposit on clothing so the store will hold it for you. Payments are made

10-5 Each store has its own layaway policy. Be sure to read the layaway agreement so you understand its terms.

each week or month for a certain amount of time. When the clothing is paid for, you can take it home.

Using checks is similar to using cash. However, when you write a check, the money is taken out of your checking account. It is then placed in the account of the person or business to whom the check is written. Writing checks is good when you are making a big purchase and do not want to carry a lot of cash. Keep in mind that you cannot write checks for more than the amount of money you have in your account.

Another way to buy clothes is with credit. **Credit** is a way to pay that lets you buy now and pay later. Credit is often used if you do not have enough cash or are buying a costly item. Credit cards are often given to people who have jobs. With your parent's permission, you may be able to use their credit cards.

You should always handle cash, checks, and credit cards carefully. Carry them in a wallet or purse. Keep your wallet or purse close to you. Do not lay them down when you are shopping. See 10-6.

10-6 Do not let your purse out of your sight when you shop. It may get stolen.

✔ Check What You Have Learned

1. If you do not have enough cash on hand, what other forms of payment can you use?
2. Why should you always handle cash, checks, and credit cards carefully?

Saving Money

There are many ways to save money when shopping for clothes. One way is to shop at sales. Sales offer clothing at reduced prices. Sales are often held to make room for new merchandise. These are usually at the end of a season. Sales can also be held to attract new customers and bring back old ones.

When you are shopping at sales, look for the original price of the clothing. This will help you decide whether or not it is a good buy. For instance, if a sweater is marked $20.98 on sale and the regular price was $23.00, you won't save much. If the original price was $30.00, the sweater is a better buy.

When you look for good buys, resist making a spur-of-the-moment purchase. Never buy anything you don't need just because it's on sale. It's not a good buy if you don't wear it. See 10-7. For instance, you may see a shirt that you like on sale. However, once you get the shirt home, you may find it doesn't match any of your other clothes. This shirt is not a good buy because you will not wear it.

Buying used clothing is another way to save money. Good quality, secondhand clothing is sometimes a better buy than poor quality, new clothing. Choose used clothes carefully. Buy only clothing that is clean and in good condition.

Before you buy clothes, always compare quality and price. This helps you find the best quality clothing at the best prices.

10-7 Even if a garment is a good buy, make sure you can wear it.

✔ Check What You Have Learned

1. Why should you find the original price of a sale item?
2. What should you check when buying used clothing?

Your Behavior When Shopping

Using good manners is important when you shop for clothes. It makes shopping more pleasant for everyone—you, the other customers, and the salesclerks. Here are a few tips to follow when shopping.

- If you bump into someone, excuse yourself.
- Carry your packages low so you can see where you're walking.
- If you stop to talk to someone, do not block aisles or doorways. Keep your voice low.
- If you shop during busy times, be prepared to wait for assistance.

If you are having trouble finding a garment you like, ask a salesclerk for help. For instance, you may be looking for a green shirt. The salesclerk may show you several green shirts. If you do not like any of them, you do not have to buy one. Say, "thank you." Then explain that you have not seen what you want but plan to shop some more.

When you buy clothing, keep your receipts. Having your receipt makes it easier for you to return or exchange an item. You should always find out if the garment you want to buy can be returned or exchanged. Sometimes you will see a sign that says, "All sales final. No returns or exchanges." Some types of clothing, such as swimsuits, cannot be returned or exchanged. You should try them on before you buy them.

When trying on clothes, try to keep them clean and in good condition. Make sure your hands are clean. If you wear makeup, wipe away any excess. If a garment feels too tight, try on a larger size. Pulling a garment to make it fit may tear it. After trying on clothes, return them to the salesclerk on a hanger or folded the way you found them.

✔ Check What You Have Learned

1. How can using good manners make shopping more pleasant for everyone?
2. Why should you keep the receipts for clothing you buy?
3. How should you handle clothes when trying them on? Give examples.

The Main Ideas

Before you go shopping, you should make a buying plan. You need to decide where to shop and how you are going to pay for the items you buy. There are many kinds of stores where you can buy clothes. Variety, quality, price, and service vary from one store to another. Buying sale clothing or used clothing can save you money if you shop skillfully. You should always use good manners when shopping.

Apply What You Have Learned

1. Look through newspapers and cut out ads showing each of the different types of stores discussed in this lesson. Make a poster using these ads. Write a caption for each one telling what kind of store it is and where it is located.
2. Make a list of three stores where you shop for clothes. Call them to find out what forms of payment they accept. If they have layaway plans, find out how much the deposit is and how long you have to finish making payments. Report your findings to the class.

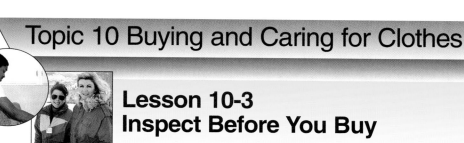

Lesson 10-3
Inspect Before You Buy

Objectives

After studying this lesson, you will be able to
➠ *define hangtag.*
➠ *tell why you should read labels and hangtags.*
➠ *show how to check for quality in clothing.*
➠ *select clothes that fit correctly.*

New Word

hangtag: *a large tag attached to a garment that is removed before the garment is worn.*

New Ideas

➠ *Labels and hangtags give you important information about garments.*
➠ *You need to check the quality of clothes before buying them.*
➠ *Clothes should fit you properly.*

When you shop for clothes, you want to get your money's worth. To do this, take a shopping list with you. This will make choosing clothes easier. Use your wardrobe inventory to make your list. Write down the clothing you plan to buy. Then list the colors and styles you need. After you find a garment that matches the qualities you listed, read the labels and hangtags carefully. Inspect the garment for quality. Then try it on to check for fit.

Read the Label and Hangtag

Garment labels are small pieces of cloth sewn into the garment. They are often found at the center back of necklines and waistlines. There may be more than one label on a garment. Be sure to read all of them.

Labels have important information that can help you decide what garments to buy. By law, the labels must state the fiber content, name of manufacturer, and country where the garment was made. Labels may state the size, brand name, and special finishes applied to the garment, too.

Care instructions are also required on many garment labels. Shoes, hats, and gloves are not required to have care labels. However, care labels must be permanently sewn in most other clothing items. A care label must list at least one safe cleaning method. In addition, the label must warn against any cleaning step—washing, bleaching, drying, or ironing—that can harm the garment. For example, if a garment cannot be bleached, the label must say so. Dry cleaning warnings must be included, too. The law requires garment manufacturers to use specific symbols to identify care instructions. See 10-8.

Clothing Care Symbols

WASH	⊔
BLEACH	△
DRY	☐
IRON	⌧
DRY-CLEAN	○

10-8 Variations of these basic symbols appear on clothing care labels to help you know how to care for your clothes.

Some garments have hangtags. A **hangtag** is a large tag attached to a garment that is removed before the garment is worn. Hangtags are not required by law. They may repeat some of the information found on the label. Hangtags may also list the size, style number, and guarantees and special features.

After you remove a hangtag, write the date, where you bought the garment, and a short description of the garment on the back. Put this in an envelope with other hangtags. Refer to these when you need information about your clothes.

✓ Check What You Have Learned

1. By law, what information must be stated on a label? What other information may be included?
2. What should you do after removing a hangtag from a garment?

Check the Quality

Quality measures how well a product is made. The quality of garments varies from store to store and even within each store. Just because garments are high priced doesn't mean they are good quality. You need to check each garment for quality.

You can judge the quality of clothing by looking at how garments are made. Before you buy a garment, look it over carefully. See 10-9. Check on both the inside and outside. To see how well a garment is made, check the following points:

- Stitches are small, even in length, neat, straight, and fastened at the ends.
- Thread color matches the color of the fabric.

10-9 Carefully inspect a garment for quality before you decide to buy it.

- Seams are even and lie flat. Wide seams lie more smoothly and take greater strain than narrow ones.
- Hems are even and lie flat. Stitching doesn't show on the outside.
- Seams and hems are wide enough to be let out if needed.
- Crotch, armhole, and pocket seams are reinforced by extra rows of stitching.
- Openings at the side or neckline allow enough room to put the garment on and take it off.
- Zippers lie flat.
- Hooks and eyes, snaps, buttons, and trims are sewn on firmly.
- Buttonholes fit easily over buttons. They are firmly stitched so they will not ravel or tear.

Sometimes a garment may not meet all of the above guidelines. It may have hanging threads and seams that need stitching. Hooks and eyes, snaps, buttons, or trims may be sewn on loosely. However, the garment can be a good buy if you are able to repair it at home. If you can't, the garment isn't a good buy. Buttons may come off and seams may rip open. You may not be able to wear the garment. Your money will be wasted.

✓ Check What You Have Learned

1. What should you check when inspecting a garment for quality?
2. When might a poorly-sewn garment be a good buy? Give an example.

Check the Fit

A garment isn't a good buy unless it fits. Good fit in a garment means it is the right size. If the length is good for you, it isn't too short or too long. If the garment fits you properly, it isn't too tight or too loose. When a garment looks good and feels comfortable, it fits you.

Clothing sizes are divided into categories. The size categories for females and males are described by different names. They are based on body measurements. If you do not know the size category best for you, ask the salesclerk for help.

Common size categories for females are Juniors, Misses, and Women's. Some garments are adapted to fit petite, large, and tall females. This can help you find clothes that fit.

Common sizes categories for males are Teen Boys' and Men's. Some clothes for males are designed for different heights and builds. They may be marked *short, slim, regular, husky,* or *tall.*

When you shop for clothes, try them on in the store. Take a parent or friend along to help you decide how they fit. Look in a full-length mirror to get the total picture. See 10-10. Check to see how

10-10 Trying on clothes may take time. However, getting a good fit is worth the effort.

the garment fits in the back as well as in the front. Salesclerks may tell you how perfect an outfit is for you. This may or may not be true. Decide for yourself.

Some clothing labels will tell you if a garment will shrink. This will affect the size you choose. For instance, cotton knits will sometimes shrink when washed. If the label does not tell you, ask the salesclerk.

✔ Check What You Have Learned

1. How do you know when a garment fits you? Give examples.
2. How can knowing the different clothing sizes help you find clothes that fit?
3. Why should you have a parent or friend come with you when you try on clothes?

The Main Ideas

Clothing labels should be read and hangtags should be saved for reference. Before buying clothes, you should check them both inside and out. The quality of a garment can be determined by how well it is made. Clothes that fit properly look better and wear better.

Apply What You Have Learned

1. Go to a clothing store. First find a garment of poor quality. Then find one of good quality. Write a short report explaining why the first garment is poor quality and the second garment is good quality.
2. Prepare a demonstration for the class showing how to check the fit of a garment. Ask classmates to model clothes that fit properly and clothes that do not fit properly. Discuss what you should look for when checking the fit of a garment.

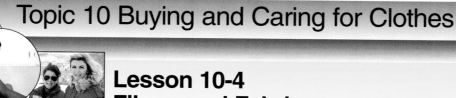

Topic 10 Buying and Caring for Clothes

Lesson 10-4
Fibers and Fabrics

Objectives

After studying this lesson, you will be able to

➡ *define* fibers, yarn, fabric, blend, *and* finish.

➡ *list traits of natural and manufactured fibers.*

➡ *give examples of how fabrics are made.*

➡ *tell why finishes are applied to fabrics.*

New Words

fibers: *hairlike strands that can be twisted together to form yarn.*

yarn: *a continuous strand of fibers.*

fabric: *cloth made by weaving or knitting yarns or by pressing fibers together.*

blend: *a combination of two or more different fibers.*

finish: *a treatment given to fibers, yarns, or fabric to improve the look, feel, or performance of a fabric.*

New Ideas

➡ *Fibers are either natural or manufactured.*

➡ *Fabrics can be made by weaving or knitting yarns or by pressing fibers together.*

➡ *Finishes are added to improve fabrics.*

You may notice that some of your clothes feel different from others. Some may keep you warmer or wrinkle easier than others. This is because clothes are made from different fibers, yarns, and fabrics. **Fibers** are hairlike strands that can be twisted together to form yarn. **Yarn** is a continuous strand of fibers. **Fabric** is cloth made by knitting or weaving yarns or by pressing fibers together. This lesson will discuss what makes fibers and fabrics different.

Natural Fibers

There are two types of fibers. One type is natural fibers. These fibers come from plants or animals. The most common natural fibers are cotton, flax, ramie, wool, and silk.

Cotton comes from cotton plants. See 10-11. The fibers are spun into yarn to make fabric. Cotton dyes easily. It is cool and comfortable to wear. Cotton wrinkles or shrinks easily unless treated with special finishes. Blue jeans, shirts, dresses, and underwear are just some of the many garments made from cotton.

10-11 When cotton plants are ripe, the soft, white cotton fibers can be picked.

Flax comes from flax plants. Like cotton, flax fibers are spun into yarn. This yarn is called *linen*. Linen is cool, comfortable to wear, and strong. Without special finishes, it will shrink and wrinkle easily. Linen is used to make dresses, skirts, pants, suits, and handkerchiefs.

Ramie comes from the stems of a plant called China grass. China grass fibers are made into ramie fibers. Ramie is shiny and strong. It is often combined with other fibers to add strength. Ramie dyes easily. It also absorbs moisture and dries quickly. Ramie can be found in sweaters, shirts, and suits along with other fibers.

Wool comes from sheep fleece. Wool fibers may be long or short. The short fibers are made into soft, fuzzy woolen yarns. The long fibers are spun into smooth, firm yarns. Wool dyes easily and holds creases well. It is warm and comfortable. It also resists wrinkles and water. Wool is often made into sweaters, skirts, coats, pants, suits, and socks.

Silk comes from the cocoons of silkworms. The fibers are long and strong. Silk is shiny and smooth and dyes easily. It is comfortable to wear. However, it can be damaged by sunlight and perspiration. It also needs to be treated with special finishes to resist water stains. Skirts, shirts, dresses, neckties, scarves, and lingerie can all be made with silk.

Clothing made from different natural fibers needs different kinds of care. Fabric made from cotton, linen, and ramie should be washed according to the care instructions on the label. Wool and silk should be dry-cleaned or hand washed.

✓ Check What You Have Learned

1. How are cotton fibers and flax fibers alike? Give examples.
2. Why do different fibers need to be cared for differently? Explain your answer.

Manufactured Fibers

The other type of fibers is manufactured fibers. See 10-12. These fibers are made from raw materials and chemicals put through a special process. Some common manufactured fibers are rayon, nylon, acrylic, and polyester.

Rayon is strong and dyes easily. It is cool, comfortable, and absorbent. Without a special finish, it may wrinkle easily. It can also be damaged by light and burns easily. Rayon is used to make garments such as shirts, blouses, dresses, and neckties.

Nylon is strong and elastic. It holds its shape well. Nylon is uncomfortable in hot weather and can be damaged by strong sunlight. It also absorbs oily stains. Swimwear, hosiery, raincoats, and skiwear are just a few garments made from nylon.

Acrylic is strong. It is warm like wool but is soft and doesn't feel scratchy. Acrylic resists wrinkles, damage from sunlight, and oils. However, it is heat sensitive. Some garments made from acrylic are sweaters, skiwear, dresses, and socks.

Polyester is strong and holds its shape. It resists wrinkles. It is uncomfortable to wear in hot weather and absorbs oily stains. Many clothes such as shirts, blouses, dresses, suits, and neckties are made from polyester.

Although most manufactured fibers are washable, rayon often needs to be dry-cleaned. Be sure to read the care instructions. Many manufactured fibers are sensitive to heat and need low temperatures when drying and ironing.

10-12 Manufactured fibers can be found in a wide variety of garments, such as this blouse and jumper.

✓ Check What You Have Learned

1. Why may clothing manufacturers choose to use manufactured fibers instead of natural fibers?
2. Why do you need to dry and iron manufactured fibers at low temperatures?

Blends

A combination of two or more different fibers is called a **blend.** Cotton, ramie, rayon, nylon, and polyester are some fibers commonly found in blends. For instance, you may have a shirt made of 65 percent polyester and 35 percent cotton.

A blend combines the good traits of two or more fibers and hides the bad traits. For instance, a 100 percent cotton shirt is comfortable to wear in hot weather but wrinkles easily. A 100 percent polyester shirt doesn't wrinkle. However, it is uncomfortable to wear in hot weather. A shirt made of a polyester/cotton blend is comfortable to wear in hot weather and doesn't wrinkle.

✓ Check What You Have Learned

1. What are two fibers commonly found in blends?
2. What is the advantage of using blends to make clothing?

Fabrics

Fabric can be made by yarns that are woven or knitted together or by fibers that are pressed together. Weaving is one of the most common ways to make fabric. Two sets of yarn are used to weave fabrics. One set of yarn goes over and under the other set at right angles. Some different types of weaves are plain, twill, and pile. Woven fabrics are usually strong and stable. They can take a lot of stress before stretching out of shape.

Knitting is done by looping one or more yarns together by machine or hand. Double knits are made by two sets of needles. This fabric is sturdy, but it may snag. Single knits are made from a single yarn. Single knits, such as hosiery, often run. Knit fabrics are comfortable to wear. They will stretch and give. See 10-13.

Nonwoven fabrics are often made from fibers that are held together with gluelike substances. Nonwoven fabrics can also be created when heat is used to melt fibers together. These fabrics are not as strong as woven or knit fabrics.

10-13 Knit fabrics are good to wear when you plan to be active.

✓ Check What You Have Learned

1. What is the difference between weaving and knitting?
2. Why are nonwoven fabrics less strong than woven or knit fabrics?

Fabric Finishes

A **finish** is a treatment given to fibers, yarns, or fabrics to improve the look, feel, or performance of a fabric. Garment labels should tell you what type of finish is used on the fabric. Below is a list of finishes you might find on garment labels.

- **Flame-resistant.** Prevents fabrics from burning easily.
- **Permanent press.** Prevents fabrics from wrinkling.
- **Wash-and-wear.** Lets fabrics dry without wrinkling.
- **Waterproof.** Prevents water from soaking into the fabric.
- **Water-repellent.** Helps fabrics resist water.
- **Preshrunk.** Prevents fabrics from shrinking more than a small amount.
- **Stain-resistant.** Helps protect fabrics from staining.
- **Soil release.** Helps soaps and detergents release soil when washing.

Knowing what each type of finish does can help you choose your clothes carefully. See 10-14. For instance, if you are buying a raincoat, you want to make sure it is waterproof. If you are buying cotton blue jeans, you want to make sure they are preshrunk.

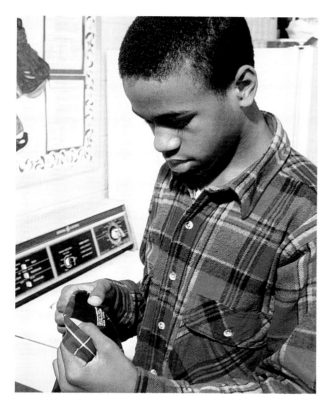

10-14 Read the label to check for special finishes.

✓ Check What You Have Learned

1. How do different finishes improve fabrics? Give examples.
2. How does knowing what each finish does help you choose clothes?

The Main Ideas

The fabrics used to make clothes are different. One reason is the type of fibers used to make a fabric. Another is the way fibers are made into fabrics. Special finishes can also be added to improve fibers, yarns, and fabrics.

⫸ Apply What You Have Learned

1. Check the labels of four of your garments. Make a list of all the fibers found in each garment. Compare your list with your classmates' lists.
2. Look in mail-order catalogs or newspapers and magazines to find examples of clothing that have the following finishes:
   - water-repellent
   - stain-resistant
   - permanent press
   - flame-resistant

   Cut out the picture and description of each of the examples. Share these with the class.

Topic 10 Buying and Caring for Clothes

Lesson 10-5
Caring for Your Clothes

Objectives

After studying this lesson, you will be able to

⟹ *define* sort, dry-clean, iron, *and* press.

⟹ *identify different types of laundry products.*

⟹ *tell how to wash and dry clothes.*

⟹ *explain the difference between washing and dry cleaning clothes.*

⟹ *demonstrate how to iron and press clothing.*

⟹ *tell how to store clothes properly.*

New Words

sort: *to group clothes according to the way you will wash them.*

dry-clean: *to clean with chemicals instead of detergent and water.*

iron: *to move an iron back and forth over fabric to remove wrinkles.*

press: *to lift and lower an iron onto an area of fabric.*

New Ideas

⟹ *Laundry products are used to help get clothes clean.*

⟹ *Clothes can be cleaned by washing or dry cleaning.*

⟹ *Caring for clothes after they are clean includes ironing, pressing, and proper storage.*

After you spend a lot of time planning and building your wardrobe, you need to take care of it. If you get a stain on your jeans, you need to remove it right away. If you buy a "Dry-Clean Only" shirt and wash it, you may not be able to wear it again. When you take good care of your clothes, they will look better and last longer.

Laundry Products

To care for your clothes properly, you need to use the proper laundry products. There are many types of laundry products to clean your clothes. The type you choose depends on the fabric in the garment and how dirty the garment is.

Prewash products are used to remove oily stains and dirt from clothes before they are washed. Prewash products are rubbed into stains and hard-to-clean areas, such as collars and cuffs. They come in liquid, spray, and stick form.

To wash the clothes, you can choose from mild or all-purpose *soaps* and *detergents*. Soaps work best in soft water. They are also milder to the skin than detergents. Mild soaps and detergents are used for delicate fabrics and baby clothes. All-purpose soaps and detergents are used for basic laundry needs. Be sure to use the correct amount of soap or detergent. See 10-15.

Liquid and dry *bleaches* are chemicals used to whiten fabrics. They also help remove stains. The correct amount of bleach must be used. Otherwise, it can damage or make holes in a fabric. Add bleach to the water before adding the clothes. Check the care label to make sure the garment can be bleached.

Fabric softeners are used to make fabrics feel soft. They also help reduce wrinkling and static electricity. Some fabric softeners are added to the wash during the wash or rinse cycle. Other fabric softeners come in the form of sheets that can be put in the dryer. If you use a fabric softener, follow the directions on the package for the best results.

10-15 The directions on the package will tell you how much soap or detergent to use.

✓ Check What You Have Learned

1. What can happen if you're not careful when using bleach?
2. What are some benefits of using a fabric softener?

Washing and Drying Clothes

To machine wash clothes, you first need to sort them. **Sort** means to group clothes according to the way you will wash them. Check care labels before you sort clothes. Sort white clothing from dark clothing. Very dark colored clothes should be sorted into another pile. If you buy a garment with a bright or deep color, such as red, wash it by itself the first time.

After you have sorted your clothes by color, check each pile to be sure that all the clothes should be washed in the same temperature water. Care labels will tell you what water temperature to use. See 10-16. Hot water is often good for light-colored and white fabrics. Warm water is good for most fabrics. Use cold water for brightly-colored and dark fabrics.

As you are sorting the garments, look for any rips, tears, or holes in the clothing. These will need to be repaired before you wash the garment.

(Clothing repairs will be discussed in Lesson 11-4, "Repairing and Altering Your Clothes.") Close all buttons, zippers, hooks and eyes, and snaps. Check pockets for any items that could ruin the garments in the wash. For instance, tissue left in a pocket can leave lint on all your other clothes.

Treat stained garments with a prewash product before washing. Soap and detergent can also be rubbed into very dirty areas. You should treat stains as soon as they occur. Otherwise they will be hard to remove. See 10-17.

Wash each pile of clothes separately. Delicate fabrics need to be washed on a gentle cycle. Very dirty clothes should be washed by themselves. Baby clothes also need to be washed separately. This prevents them from coming into contact with germs from the regular family wash.

Clothes can be dried using an automatic dryer. Check the care label to see how a garment should be dried. Use the correct setting on your dryer for

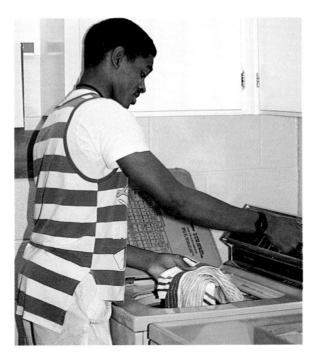

10-16 Be sure to choose the correct water temperature for the clothes you are washing.

10-17 Most stains can be removed. Here are the removal methods for a few common stains.

the fabric. If your clothes are overdried, the fabric may be damaged. Remove clothes from the dryer as soon as they are dry. Hang any garments you can on hangers. Then smooth out collars, cuffs, and seams with your hands to help get rid of wrinkles.

You may choose to line dry clothes. You can do this by hanging them outdoors on a clothesline. You can also hang them indoors over a bathtub or in a shower.

✓ Check What You Have Learned

1. What are three things you should do as you sort clothes?
2. What are two ways clothes can be dried?

Dry-Cleaning Clothes

Some garments you buy may need to be dry-cleaned. **Dry-clean** means to clean with chemicals instead of detergent and water. If the care label says "Dry-Clean Only," the garment may be ruined if machine washed.

Garments made of silk or wool often need to be dry-cleaned. Garments that have decorative trims, such as beads and sequins, may also require dry cleaning.

Dry cleaning can be done by a professional dry cleaner. Professional dry cleaners remove

290

stains as well as doing general cleaning. If you have a stain or spot, tell your dry cleaner about it so the stain can be removed. Some fabrics, such as fur, leather, or suede, need to be dry-cleaned differently. The care label should tell you how.

Many "Dry-Clean Only" clothes can be cleaned in a coin-operated dry cleaning machine. This method costs less than having clothes professionally dry-cleaned. However, stains will not be treated. Sometimes you can use a coin-operated machine yourself. Other times, a helper will operate the machine for you. If you use a coin-operated machine, follow the directions carefully.

✓ **Check What You Have Learned**

1. What is the difference between dry cleaning and washing clothes?
2. What are the two ways you can dry-clean clothes?

Ironing, Pressing, and Storing Clothes

Ironing and pressing are two ways to remove wrinkles from garments. **Ironing** is moving an iron back and forth over fabric. **Pressing** is lifting and lowering an iron onto an area of fabric. Pressing is good for fabrics such as knits and wools. It prevents the fabrics from stretching.

Most irons have different temperature settings for different fabrics. See 10-18. Some fabrics melt or burn if the iron is too hot. If you are not sure about the right setting for a fabric, check the care label.

When removing wrinkles from a garment, first press small areas, such as cuffs. Then iron the larger areas, such as shirt backs. You should press dark fabrics and wools on the wrong side. This will keep the fabric from shining.

After clothes have been washed, dried, and ironed or pressed, they need to be stored properly. Properly stored clothes stay neat and are always ready to wear. You should hang clothes such as skirts, pants, blouses, shirts, and dresses on hangers. Clothes such as sweaters and knits should be folded and stored flat on shelves or in drawers. Do not crowd stored garments together. They may become damaged, wrinkled, or stretched out of shape.

10-18 Choose the correct temperature when ironing.

If you live in a part of the country where seasons change, you may need to store some of your clothes during the summer or winter. Store your clothes in dry, cool places away from sunlight. Make sure your clothes are clean before you store them. Stains you don't notice may become worse over time. You also need to be careful of fabric-eating insects. You can use moth repellents and insect sprays to keep them away from your clothes.

The Main Ideas

Caring for your clothes is very important. When you wash, dry, iron, press, and store your clothes properly, they will look better and last longer. You should always follow the care instructions and use the right laundry products. This will prevent your clothes from being damaged and will keep them in good shape.

Apply What You Have Learned

1. Go to a store and look at the laundry products available. Write down which ones are prewash products, soaps, detergents, bleaches, and fabric softeners. Read the instructions on the labels to see how they are used.
2. Call two local dry cleaners. Ask for the price of dry-cleaning garments, such as pants, coats, and dresses. Ask if they have coin-operated dry cleaning machines. Compare prices between the two stores.

Case Study

Read the story below and look at Lesson 10-2 again.
Then answer the questions below.

Shopping Skillfully

Eleanor will be starting a new school year soon. She and her mother have talked about the clothes she has and those she will need. Mrs. Evans plans to sew some skirts and blouses for Eleanor. However, Eleanor still needs shoes, blue jeans, shirts, sweaters, and a dress.

"I'd like to go shopping on Thursday," said Mrs. Evans. "That's when I have the most time. Also, the stores are not as crowded during the week. Do you have any activities planned for Thursday?"

"No, Mom. Thursday is fine," said Eleanor. "I like to shop. Are we going to shop at Bender's Department Store?"

"No, Eleanor," said Mrs. Evans. "We're going to shop at Murray's."

Eleanor asked, "Why do we have to shop at Murray's? Bender's is a neat store. They have great clothes. Can we please go to Bender's?"

"Bender's is nice, but their prices are too high. We can't afford to shop there. Murray's has better prices, and they carry the styles you like," said Mrs. Evans.

"But, Mom. Betty's mom took her to Bender's last week," said Eleanor. "I want to have nice clothes like Betty."

"Eleanor, you do have nice clothes like Betty's," said Mrs. Evans. "Remember when we found the same jacket at Murray's that Betty got at Bender's and it cost a lot less? Do you have your shopping list?"

"Yes, Mom. Here it is," said Eleanor as she handed the list to her mother.

Mrs. Evans took the list and began writing down prices next to each item. "This is what we can spend on each item," she said. "We should be able to find the clothes you want at prices we can afford. If we can find good quality clothes on sale, we might save some money. I'm going to pay with cash instead of using my credit cards."

To Discuss

⟹ 1. What steps are Eleanor and Mrs. Evans taking to make a buying plan?

⟹ 2. What factors have influenced Eleanor's decision about where to shop?

⟹ 3. How will Eleanor and Mrs. Evans benefit from making a buying plan?

Topic 10 Review

Topic Summary

To build a wardrobe, you first need to consider your clothing needs. Based on these needs, you can make a plan. Taking a wardrobe inventory can help you do this. The inventory will let you know what clothes and accessories you have and what you still need.

After you plan your wardrobe, you need to make a buying plan. This consists of deciding where to shop and how to pay for your clothes. You should think about variety, quality, price, service, and location as you make up your mind.

When you have a buying plan, you will be more organized. This will give you time to look for the best buys. Another way to get the most for your money is to inspect clothes before you buy them. Read labels and hangtags. Check the quality and the fit. Clothes that fit properly and are of high quality look better and wear better.

Knowing about fiber and fabric choices in clothing can help you make good shopping decisions. Each fiber has a different trait. Knowing what these traits are can help you choose clothes that are right for you and your activities.

Taking good care of your clothes will help them look better and last longer. Caring for your clothes includes sorting, washing, drying, ironing, pressing, and storing. Be sure to follow the care instructions and use the right laundry products. This will keep your clothes from being damaged and will keep them in good shape. Sometimes you may need to dry-clean your clothes instead of washing them. Washing can ruin these clothes.

1. Match the clothing with the factor that affects the clothing need.
   a. Ski jacket.   1. Activities.
   b. School   2. Standards of dress.
      uniform.   3. Climate.
   c. Track shoes.
2. Explain the difference between a fad and a classic.
3. What are two advantages of taking a wardrobe inventory?
4. List five different types of clothing stores. List one advantage of shopping at each. Then list one disadvantage of shopping at each.
5. What are three factors you should consider when deciding where to shop?
6. True or false. When you are shopping for clothes, you should decide how to pay when you're at the cash register.
7. True or false. A garment is a good buy if the sale price is $25 and the regular price was $40.
8. List three ways to save money when shopping for clothes.

9. What is the difference between a label and a hangtag?
10. What are three guidelines that should be met when checking quality in a garment?
11. What are three ways to make fabric?
12. What finishes should you look for when buying these items?
    a. Boots.
    b. Children's sleepwear.
    c. Blue jeans.
    d. Work clothes.
13. What are two benefits of using a fabric softener?
14. True or false. You need to treat stains as soon as they occur.
15. What could happen if you wash clothes labeled "Dry-Clean Only?"
16. (Ironing/Pressing) is moving the iron back and forth over the fabric to remove wrinkles.
17. List three hints for storing clothes.

Vocabulary Quiz

Match the definitions in Column A with the terms in Column B.
Write your answers on a separate sheet of paper.

Column A

1. A way to pay that lets you buy now and pay later.
2. A larger tag attached to a garment that is removed before wearing.
3. Cloth made from fibers or yarns.
4. Hairlike strands that can be twisted together to form yarn.
5. To group clothes according to the way you will wash them.
6. The design of a garment.
7. A style that is popular at the current time.
8. A style that is popular for only a short time.
9. A treatment given to fibers, yarns, or fabrics to improve the look, feel, or performance of a fabric.
10. To clean with chemicals instead of detergent and water.
11. To lift and lower an iron onto a small area of fabric.
12. A list of items on hand.
13. All the clothes and accessories you have to wear.
14. A combination of two or more fibers.

Column B

a. Style.
b. Fashion.
c. Fad.
d. Inventory.
e. Credit.
f. Accessory.
g. Fibers.
h. Wardrobe.
i. Fabric.
j. Finish.
k. Sort.
l. Iron.
m. Dry-clean.
n. Blend.
o. Press.
p. Hangtag.
q. Label.

Topic 11 Learning to Sew

Lesson 11-1
Sewing Basics

Objectives

After studying this lesson, you will be able to
- *define* serger *and* ravel.
- *explain the benefits of sewing.*
- *identify the parts of a sewing machine.*
- *list the basic sewing tools.*
- *describe how to behave when you are in the sewing lab.*
- *demonstrate how to work safely with others in a sewing lab.*

New Words

serger: *a type of sewing machine that uses an overlock stitch to prevent seams from raveling.*

ravel: *when threads pull out of the cut edges of a fabric.*

New Ideas

- *Use and care manuals tell you how to run and care for your sewing machine.*
- *Sewing tools are used to measure, mark, cut, and sew fabric.*
- *You need to help keep the sewing lab clean and neat.*
- *Safe sewing habits can protect you and your classmates from accidents.*

Sewing can be both fun and useful. You can make clothes or gifts for yourself or your family and friends. You can make these special by choosing the styles and colors you want. This will save you money. You can also repair your clothes.

Before you start sewing, you need to learn some basics. You need to learn how a sewing machine works and which tools to use. You should also become familiar with working in a sewing lab and following the safety rules. You can change clothes you have by redesigning or recycling them.

The Sewing Machine

Sewing machines make sewing easier. All sewing machines make straight stitches and most make backstitches. Some also make buttonholes and decorative stitches. Read your *use and care manual* to find out what kinds of stitches your sewing machine can make.

Sewing machines have many parts. Each of these parts performs a different task. Read the use and care manual to locate the parts on your sewing machine. See 11-1. You can also find out how these parts work. The use and care manual will also tell you how to set up, store, and care for your sewing machine.

Before you begin a sewing project, you should learn how to thread the sewing machine and make stitches. You should also learn how to control the speed and stop at the desired point. Somebody may show you how to do these tasks. You can also read the use and care manual to learn how.

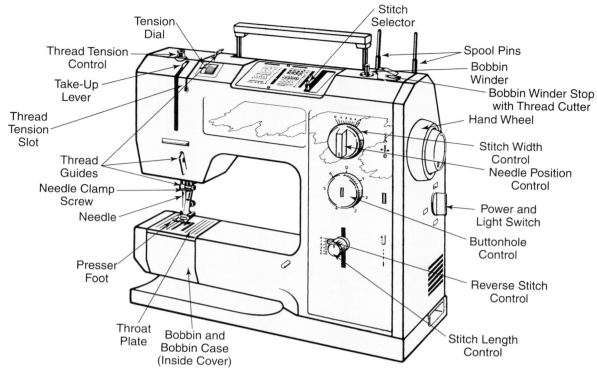

Tension Dial

Stitch Selector

Thread Tension Control

Spool Pins

Bobbin Winder

Take-Up Lever

Bobbin Winder Stop with Thread Cutter

Thread Tension Slot

Hand Wheel

Stitch Width Control

Needle Position Control

Thread Guides

Needle Clamp Screw

Power and Light Switch

Needle

Buttonhole Control

Presser Foot

Reverse Stitch Control

Throat Plate

Bobbin and Bobbin Case (Inside Cover)

Stitch Length Control

11-1 While all sewing machines are not alike, they have the same basic parts.

A different type of sewing machine is a **serger.** It uses an overlock stitch to prevent seams from raveling. **Raveling** is when threads pull out of the cut edges of a fabric. Sergers use from two to five spools of thread and sew faster than conventional sewing machines. Sergers cannot make buttonholes or insert zippers. Therefore, they are often used along with conventional sewing machines.

✔ **Check What You Have Learned**

1. What information can you find in your sewing machine's use and care manual?
2. How are sergers different from conventional sewing machines?

Sewing Tools

Before you begin sewing, you need to become familiar with the sewing tools. They can be used to measure, mark, cut, and sew fabric. See 11-2. Measuring tools include tape measures and sewing gauges. Marking tools include tracing wheels, dressmaker's carbon, and tailor's chalk and pencils. Cutting tools include shears, scissors, seam rippers, and pinking shears. Sewing tools include needles, pins, pincushions, and thimbles.

Collect all the tools you need before you begin to sew. This will save you from having to stop your work to look for them. When you are finished sewing, put your tools away. This way, you'll know where they are the next time you sew.

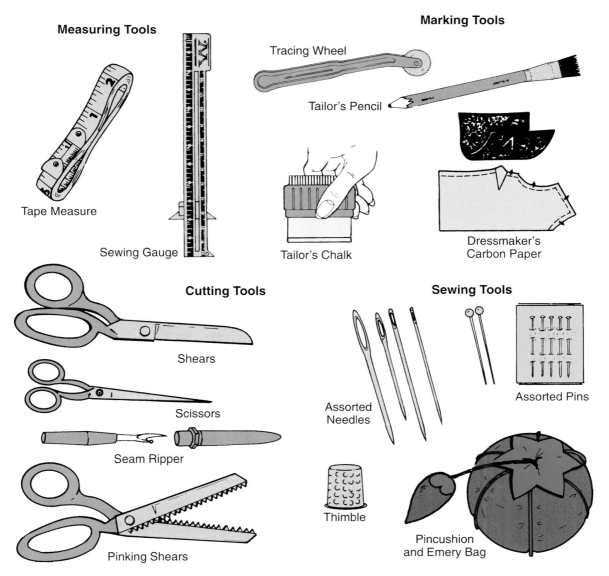

Measuring Tools

Tape Measure

Sewing Gauge

Marking Tools

Tracing Wheel

Tailor's Pencil

Tailor's Chalk

Dressmaker's Carbon Paper

Cutting Tools

Shears

Scissors

Seam Ripper

Pinking Shears

Sewing Tools

Assorted Needles

Assorted Pins

Thimble

Pincushion and Emery Bag

11-2 Sewing tools are used to perform many tasks. These tasks help make sewing easier.

✓ **Check What You Have Learned**

1. What are the four different types of sewing tools?
2. Why should you collect all your sewing tools before you begin sewing?

The Sewing Lab

When you sew at school, you need to make the most of your time in the sewing lab. Start working when the class begins. Work neatly at your table or desk. Label your sewing tools, pattern pieces, and guide sheet. This will keep them from getting mixed up with your classmates' tools and supplies. You should also write your name on pieces of paper and pin them to your fabric pieces.

When you are in the sewing lab, you need to think about your classmates. Sometimes you may have to share a sewing machine with a partner. Wait patiently until he or she is done. You may be able to do other work while you wait. You may also have to wait to use the iron. When it is your turn, use it quickly. If you need help from the teacher, be patient. He or she may be busy helping other students. See 11-3.

Help clean up at the end of the sewing lab. Be sure to clean the area around your sewing machine. Pick up fabric scraps, threads, and pins. Return

11-3 Your teacher may have to help many students. Work on other tasks while you wait your turn.

classroom tools to the proper place. Put your supplies and tools in a tote tray and store it in the assigned place.

You may also be assigned a cleanup task. You may have to put away or cover the sewing machines, sweep the floor, or put away the iron and pressing tools. These tasks help prepare the room for the next group of students.

✔ Check What You Have Learned

1. Why do you need to label your tools and supplies? How should they be stored?
2. Why is it important to clean your sewing area at the end of a sewing lab?

Working Safely

There are a lot of tools in the sewing lab. To protect yourself and your classmates, you need to use them carefully. Below are some tips for working safely in the sewing lab.

- Operate sewing machines carefully.
- Place pins in pincushions. Do not hold pins or needles in your mouth. You could swallow them.
- Store scissors and shears in a safe place.
- Keep the blades of scissors and shears closed when you're not using them.
- Hand scissors to other people with the handle turned toward them. See 11-4.

11-4 Be sure to follow good safety practices in the sewing lab. Handle sharp objects carefully.

- Test the heat of an iron on a scrap of fabric. Never touch the iron with your hand. You may burn yourself.
- Rest the iron on its heel. Never rest it face down.
- Turn off the iron when you are finished using it. Otherwise it may get too hot and a fire may start.
- Unplug the iron at the end of class. Let it cool before you empty the water. The steam could burn you.

✓ Check What You Have Learned

1. What are some tips for working safely in the sewing lab? How can they help prevent you from getting hurt?
2. Why shouldn't you test an iron with your hand?

The Main Ideas

When you sew, you need to use the proper sewing tools. You also need to understand the parts of a sewing machine and how it works. In the sewing lab, your work area, tools, and supplies must be carefully used, cared for, and shared. Safety rules must be followed to prevent accidents.

Apply What You Have Learned

1. With a classmate, make up a game to identify the different parts of a sewing machine and the tasks they perform. Be creative. Play this game with your classmates.
2. In small groups, make a list of rules to follow in your sewing lab. These should be both safety rules and rules for working with others. Brainstorm ideas to promote these rules. As a class, decide on the best one. Use this idea in your sewing lab.

Topic 11 Learning to Sew

Lesson 11-2
Preparing to Sew

Objectives

After studying this lesson, you will be able to
- ⟹ *define* pattern, guide sheet, grain, notions, *and* selvage.
- ⟹ *identify your correct figure type.*
- ⟹ *choose a pattern for your project.*
- ⟹ *explain the information on pattern envelopes and guide sheets.*
- ⟹ *choose the correct fabrics and notions for your project.*
- ⟹ *demonstrate how to correctly lay out, pin, cut, and mark a pattern.*

New Words

pattern: *a set of guidelines for making a garment or project.*
guide sheet: *a sheet that gives directions for cutting and sewing a project.*
grain: *the direction yarns run in a fabric.*
notions: *items other than fabric that become part of a garment or project.*
selvage: *the smooth, tightly-woven edge of a fabric.*

New Ideas

- ⟹ *You can select a pattern suited to your figure type.*
- ⟹ *Pattern envelopes and guide sheets give important sewing information.*
- ⟹ *Selecting the correct fabric and notions is important.*
- ⟹ *You need to correctly lay out, pin, cut, and mark patterns.*

A sewing project should be well planned. For this to happen, you need to follow certain steps. This will help you make sure your project turns out right. This lesson will discuss the steps you need to follow when preparing to sew.

Choosing a Project

The first step you need to take is to choose a project. See 11-5. When you are choosing a project, you need to think about your sewing skills. You also need to think about the time it will take you to make the project.

If you are a beginning sewer, you should choose an easy project. Pillows, sweatshirts, stuffed animals, and gym bags are good ideas for first projects. They do not take long to make, and the directions are easy to follow. As your sewing skills increase, you can make more advanced projects.

11-5   Choose an easy project, such as a pillow, the first time you sew.

You may or may not be able to choose your first project. Your teacher may decide that everyone in the class will make the same project. You can make your project different from your classmates' by selecting different fabrics and designs. You may be able to add your own details.

✔ Check What You Have Learned

1. What two factors do you need to keep in mind when choosing a sewing project?
2. How can you make your project different from your classmates'? Give examples.

Choosing a Pattern

After you choose a project, you need to choose a pattern. A **pattern** is a set of guidelines for making a garment or project. To find a pattern you like, look through pattern catalogs. See 11-6. Pattern catalogs are divided into different sections. They include patterns for women, juniors, girls, men, boys, children, toys, crafts, and household items.

If you are making a garment, you will need to choose a pattern that will fit you. To do this, you first need to determine your figure type. Figure types are based on height and body measurements. Because it is hard to measure yourself correctly, have your teacher or a classmate measure you. Then, compare your measurements with figure type charts in the back of pattern catalogs. Decide which figure type is the most like yours.

Once you know your figure type, you can choose the correct pattern size. Compare your measurements with the different sizes for each figure type. Then choose the pattern size closest to your own measurements.

11-6   Select a pattern designed for your figure type.

✔ Check What You Have Learned

1. Why do you need to have someone else take your measurements?
2. How can you determine your figure type? How can you choose the correct pattern size?

The Pattern Envelope

The front and back of the pattern envelope can give you a lot of information. The front of each envelope lists the size, pattern number, and the name of the pattern company. It also has pictures of the project. See 11-7. Sometimes more than one style or garment is shown. For instance, there may be a picture of both shorts and sweatpants.

The back of the pattern envelope has more detailed information than the front. This information tells you what supplies you need and what amount of fabric to buy. It also gives you descriptions of how the project will look when it is done. See 11-8.

Be sure to read the pattern envelope before you buy your sewing supplies. This way you will be sure to buy the correct amounts.

11-7 The front of a pattern envelope shows how the finished garment or project will look when completed.

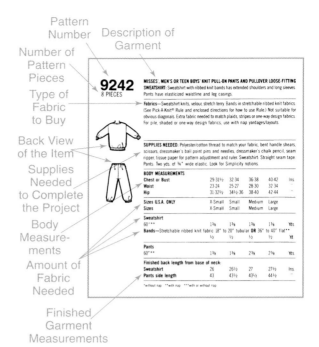

Pattern Number

Description of Garment

Number of Pattern Pieces

Type of Fabric to Buy

Back View of the Item

Supplies Needed to Complete the Project

Body Measurements

Amount of Fabric Needed

Finished Garment Measurements

11-8 Important information about your project can be found on the back of a pattern envelope.

✓ Check What You Have Learned

1. What information can you find on the front of a pattern envelope? What information can you find on the back?
2. Why should you read the pattern envelope before buying sewing supplies?

Inside the Pattern Envelope

A **guide sheet** is a sheet included with a pattern that gives directions for cutting and sewing a garment or project. The front of the guide sheet tells you which pattern pieces you need for your project. It gives you cutting layouts and directions for preparing and marking the fabric. Some basic sewing instructions are also included.

The back of the guide sheet gives you directions for putting the pattern pieces together. Detailed sewing instructions are also included.

Look at the front of the guide sheet to see which pattern pieces you need for your project. Cut these pattern pieces out of the tissue paper pattern sheets. Do not trim them. This will be done when you cut the fabric. Put the pattern pieces you are not using back in the envelope.

Look at the markings on the pattern pieces you are using. They are guides on pattern pieces for making a garment or project. There are two types of pattern markings. Some help you lay out and cut the pattern. Others help you construct the project. See 11-9.

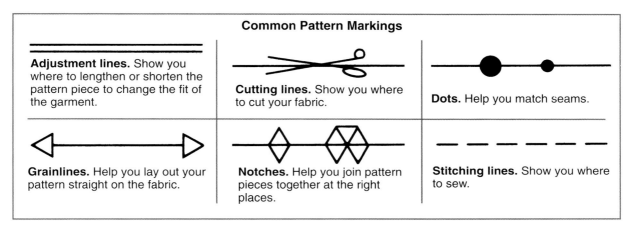

Common Pattern Markings

Adjustment lines. Show you where to lengthen or shorten the pattern piece to change the fit of the garment.

Cutting lines. Show you where to cut your fabric.

Dots. Help you match seams.

Grainlines. Help you lay out your pattern straight on the fabric.

Notches. Help you join pattern pieces together at the right places.

Stitching lines. Show you where to sew.

11-9   These are a few common markings you will see on your pattern pieces. Other markings are explained in the guide sheet.

✓ Check What You Have Learned

1. What information can you find on the front of a guide sheet?
2. What are two types of pattern markings? What are their functions?

Choosing Fabric and Notions

Once you have selected a pattern, you need to choose the fabric and notions. Before you choose the fabric, read the back of the pattern envelope carefully. See what type of fabric is suggested.

You can choose either woven or knit fabrics. Whichever kind you choose, make sure it has a firm weave. Fabric with a loose weave can stretch out of shape. The edges may ravel.

As a beginning sewer, there are many types of fabric you should avoid buying. Fabrics that are slippery, flimsy, stiff, or heavy may pucker, slip, or be hard to sew. Fabrics with stripes, plaids, or large prints need to be matched at the seams. You need to buy extra fabric for one-way designs, such as corduroy, velour, or terry cloth. When you lay out pattern pieces on one-way fabrics, all the pattern pieces must run the same direction.

Once you have chosen a fabric, you need to make sure the grain is straight. **Grain** is the direction yarns run in a fabric. Fabrics should be *on-grain*. This means that the lengthwise and crosswise yarns are at right angles to each other. Fabrics that are on-grain are easier to cut and sew than fabrics that are *off-grain*. See 11-10. Finished garments will hang right and keep their shape.

If you buy fabrics that are off-grain, they can be straightened by pulling on the two shortest corners. However, some fabrics have finishes that lock the fabric in place. These fabrics will return to their locked shape even after you straighten them.

Check the fabric you buy to see if it has been preshrunk. This information can be found on the end of the fabric bolt along with the care instructions. If the fabric has not been preshrunk, you need to wash it before you lay it out.

You will also need to buy notions to complete your project. **Notions** are items other than fabric that become part of a garment or project. The most common notions are the following:

On-Grain Fabric

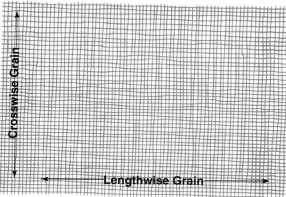

Off-Grain Fabric

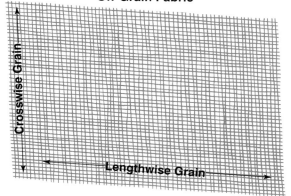

11-10 Always check to make sure the fabric you buy is on-grain.

- thread
- fasteners (buttons, snaps, hooks and eyes, zippers, and hook and loop tape)
- elastic
- seam binding or hem tape
- interfacing

Buy all the fabric and notions for your project at the same time. This way you will know that the thread, buttons, zipper, and seam binding match the fabric. You also will not have to stop working on your project to buy extra notions.

Laying Out, Pinning, Cutting, and Marking

Once you have chosen your pattern and fabric, you can begin laying them out. Cutting layouts show you how to place the pattern pieces on the fabric. There is a layout for each view, fabric width, and size. Find the layout for your garment or project. Draw a circle around it.

To lay out pattern pieces, first place the fabric on a tabletop. Then fold it according to the directions in the guide sheet. After that, place each pattern piece on the fabric following the cutting layout. Check this carefully several times to make sure the pattern pieces have been placed correctly.

Make sure the grainlines on the pattern pieces are placed on the grain of the fabric. The grainline should be even with the selvage. A **selvage** is the smooth, tightly-woven edge of a fabric. Use a yardstick or measuring tape to check that the grainline is even with the selvage.

The next step is to pin the pattern pieces to the fabric. See 11-11. Pins should be placed along the grainline. They should be placed at right angles to the pattern edge every three to four inches. If you place pins too close together, the fabric will not lie flat. Pins placed too far apart can cause the fabric and pattern to slip when you are cutting. Pins

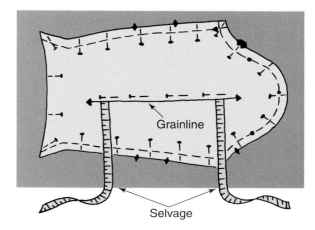

11-11 Pattern pieces need to be correctly placed and pinned.

should also be placed diagonally at each corner of the pattern piece. Never start cutting until all the pattern pieces are correctly placed and pinned.

To cut out pattern pieces correctly, let your scissors glide across the table. Do not pick the fabric up to cut around the pattern. Cut around notches.

Before you sew, markings, such as darts and dots, need to be marked on the fabric. This should be done before you unpin the pattern pieces from the fabric. Be careful when marking the wrong side of the fabric. Mark a scrap of fabric first to make sure the marks do not show on the right side.

The Main Ideas

As a beginning sewer, you should start with a simple project. You may need to choose a pattern for this project. If you are making a garment, choose one that will fit you. Make sure to read the pattern envelope for information about the project. Inside the pattern envelope, you will find the guide sheet and pattern pieces. After you have selected a pattern, you need to choose fabric and notions. Then you need to lay out, pin, cut, and mark the fabric.

Apply What You Have Learned

1. Ask your teacher, a parent, or a classmate to take your body measurements. Then compare your measurements with a figure type chart in the back of a pattern catalog. Identify which figure type and size is best for you.
2. Demonstrate to the class one of the following tasks:
   - straightening fabric
   - preparing fabric for lay out
   - laying out and pinning a pattern
   - transferring markings to fabric

Topic 11 Learning to Sew

Lesson 11-3
Sewing Your Project

Objectives

After studying this lesson, you will be able to
➠ *define* seam, basting, *and* shank.
➠ *demonstrate how to machine stitch.*
➠ *make different hand stitches.*
➠ *show how to sew seams.*
➠ *tell how to attach different fasteners.*

New Words

seam: *a row of permanent stitches used to hold two pieces of fabric together.*
basting: *sewing fabric pieces together with long, loose, temporary stitches.*
shank: *a short stem that holds a button away from fabric.*

New Ideas

➠ *You can make stitches by machine or hand.*
➠ *Well-made seams have certain traits.*
➠ *Fasteners need to be attached securely.*

After you have completed all the sewing preparation steps, you need to sew your project. There are certain skills you need to have to make your project turn out right. They include making good stitches and seams. Attaching fasteners correctly is also important.

Making Stitches

There are two types of stitches. Some are temporary. Others are permanent. Temporary stitches are removed from the fabric after a short time. Permanent stitches are left in the fabric. They hold the fabric pieces together securely.

Stitches can be made by machine or by hand. Machine stitching is quicker and stronger than hand stitching. To learn to make machine stitches, read your use and care manual. You should learn how to make straight seams, curved seams, and to turn corners. These are some of the basic stitching skills you will need to have to sew well.

Hand stitching lets you have more control over the fabric and stitches than machine stitching. Some common hand stitches are the basting stitch, hemming stitch, backstitch, and slip stitch. See 11-12. Hand stitching is used for temporary stitching, hemming, and attaching fasteners. When hand stitching, use a single thread with a knot at the end.

Hand Stitches

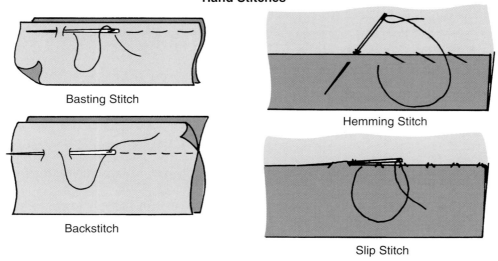

Basting Stitch

Hemming Stitch

Backstitch

Slip Stitch

11-12 Each hand stitch is sewn a little differently than the others.

✔ **Check What You Have Learned**

1. What is the difference between temporary and permanent stitching? Which one is stronger?
2. Why do you have more control over the fabric and stitches when you hand stitch?

Seams

Stitches are often used in sewing to make seams. A **seam** is a row of permanent stitches used to hold two pieces of fabric together. Seams should have strong, even stitches. They should be flat, smooth, and straight.

To make a seam, place the right sides of the fabric pieces together. Match the edges and notches. Then pin the pieces together and stitch the seam. Most seams are sewn ⁵/₈ inch from the edge of the fabric. See 11-13.

You can also baste the pieces together before stitching. **Basting** is sewing fabric pieces together with long, loose, temporary stitches. Basting can be done by machine or by hand. After fabric pieces have been basted together, stitch the seam.

Each permanent stitch should begin and end with a few small backstitches. This will secure the

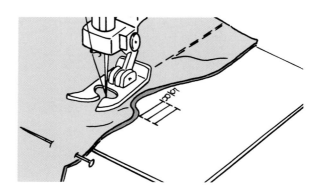

11-13 On the throat plate of the sewing machine, there is often a marking showing ⁵/₈ inch.

stitching. The backstitches can be made by machine or by hand.

After seams are stitched, press them according to the directions in the guide sheet. Pressing keeps the seams flat and smooth. Always press on the wrong side of the fabric.

Seam edges need to be finished to prevent raveling. There are many different types of seam finishes. Some are shown on your guide sheet. Different types of seam finishes are good for different types of fabrics. Your teacher can help you decide which type is best for your fabric.

✓ Check What You Have Learned

1. What are the traits used to describe a well-made seam?
2. What can happen if you forget to backstitch at the beginning and end of a seam?

Attaching Fasteners

Fasteners need to be sewn on securely because they are used so much. Always use a double thread with a knot at the end. This will help attach them more securely.

Before sewing on buttons, make sure they are the correct size and color. Select thread that matches the buttons. If you are sewing a button on heavy fabric, like a coat, use button thread.

Buttons need to have a shank when they are sewn onto fabric. A **shank** is a short stem that holds the button away from the fabric. Shanks prevent the fabric under the button from tearing. They also help hold buttons on firmly.

Some buttons are made with shanks. Other buttons, called *sew-through buttons,* need to have a shank made when they are attached. See 11-14.

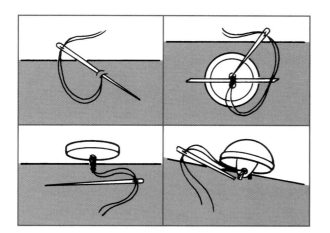

11-14 Before you sew on a button, make sure it is in line with the buttonhole.

Follow these steps for sewing on buttons.

1. Make several small stitches to secure the thread in the fabric where you want the button to be placed. Insert the needle through one of the holes on the underside of the button. Pull the thread through to the top of the button.

2. Place a pin on top of the button. If you are sewing on heavy fabric, use a toothpick. This helps produce a shank when you stitch on a sew-through button. Push the needle down through the second hole and back up the first hole. Repeat this four or five times.

3. Remove the pin or toothpick when you are finished. Then pull the button up. Wrap the thread around the loose threads underneath the button four or five times. This creates the shank.

4. Push the threaded needle to the back of the fabric. Make several small stitches through the thread loop. This will fasten the thread.

5. If your button already has a shank, simply sew it following steps 1 and 4.

Snaps are used to hold overlapping edges flat. See 11-15. They do not stay fastened under stress.

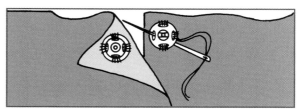

11-15 Mark where you want the snap parts to be placed. Make sure these marks meet so the fabric will lie flat when snapped.

Hand stitch the snap parts on with a series of small stitches. Be careful that the stitches don't show on the right side of the fabric.

Hooks and eyes are used to fasten waistbands and neck edges. See 11-16. Hooks and eyes can take more strain than snaps. Hand stitch hooks and eyes on with several short stitches. Make sure the stitching doesn't show on the outside of the fabric.

Hook and loop tape can be attached by following the directions on the package. Zippers should be inserted according to the directions in your guide sheet.

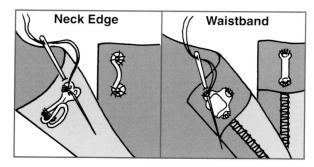

11-16 Different types of hooks and eyes are used for neck edges and waistbands.

✓ Check What You Have Learned

1. Why should you use a double thread when sewing on fasteners?
2. What are the steps for sewing on a button without a shank? For sewing on a button with a shank?

💡 The Main Ideas

Sewing projects often need to be both machine and hand stitched. Some stitching is temporary and some is permanent. Once you know how to make stitches, you can make good, strong seams. These hold your fabric together. Fasteners also need to be attached securely and correctly.

▶ Apply What You Have Learned

1. On a piece of paper, draw straight lines, curved lines, and corners. Practice your machine stitching following these lines. Stitch without using thread.
2. Demonstrate how to make a seam. Stitch two scraps of fabric together following the directions in this lesson. Be sure to press and finish the seam.
3. Choose two of the four hand stitches described in this lesson. On scraps of fabric, make samples of these two stitches.

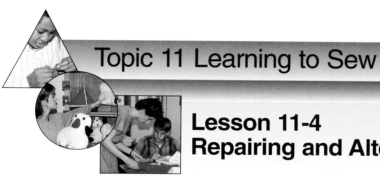

Lesson 11-4
Repairing and Altering Your Clothes

Objectives

After studying this lesson, you will be able to

➡ *define* alterations, redesign, *and* appliqué.

➡ *explain the advantages of repairing and altering your clothes.*

➡ *demonstrate how to make clothing repairs.*

➡ *describe how to make clothing alterations.*

New Words

alterations: *changes made in the size, length, or style of a garment so it will fit properly.*

redesign: *to change the appearance or function of a garment.*

appliqué: *to sew one or more pieces of fabric to a large piece of fabric or a garment.*

New Ideas

➡ *Some common clothing repairs are fixing fasteners, rips, and tears.*

➡ *You can alter hems and seams to make your clothes fit better.*

➡ *You can redesign and recycle garments to extend the use of your clothes.*

Do you have clothes in your closet that need to be repaired? Many times you can make these repairs yourself. When you make your own clothing repairs, your clothing will last longer. Your clothing money will go further.

You can also stretch your clothing budget by making alterations to your clothes. **Alterations** are changes made in the size, length, or style of a garment so it will fit properly. They include changing hems and seams.

Repairing Fasteners

Sometimes fasteners may come loose. They may also break. Resew fasteners when they become loose. If they fall off and you lose them, they will need to be replaced. Follow the directions for attaching fasteners in Lesson 11-3, "Sewing Your Project."

If a button falls off and you loose it, check to see if you have any extra buttons that match. Some clothes come with extra buttons when you buy them. If you cannot find an identical button, you may have to replace all the buttons on the garment. This is why you should resew loose buttons before they fall off.

If a zipper breaks, you need to replace it. Be sure to buy a new one that is the same color and size as the old zipper. See 11-17. Follow these steps to replace a zipper.

1. Remove the broken zipper carefully, using a small pair of scissors or a seam ripper. Be careful not to cut the fabric. (If you are replacing a zipper on a garment with a waistband, you will have to remove some of the stitching in the waistband.)

2. Press the zipper area flat.

3. Pin the new zipper in place, following the directions on the zipper package.

4. Baste and then stitch the zipper along the old stitching lines.

5. Press well.

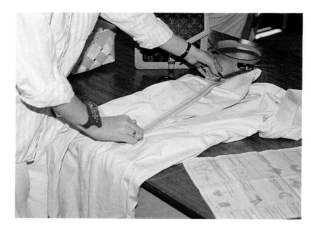

11-17 It is important that your new zipper matches your garment as closely as possible.

✔ **Check What You Have Learned**

1. Why is it important to resew loose buttons before they fall off?
2. If you have a garment that needs to have the zipper replaced, what steps should you take?

Repairing Rips and Tears

If you rip a seam, repair it right away. Rips are easier to repair when they are small. To fix a rip, turn the garment inside out and pin the seam together. Then stitch the seam, going past the ripped area a little on each end. Try to match the color of the thread to the garment. If this is not possible, use thread a shade darker.

You can repair seams by machine or by hand. If you hand stitch, make small stitches. Make sure the stitching isn't too tight. This could cause the threads to break. Seams that receive a lot of stress need to be stitched twice. These seams include crotch seams in pants and armhole seams in shirts.

When your clothing gets torn, it can be fixed using iron-on mending tape. First clip any frayed threads. Then apply iron-on mending tape to the inside of the garment. Be sure to also follow the directions on the package.

Another way to fix tears is to patch them. You can buy patches. You can also cut patches out of fabric scraps. Make sure they match the color of the fabric. Patches are often sewn on the outside of the garment by machine or by hand.

✔ **Check What You Have Learned**

1. Why do you need to repair ripped seams right away?
2. What are the two ways to repair torn clothes? How do these methods differ?

Altering Hems

Sometimes you may buy clothes that are too long or too short. You may have clothes that you want to make longer or shorter. You can make these changes by altering the hem. See 11-18.

Before you lengthen a garment, make sure there is enough fabric in the hem to lengthen it. If there isn't, you can buy hem facing to extend the hem. This can be sewn on the edge of the hem. To shorten a garment, you may need to trim away some of the fabric.

How to Alter Garment Hems

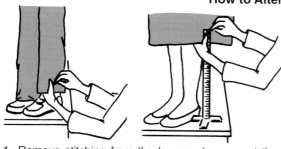

1. Remove stitching from the hem and press out the crease. Try on the garment. Have someone mark the hem with a pin line. Use a yardstick to be sure all pins are the same distance from the floor.

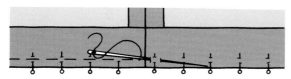

2. Turn up the hem on the pin line. Pin the hem in place and press the fold. Then baste close to the fold. Remove the pins.

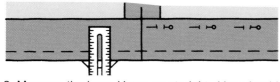

3. Measure the hem. Hems on straight skirts should be 2½ inches wide. Hems on pants and flared skirts should be 1½ inches wide. The hem should be even all the way around. If it isn't, make a pin line the same distance from the fold all the way around.

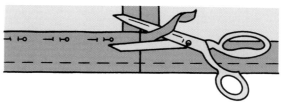

4. Cut the fabric along the pin line. Remove the pins.

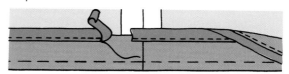

5. Machine stitch seam tape to the raw edge of woven fabrics that ravel. Knit fabrics do not need seam tape.

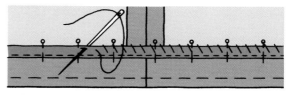

6. Pin the hem edge in place. Hand stitch the hem edge to the garment. Use the hemming stitch for hems on woven fabrics. Use the slip stitch for hems on knitted fabrics. Be careful that the stitching doesn't show on the right side of your garment.

7. Remove the pins and basting. Press well.

11-18 To make sure your new hem looks good, follow these steps very carefully.

> **✔ Check What You Have Learned**
>
> 1. If you have a garment that is too long or short, what steps should you take to change the hem?
> 2. Why do you need to stitch seam tape to the edges of woven fabric that ravels?

Altering Seams

Sometimes your clothes may be too big or too small. Instead of getting rid of them or giving them away, you may be able to make alterations. Some alterations are easy to make. You may just need to move a button or a hook.

Other alterations can be more demanding. You may need to take in or let out the seams. This will make the garment smaller or larger. These changes mean adjusting the sides or the front and back of the garment.

To alter seams, first pin the new seams in place. See 11-19. Then try on the garment to check the fit. When the fit is right, sew the new seams. When you let out a garment, sew the new seam in the old seam allowance. When you are taking in a garment, sew outside the old seam allowance. After you have sewn the new seams, remove the old stitching and press well.

11-19 Before you pin the new seams, make sure you are letting out or taking in the correct amount of fabric.

> **✔ Check What You Have Learned**
>
> 1. Why may you need to take in or let out a garment? Give examples.
> 2. Why should you check the fit of the garment before you sew the new seams?

Redesigning and Recycling Clothes

Using basic sewing skills, you can redesign or recycle your clothes. To **redesign** clothing is to change the appearance or function of a garment. For example, if you have a pair of jeans that are too short, you could redesign the jeans into cut-offs. You also could make a completely new item by recycling the jeans into a backpack. To do this, cut off the legs below the crotch, turn the garment inside out, and sew the legs together. Use the rest of the fabric to make a top flap and straps.

Other examples of redesigning your clothes include sewing a patch or appliqué onto something you already have. To **appliqué** means to sew one or more pieces of fabric to a large piece of fabric or a garment. An appliqué can be a colorful trim. Alan appliquéd a design of his school mascot to his jacket. An appliqué also can cover a rip or stain. Katie made an appliqué for a stained skirt out of material that matched a blouse.

T-shirts are fun to redesign. You can use fabric paint and create a unique shirt. You can color a white T-shirt by dyeing it. You can create a special design through a process called *tie-dyeing*.

When you recycle clothes, you give an old garment a new use. The simplest way to recycle clothing is to give your outgrown garments to another person. Many families and friends give clothes that no longer fit to other family members and friends. Mary used her grandfather's discarded jacket and recycled it with decorative trim.

You also can donate your clothes to a charity or sell them at a yard sale. You can sell your clothing in a consignment shop and receive a portion of the sale price.

Recycling also can mean finding a new use for old clothes. You can use the fabric of old clothes to make pillows, stuffed animals, or clothes for children. You can use soft, cotton garments, such as T-shirts, for cleaning. Some communities offer recycling drop-offs for clothes.

Both redesigning and recycling clothing extend the use of your clothes and reduce waste. By using these practices, you are helping the environment and saving money. You also may enjoy making creative projects.

✓ Check What You Have Learned

1. What is the difference between redesigning and recycling clothing?
2. What organizations in your community accept donations of used clothing?

💡 The Main Ideas

It is important to know how to repair and alter your clothes. You can save money. You can also make your clothes last longer. Repairing fasteners, rips, and tears are easy tasks. To make your clothes fit better, you can alter hems and seams. Redesigning and recycling clothes can increase the amount of clothing you have and reduce waste.

⏭ Apply What You Have Learned

1. Prepare a demonstration on how to make simple clothing repairs. Use fabric scraps to show how to repair fasteners, rips, or tears. Include the steps you need to take to correctly make the repair.
2. Look through your closet and drawers at home. Find a garment that needs to have the hem altered. Bring the garment to class and make the alterations. Follow the directions given in this lesson.
3. Create a pamphlet showing the benefits of recycling clothing. Include specific suggestions for others to use.

Case Study

Read the story below and look at Lesson 11-2 again. Then answer the questions below.

A Sewing Project

Mel and Jay were eating pizza at Mel's house one Friday night. Jay was telling Mel about how he has to make a project in sewing class at school.

"Can you believe it, Mel?" Jay asked. "I don't want to make a project. I don't know how to sew. My project will probably turn out all wrong."

"Actually, sewing is pretty easy," Mel said. "I took sewing last year at the school I went to before my family moved here."

"You did?" Jay asked. "I didn't know that other schools required sewing classes."

"Sure. I didn't like the idea at first either," Mel said. "But my teacher, Ms. Lee, made sewing fun and easy."

"What projects did you have to make?" Jay asked.

"My first project was a stuffed bear," said Mel. "I used a kit that came with all the pieces. I didn't have to buy anything except the kit. It was really fun to make, and the directions were easy to follow. I was really excited to make the next project."

"What was your second project?" Jay asked.

"I made a gym bag. That may sound hard, but it really wasn't," Mel said. "I also got to go to the fabric store and choose the pattern and fabric that I wanted. I like the style and colors I chose better than any I've seen in the stores."

"My teacher said that we'll have to make a project with a zipper," said Jay. "That's what sounds hard to me."

"I thought so, too," Mel said. "But after I made my gym bag, applying zippers is easy. Don't worry. Your teacher will help you if you have problems."

To Discuss

➡ 1. What can Jay do to overcome his fear of sewing?

➡ 2. How do you think Mel's advice to Jay is helping Jay feel better about sewing class?

➡ 3. What are three sewing projects Jay might choose?

Topic 11 Review

Topic Summary

Sewing can be fun. It can also save you money. You can make clothes and other items, such as gym bags or stuffed toys, for yourself. You can make gifts for family and friends. You can also repair and alter your clothes.

If you are a beginning sewer, you first need to learn the basic sewing skills. You need to know the parts of a sewing machine and the different types of sewing tools used. When you are in the sewing lab, you need to learn to use your time wisely and work well with others. You also need to work safely to prevent accidents.

The next step is to plan a project and prepare to sew it. Your first project should match your sewing skills. Look in pattern catalogs to find a pattern for a project you have the skills to make. If you are making a garment, make sure you choose a pattern that is the correct size.

After you have selected a pattern, you need to choose the fabric and notions. The pattern envelope gives important information about choosing supplies and making the project. Directions in the guide sheet will tell you how to lay out, pin, cut, and mark the fabric.

When you sew, you may use machine stitching or hand stitching. Machine stitching is strong and permanent. It is good for making seams. Hand stitching is temporary and lets you have more control over the fabric and stitches than machine stitching. It is good for sewing on fasteners and making hems.

Repairing and altering your clothes will make them last longer. Some common clothing repairs include fixing fasteners, rips, and tears. You can alter hems and seams to make your clothes fit better. Redesigning and recycling clothes extends their use.

To Review

Write your answers on a separate sheet of paper.

1. List three benefits of sewing.
2. What are the four types of sewing tools?
3. List three hints for working safely in the sewing lab.
4. Figure types are based on
   a. Height.
   b. Weight.
   c. Body measurements.
   d. Fabric needed.
   e. Both a and c.
5. True or false. It is easy to take your own body measurements.
6. What are two items found on the front of a pattern envelope?
7. List three items found on the back of a pattern envelope.
8. Draw symbols for the following pattern markings:
   a. Notch.
   b. Grainline.
   c. Stitching line.
   d. Cutting line.
9. Be sure to buy fabrics that are (on-grain/off-grain).

10. Which of the following are examples of notions?
    a. Zippers and seam binding.
    b. Needles and pins.
    c. Scissors and shears.
    d. Patterns and fabric.
11. What are two advantages of machine stitching and two advantages of hand stitching?
12. How far are most seams sewn from the edge of the fabric?
13. Press seams on the (right/wrong) side of the fabric.
14. True or false. Use a double thread when sewing on a button.
15. What are two advantages of repairing and altering your clothes?
16. True or false. Use a contrasting color of thread when sewing rips.
17. List two ways to repair tears.
18. What are two alterations you can make to your clothes?

Vocabulary Quiz

Match the definitions in Column A with the terms in Column B.
Write your answers on a separate sheet of paper.

Column A

1. When threads pull out of the cut edges of a fabric.
2. The direction yarns run in a fabric.
3. Items other than fabric that become part of a garment or project.
4. A sheet that gives directions for cutting and sewing a project.
5. A row of permanent stitches used to hold two pieces of fabric together.
6. Sewing fabric pieces together with long, loose, temporary stitches.
7. Changes made in the size, length, or style of a garment so it will fit properly.
8. A short stem that holds a button away from fabric.
9. A set of guidelines for making a garment or project.
10. A type of sewing machine that uses an overlock stitch to prevent seams from raveling.
11. To change the appearance or function of a garment.
12. To sew one or more pieces of fabric to a large piece of fabric or a garment.

Column B

a. Serger.
b. Ravel.
c. Notions.
d. Pattern.
e. Grain.
f. Seam.
g. Shank.
h. Basting.
i. Selvage.
j. Alterations.
k. Guide sheet.
l. Appliqué.
m. Redesign.

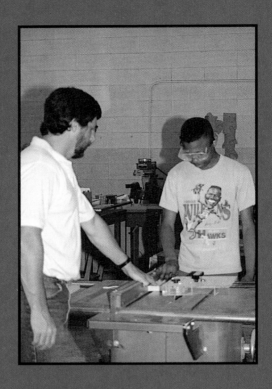

Unit 5
The World of Work

You learn many skills you will need in your future workplace at school.

Topic 12 Learning About Work

Lesson 12-1
Questions About Work

Objectives

After studying this lesson, you will be able to

- → *define work, fringe benefit, job, and career.*
- → *give examples of how working benefits you and your community.*
- → *explain the difference between a job and a career.*
- → *tell how decisions about work will affect a person's future.*

New Words

work: *what a person does to earn money.*
fringe benefit: *reward of a job other than income, such as paid vacations and health insurance.*
job: *a position held by a worker.*
career: *a series of related jobs a person holds over time.*

New Ideas

- → *Work benefits you and your community.*
- → *Some people have a series of jobs; others pursue a career.*
- → *Your decisions about work will affect your future.*

You see people working every day. You have probably thought about what kind of work you would like to do some day. However, you may have a number of questions about what work will mean in your life. This lesson will attempt to answer some of those questions.

Work is energy that is spent in order to complete a task. In this sense, work can mean anything a person does. You work when you mow the lawn or do homework. Jogging three miles is work. In this unit, **work** is described as what a person does to earn money.

Why Work?

One of your first questions about work may be, "Why should I work?" There are many reasons for working. All jobs serve some purpose and are worthwhile. See 12-1. Think of all the jobs you have seen today. Perhaps you rode the bus to school. The bus driver performed a worthwhile job. Can you think of other workers you have seen today? Think of the reasons each job is worthwhile.

Working has many personal benefits. Work can give you a sense of *dignity* or self-worth. It can provide you with a sense of pride, success, and independence.

Lamont is a social worker who works with child abuse cases. He has a strong desire to help children. He wants to provide a service to society. The feeling that he is helping others is a reward of his job.

12-1 This woman provides a valuable service through her job as a child care worker.

Working can give you a sense of identity. Your job gives you a "place" in your community. You may be known as a hairstylist, doctor, dance teacher, salesperson, or by some other title. See 12-2.

Earning an income is another important benefit of having a job. Income is the money you earn. You can use your income to buy items you need and want.

Besides income, many workers earn other benefits, called **fringe benefits.** Fringe benefits include paid vacations, health insurance, life insurance, bonuses, and retirement funds.

Friendship can be a benefit of work, too. Sharing experiences with coworkers can give you a chance to make new friends.

You are not the only one who benefits when you work. Your community also benefits. Your working helps the flow of money and creates the need for jobs in your community. You use the money you earn to buy products and services. Some of the money you spend is used to pay the people who make the products and offer the services. You provide work for others when you spend your money in this way. See 12-3.

12-3 Communities benefit when people work. When you are able to buy local products, you help others in your community.

12-2 This man's job as a photographer gives him identity in his community.

Your community further benefits when you pay taxes on your income. Taxes are used to help support public resources in the community. These resources include schools, fire and police protection, hospitals, and libraries.

Job or Career?

Do you want to hold a series of unrelated jobs, or do you want to pursue a career? A **job** is a position held by a worker. A **career** is a series of *related* jobs a person holds over time.

Each job in a career builds on the knowledge and experience gained in the job before. Suppose you decide on a career in food service. You may start with a job as a waiter. Then you may get a job as a cook. With some classes or special training, you may advance to pastry chef. Your hard work and experience may one day land you a job as executive chef.

A career involves your feelings toward work as well as what you do. A career requires setting goals. You have to be willing to get the training needed to help you get your first job. Then you have to stick with the job to get the experience needed to advance to the next job. See 12-4. Pursuing a career takes dedication, time, and hard work. However, you will be rewarded with a higher job status and a sense of accomplishment. You are also likely to earn more money than if you held a number of unrelated jobs.

In the past, many people had only one career. Today, people are more flexible. Many people change careers in their lifetimes. For instance, Pam always wanted to be a kindergarten teacher. She went to college for four years to get her teaching degree. After teaching for eight years, she decided to stop teaching and sell real estate. She changed her career in education to a career in sales.

Changing careers will require more training. Pam had to take classes and get a real estate license. However, she felt the challenge of doing something new was worthwhile.

12-4 If this young man sticks with his job, he may one day become a hardware store manager.

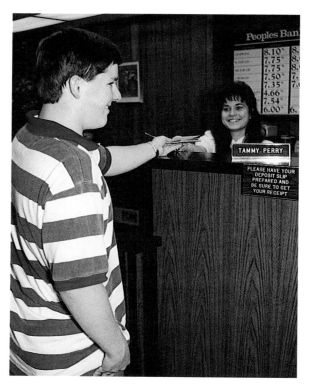

Check What You Have Learned

1. Why is your attitude important to pursuing a career?
2. What is a career that interests you? What are four related jobs that career might include?

How Will Work Affect You?

Your decision about a job will affect your future lifestyle. Your lifestyle is the way you live. This means your job will affect your income, how you spend your time, and where you live. It will even have some effect on whom your friends will be. How can a job do all of this?

Your choice of jobs will affect how much money you will make. The amount of income you have impacts what goods and services you can buy. See 12-5.

How often you are paid will also be controlled by your job. You may be paid every week, every other week, or once a month. You might even be paid every time you complete a job. The way you are paid will affect how you will have to budget your money.

Hilary is a professional dancer in a large city. She is paid each time she performs. The number of performances varies from month to month. She has to carefully plan how she will pay for her living expenses. When Hilary is working, she must save part of her money. This takes care of her expenses when she is not working.

Your job will control how you use your time. The hours you work will depend on your job. Many people work the same hours every week. However, some jobs have schedules that change from one week to the next. You might work at night or during the day. Some jobs require that you take work home. The amount of time you spend working will affect how much time you can spend doing other activities.

Working affects your decision about where to live. Some jobs require that you live in a certain area. Even if you are free to live anywhere, you may want to live near your job. This will allow you to avoid long drives to and from work.

You are likely to become friends with some of the people who work with you. Therefore, your job may even affect who your friends will be. See 12-6.

12-5 Your job will affect how much income you can save as well as how much you can spend.

12-6 Most people form friendships with some of their coworkers.

✓ Check What You Have Learned

1. What difference might it make in your life if you got paid monthly instead of weekly?
2. How can your job have an effect on whom your friends will be?

💡 The Main Ideas

There are many reasons for working. These reasons include benefits for both you and your community. You need to decide if you would rather hold a series of unrelated jobs or pursue a career. Your lifestyle will be directly affected by your choice of jobs.

▌▌▌▌➡ Apply What You Have Learned

1. Make a collage that illustrates personal and community benefits of working.
2. Interview an older person who has a career that interests you. Ask questions to find out what jobs he or she has held throughout the career. Also find out how his or her choice of careers affected his or her lifestyle. Share your findings in class.

Lesson 12-2
Work Trends

Objectives

After studying this lesson, you will be able to
⇒ *define* trend *and* entrepreneur.
⇒ *list social and technological trends that will affect future jobs.*
⇒ *describe opportunities for entrepreneurship.*

New Words

trend: *a general pattern of events.*
entrepreneur: *a person who starts and manages his or her own business.*

New Ideas

⇒ *Trends in society and technology affect the workplace and jobs.*
⇒ *Entrepreneurship is a growing trend in the world of work.*

What kind of job will you have in 25 years? Describing your future job may be hard because it may not have been invented yet. Many of the jobs today were not around 20 years ago. Some of today's jobs will not be around in the future. The demand for certain jobs changes as society changes.

Predicting your future career is not easy. However, you can be aware of certain trends that will affect the workplace. This awareness might give you a clue about what the world of work may have in store for you.

Trends That Will Affect Jobs

The demand for certain jobs is affected by changes in society and technology. These changes are seen as trends. A **trend** is a general pattern of events. By studying trends that will affect jobs in the future, you can make better career choices. See 12-7.

Listed below are some of the social trends that will affect jobs in the future.

- With more women working outside the home, the need for child care will keep increasing. More jobs related to child care will be created. See 12-8.
- Keeping up with the changing society will create a greater need for communication skills. Many jobs will require that workers have good reading, writing, and speaking skills. Taking classes that focus on communication will help you with your future jobs.
- The number of service jobs will increase. These jobs involve helping people.

12-7 Reading the newspaper can help you keep up with trends that may affect the job market.

12-8 The need for child care services will continue to increase as more and more mothers enter the workplace.

They include repair people, fire fighters, police officers, bus drivers, and restaurant workers.

- More people are living longer. Therefore, more jobs related to services for older people will be created.

- More people will choose to work in their homes. They may use home computers that are connected to an office by phone lines.
- Working hours will be more flexible. You may be able to choose your work hours.

Technological trends also affect the job market. The following shifts in the world of work are a result of advances in technology:

- Fewer jobs will be open to unskilled workers. Machinery, robots, and technical processes will replace many unskilled workers.
- High-tech items, such as computers, lasers, and satellites, are being used more in the workplace. More workers with technical skills will be needed to run these devices.
- Increased use of computers will allow workers to complete their work faster. Use opportunities to learn computer skills while you are in school. See 12-9.

12-9 The computer skills you learn in school will be useful in almost any career you choose.

Entrepreneurship

Another trend that will affect work is that more people are becoming entrepreneurs. An **entrepreneur** is a person who starts and manages his or her own business.

Entrepreneurs find needs for certain products and services. Then they start businesses to supply those products and services. For instance, today more women are working outside the home. As a result, there is a need for housecleaning services for families. A person who sees this need and begins such a service would be an entrepreneur. See 12-10.

People choose to become entrepreneurs for many reasons. They like being in charge and making their own business decisions. They feel they can use their skills better than an employer would. Perhaps they believe they can make more money by working for themselves.

You don't have to be an adult to become an entrepreneur. Many teens have successfully started businesses. Lawncare services and children's party planning are just two examples.

Lia's business is another example. Lia is 13 years old, and she loves animals. She started a pet-sitting service to care for animals while their owners are away. She feeds, brushes, and walks the animals. Her special effort causes her clients to favor her over the local kennel.

Do you think you might like to become an entrepreneur? If you are interested in starting your own business, keep the following tips in mind:

- Choose a business you will enjoy.
- Offer a service or product that is needed by your community.

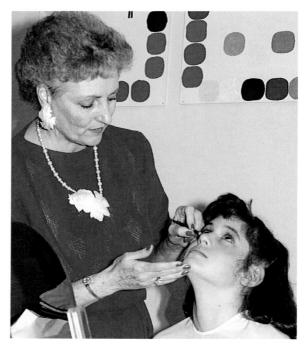

12-10 An entrepreneur with a color consulting business shows customers how they can use color to enhance their appearance.

- Research the requirements of your proposed business before you begin. Try to talk to people who have similar businesses.
- Decide on a fair price for your service or product. Do not undervalue yourself but do not overcharge either. See 12-11.
- Assume responsibility for this job just as if you were working for someone else.

12-11 This young entrepreneur is making shirts to sell. She has to choose a price for her products that customers will be willing to pay.

✔ Check What You Have Learned

1. Why do some people choose to become entrepreneurs?
2. Why should you research the requirements for your proposed business before you begin?

💡 The Main Ideas

In order to make wise decisions about work, you need to look at work trends. Social and technological trends affect the workplace and working conditions. These trends also affect the kinds of jobs that will be available to you. One job trend that might affect you is entrepreneurship.

⫸ Apply What You Have Learned

1. Look through today's newspaper. Find an article that is related to one of the trends discussed in this lesson. Share your article with the class.
2. Make a list of services that are needed in your community. Write a one-page report on how an entrepreneur could provide one of the services you listed.

Lesson 12-3
What Will You Do?

Objectives

After studying this lesson, you will be able to

➥ *define* interest inventory, aptitude, occupation, *and* career plan portfolio.

➥ *give examples of ways to learn about interests and aptitudes.*

➥ *identify sources of information about careers.*

➥ *explain how setting goals can help you choose a career and get it.*

➥ *describe how a career plan portfolio can help you reach your career goals.*

New Words

interest inventory: *a test that shows areas in which a person seems to have the most interest.*

aptitude: *a natural skill.*

occupation: *a job or position held by a worker.*

career plan portfolio: *sample of materials relating to a person's career plan.*

New Ideas

➥ *Identifying your interests and skills can help you choose a career you will enjoy.*

➥ *Learning about many careers can help you decide which one is right for you.*

➥ *Setting goals can help you enter the career of your choice.*

➥ *Making a career plan can assist you in entering the career of your choice.*

Preparing to enter the world of work involves matching yourself to a career. You need to think about what your interests and skills are. Then you need to find out what types of jobs would use those interests and skills.

Who Are You?

The first step in deciding on a career is learning about yourself. What do you like to do best? What are your special talents? What do you value? What kind of lifestyle do you want to have when you are older? Answering these questions can help you decide what type of career would be right for you.

You are likely to enjoy a job you find interesting. See 12-12. To help you find such a job, you may want to take an **interest inventory.** This is a test that will show you areas in which you seem to have the most interest. For instance, an interest inventory might suggest whether you prefer working with your hands or your mind. It may show whether you like working indoors or outside. Some questions may reveal if you prefer working alone or with others. Your guidance counselor can give you an interest inventory.

You are likely to do your best work if you select a job for which you have an aptitude. An **aptitude** is a natural skill. For instance, suppose you have an aptitude for spelling. You may work well as a proofreader. (A proofreader is someone who finds misspelled words in written work.)

Your counselor can give you an aptitude test. This test can show you if you have a natural talent for doing certain tasks. See 12-13. Learning what

12-12 Someone who is interested in nutrition may enjoy working as a dietitian.

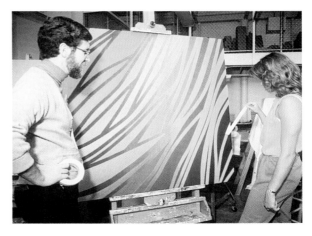

12-13 If you are creative and express yourself well through painting, you have an aptitude for art.

your aptitudes are can help point you toward a career you will enjoy.

Your values will also affect the kinds of jobs that appeal to you. Suppose you value time with your family. You may be happier in a job that does not require a lot of traveling. If change is something you value, you may want a job with varied tasks.

✓ Check What You Have Learned

1. Why should learning about yourself be the first step in deciding on a career?
2. What is one of your aptitudes? What job might let you use this aptitude?

Exploring Careers

The second step in choosing a career is to explore what kinds of jobs are available. You can get information about jobs from a number of sources. You can get help from your guidance counselor. Career and family and consumer sciences classes will give information. Your school and public libraries can assist you. You can also talk to people who have jobs that interest you.

Two books can help you gather information about **occupations,** or jobs. *The Dictionary of Occupational Titles* (DOT) describes over 35,000 jobs. It explains the type of work, training needed, physical demands, and work setting. *The Occupational Outlook Handbook* describes about 200 of the most common jobs. It lists job requirements, places of work, and income. It also predicts future needs for each job. Both books are published by the U.S. Department of Labor. They can be found in most libraries.

As you explore careers, find out what the work is like in each job. Ask about the type of preparation required. Decide if you have the traits needed for the job. In this way, you can decide which jobs appeal to you. See 12-14.

Career decisions, just like other decisions, involve making trade-offs. For instance, one job that interests you may require a college degree. Another job you like may require a two-year training program. Before you decide which job you want, think about the good and bad points of each job. The first job may pay better than the second. However, in order to earn the higher income, you have to attend school for four years instead of two. This is a trade-off. Think about trade-offs when you are planning your future. This will help you make decisions that are best for you.

12-14 Someone who enjoys working with infants and is interested in medicine may want to explore a career as a neonatal nurse.

✓ Check What You Have Learned

1. What are three occupations that appeal to you? How can you gather information on these jobs?
2. What kinds of information should you try to find out about careers that interest you?
3. What is an example of a trade-off involving a job choice?

Setting Career Goals

Once you've gathered facts, you'll be ready to think seriously about what you want in a job. You will be ready to set career goals.

Your goals will help you decide which of the careers you've explored is right for you. You may have a goal to improve the way machines work. If so, you might choose a technical career. You may have a goal to help other people. To meet this goal,

you will want to choose a service career. Whatever your goals are, you can find a career that will help you meet them.

You can set short-term goals to help you reach your career goal. From the facts you've gathered, you know what type of training and background you need. Setting goals can help you get them. See 12-15. You may want to revise your goals along the way. However, having goals will help you begin your career path.

12-15 Set goals to get the education you need to achieve your career plans.

Randall is a forester in a state park. When he was young, Randall researched the requirements of being a forester. He found he needed a college degree in forestry. To reach his career goal of being a forester, Randall had to set short-term goals. First, he had to find a college that offered this degree. Then he had to apply and get accepted at that college. Randall had to finish high school. He had to find a way to pay for college. He also had to study to pass his college courses. These are just some of the short-term goals that helped Randall reach his career goal.

Try to set realistic career goals. Ask for help. Your counselor is trained to help you learn about jobs and their requirements. See 12-16.

When you first set your career goals, it will be helpful to develop a **career plan portfolio**. This is a sample of materials relating to your career plan. It could be a folder you develop as you research different career opportunities. You might include the following in the portfolio:

12-16 Talk to teachers and guidance counselors about jobs suited to your interests, aptitudes, and goals.

- results of interest inventories and aptitude tests
- research on various careers
- list of courses you would need to take in high school to prepare for listed careers
- list of places where you could get further education/training after high school
- notes from people whom you have interviewed about possible careers
- recommendations from guidance counselors and teachers
- a list of all jobs you have held

This career plan portfolio will probably change as you complete your education. It is a way of organizing your career information. It will help you reach your career goals.

✓ Check What You Have Learned

1. What is one of your goals for the future, and what career can help you reach that goal?
2. How can setting short-term goals help you get the career you want?
3. What could you include in your career plan portfolio?

The Main Ideas

You can take tests to help you identify your interests and aptitudes. Learning about many careers will help you choose one that relates to your interests and aptitudes. Setting goals will help you enter the career you choose. Guidance counselors are trained to help you with each of these steps. A career plan portfolio can help you organize your career goals.

⫸ Apply What You Have Learned

1. Divide a sheet of paper into two columns. In the first column, make a list of all your interests and aptitudes. (You may ask your family and friends to help you complete your list.) In the second column, list jobs that require the interests and aptitudes you have.
2. Make a poster illustrating all the jobs you have seen performed in the last week. Under each illustration, write how you could find out more information about that job.
3. Develop a career plan portfolio. Include the information suggested in this lesson.

Lesson 12-4
Careers in Family and Consumer Sciences

Objectives

After studying this lesson, you will be able to
- ⇒ *define* job cluster, family and consumer sciences, entry-level job, skilled-level job, *and* advanced-level job.
- ⇒ *give examples of jobs in each of the seven areas of family and consumer sciences.*
- ⇒ *explain how a worker can advance to jobs at different levels.*

New Words

job cluster: *a group of jobs that requires some of the same skills and knowledge.*

family and consumer sciences: *a field that helps people improve their quality of life.*

entry-level job: *a job that requires the least amount of training.*

skilled-level job: *a job that requires some training beyond high school.*

advanced-level job: *a job that requires a four-year college degree or an advanced degree.*

New Ideas

- ⇒ *Careers are offered in each of the seven fields of family and consumer sciences.*
- ⇒ *Jobs are grouped in three main levels of training and experience.*

There are many choices of jobs. Learning about each one is almost impossible. You may find it easier to look at job clusters. A **job cluster** is a group of jobs that requires some of the same skills and knowledge. Jobs within a cluster all relate to the same field of work, such as business or health care.

The Family and Consumer Sciences Cluster

One job cluster is family and consumer sciences. **Family and consumer sciences** is a field that helps people improve their quality of life. Family and consumer sciences includes careers in seven main areas. Foods and nutrition, housing, and clothing and textiles are part of family and consumer sciences. Child development, family relations, consumer education and management, and education and communications are family and consumer sciences areas, too.

Foods and nutrition. People who work in restaurants work in foods and nutrition. Hosts greet you and waiters wait on you. Chefs prepare food for you. See 12-17. Chefs may have helpers who prepare pastries or salads. Buspeople clear tables and dishwashers wash dishes. Managers make sure all the jobs are done.

Hospitals, ad firms, and labs have jobs for people in foods and nutrition, too. For instance, a dietitian plans meals for hospital patients. A food stylist arranges food for ad photos. A food technician works in a lab to create recipes and test foods.

12-17 A cook is just one of many jobs in the foods and nutrition area of the family and consumer sciences cluster.

12-18 This architecture student is preparing to begin a career in housing.

Today, keeping fit and eating right has become a social trend. Eating more meals away from home is also a trend. Therefore, there is a demand for people to work in foods and nutrition.

For a career in foods and nutrition, you need an interest in food. You need to be able to get along well with others, too. Some jobs require math skills to figure amounts of ingredients and nutrients. Careers in nutrition demand a science background. Some jobs call for artistic skill. Others involve long working hours.

Housing. People who work in housing might sell, design, decorate, or care for homes. Real estate agents assist people in buying and selling homes. Architects design the structures of houses and other dwellings. See 12-18. Interior designers plan and design the interiors of homes. They suggest color schemes and furniture to make homes appealing. Housekeepers keep homes clean.

Housing is a basic physical need. Therefore, people will always be needed to work in housing careers. If you are interested in housing, you should learn the basic principles of art and design. An eye for detail is also helpful in this field.

Clothing and textiles. Careers in clothing and textiles deal with clothes and fabrics. Fashion designers create the clothing styles people wear. Textile designers create fabric textures and patterns. Textile researchers test fabrics for certain

qualities, such as strength. Tailors make clothes. Buyers purchase clothes for stores to sell to consumers. Salesclerks sell clothes, and dry cleaners clean them. See 12-19.

Clothing, like food and housing, is a basic need. Therefore, people will always be needed to work in this area. Many clothing and textile careers require a command of color and design. Researchers need a science background. Tailors need good eye-hand coordination. Buyers and salesclerks need strong communication skills.

12-19 Salesclerks help customers find the right size clothes.

Child development. If you baby-sit, you already have a job in child development. Jobs in child development involve working with and designing products for children. Directors, teachers, and teaching assistants work in child care centers. See 12-20. Recreation workers plan and direct children's activities at camps, parks, and playgrounds. Child welfare workers work with children who are abused or neglected. People who write children's books and design children's toys also work in this field.

12-21 Counselors help individuals and families solve problems.

12-20 Teachers in child care centers plan and lead learning experiences for children.

With more parents working outside the home, more children need child care. If you want to work in this field, you need to enjoy children. You need to understand how children grow. You should know about nutrition and first aid. Patience and creativity are other traits that will help you care for children.

Family relations. Family relations workers help people and families manage daily tasks and crises. Home companions visit people who have trouble performing household tasks by themselves. They provide company and help their clients with day-to-day chores. Counselors may help children, teens, adults, older people, couples, or families deal with problems. See 12-21. Hot line operators are trained to handle crisis calls from people. People who direct events at senior citizens' centers also work in this field.

As long as families have problems, family relations workers will be needed. To work in this field, you need good communication skills. You need to get along well with people. You also need to have a warm, caring personality.

Consumer education and money management. Consumer education jobs teach people how to use their money wisely. Bank counselors help customers set up budgets. Financial advisors help people invest their money to meet future goals. Some stores hire comparison shoppers to check prices in competing stores. Consumer service agents handle consumer complaints. See 12-22. Credit managers approve credit forms and make sure bills are collected. Credit counselors advise families on paying their debts.

Many people need help managing their incomes. To succeed in this field, you need to know about business. Many jobs require math skills. Communication skills are also vital in many jobs.

Education and communications. Although there are several entry-level and skilled-level jobs in education and communications, most require a college degree. This major in college offers a general background in all areas of family and consumer sciences subject matter. You would study each of the areas discussed in this lesson. You can teach family and consumer sciences in a middle or high school. You would also be qualified to be a cooperative extension agent. Some extension agents work with young people in organizations such as 4-H and FHA. Others teach adults. With a graduate degree, you can teach at a community college or at a university.

The family and consumer sciences cluster includes a broad range of careers. If any of these careers interests you, find out more about it. Ask your guidance counselor or do library research. You may decide that a career in this field is right for you.

12-22 Consumer service representatives help consumers resolve complaints.

✓ Check What You Have Learned

1. Choose one of the areas of family and consumer sciences. What factors create a need for people to enter careers in that area?
2. What are three jobs related to that area of family and consumer sciences?
3. What traits do you need to enter a career in that area?

Job Levels

When you research a job cluster, you will find three main levels of jobs. **Entry-level jobs** require the least amount of training. You can get some entry-level jobs while you are still in high school. Other entry-level jobs require a high school diploma.

Skilled-level jobs require some training beyond high school. These jobs involve more skills than entry-level jobs. Technical schools, junior colleges, or military training prepares many workers for skilled-level jobs. Some entry-level workers receive enough training and practice on the job to advance into skilled-level jobs.

Most **advanced-level jobs** require a four-year college degree or an advanced degree. Some workers advance to this level from skilled-level jobs. Advanced-level jobs often require management skills.

The three main levels of jobs within a job cluster offer chances to advance. You may be able to start in an entry-level job and work your way up. See 12-23. For a review of job opportunities in family and consumer sciences, see 12-24.

12-23 In the area of child development, a playground attendant is an entry-level job. A teacher's assistant is a skilled-level job. A teacher of young children and a child care director are advanced-level positions.

Family and Consumer Sciences			
Major Categories	**Entry-Level Jobs**	**Skilled-Level Jobs**	**Advanced-Level Jobs**
Foods and Nutrition	Busperson Dishwasher Cook's helper Short-order cook Waiter Host	Food service manager Food purchaser Sanitation supervisor Quality control supervisor Chef or chief cook Restaurant owner	Dietitian Executive chef Marketing executive Caterer Food technologist Product developer
Housing	Upholsterer's helper Designer's aide Home lighting aide Home furnishings salesperson	Drapery/slipcover maker Home lighting designer Real estate agent	Home furnishings buyer Interior designer Public housing consultant Home planning specialist Facilities planner
Clothing and Textiles	Salesclerk Alterationist's assistant Laundry attendant Display assistant Clothing repair specialist Fabric salesperson	Sewing machine operator Presser/finisher Store manager Dry cleaner Alterationist Tailor/reweaver	Fashion or textile designer Marketing specialist Display artist Researcher or tester Clothing consultant Merchandise manager

Child Development	Baby-sitter
	Parent's helper
	Nursery school aide
	Child care center aide
	Playground assistant
	Camp counselor's aide
		Playground director
		Teacher's aide
		School food service worker
		Scout leader
		Recreational leader
			Nursery school teacher
			Designer of children's
			  clothing, furniture, or toys
			Child care center or
			  preschool administrator
			Child welfare worker
			Parent educator

Family Relations	Homemaker's aide
	Caseworker's aide
	Senior citizens'
	  center aide
		Hot line counselor
		Counseling paraprofessional
		Senior citizens' center
		  staff worker
		Youth services worker
		Homemaker services
		  director
			Social worker
			Crisis center counselor
			Family/marriage therapist
			School counselor
			Family health counselor

Consumer Education and Money Management	Consumer affairs aide
	Office worker
	Consumer product tester
	  assistant
		Consumer service
		  representative
		Credit bureau research
		  clerk
		Loan officer assistant
		Bank teller
		Collection agent
			Retail credit manager
			Money investment
			  advisor
			Consumer affairs director
			Loan officer
			Consumer product
			  specialist
			Financial planner

Education and Communications	Baby-sitter
	Nursery school assistant
	Youth counselor
		Teacher's aide
		4-H leader
			Middle school/junior high
			  or high school family and
			  consumer sciences teacher
			Family and consumer
			  sciences professor
			Cooperative extension agent
			Adult educator
			Journalist

12-24 Family and consumer sciences offers a wide range of job opportunities from entry-level to advanced-level jobs.

The Main Ideas

Careers in the family and consumer sciences job cluster are involved with helping people improve their quality of living. This cluster includes jobs in foods and nutrition, housing, and clothing and textiles. It also includes jobs in child development, family relations, consumer education and management, and education and communications. Depending on their training and experience, workers may fill entry-level, skilled-level, or advanced-level jobs.

Apply What You Have Learned

1. As a class, plan an assembly on careers related to family and consumer sciences. Use the Yellow Pages to come up with a list of people your teacher could invite to speak. Your list should include representatives from each of the seven main areas of family and consumer sciences. Prepare questions for the speakers to answer about their current jobs. Also ask them about their training and past job experiences.
2. Explore any job cluster that interests you. Make a list of the entry-level, skilled-level, and advanced-level jobs found in this cluster. Write a short report explaining how you could receive training for the skilled- and advanced-level jobs.

Case Study

Read the story below and look at Lesson 12-3 again. Then answer the questions below.

Thinking About the Future

Keith has been talking to his parents about preparing for a career. He has made an appointment with the seventh grade guidance counselor, Mr. Linsky, to talk about his future.

"Keith, I'm glad that you came to see me," Mr. Linsky said. "This is a good time for you to start thinking about your future."

"I want to talk to you because my dad says he would like me to become a lawyer," Keith said. "I want to find out what other jobs there are. I also want to know which one is the right one for me."

Mr. Linsky handed Keith a sheet of paper. "Here's an outline of what I can do to help you. I want you to read this over before we meet again," said Mr. Linsky. "At that time, I can give you an aptitude test. This test will show you if you have a natural talent for doing certain tasks. It will help point you toward a career that you will enjoy."

"My dad's a construction worker. I like to watch him build the buildings," said Keith. "I thought I might like to design buildings. Dad says architects design buildings. Would this test tell me if I'd be a good architect?"

"This test can help you know if you have the skills needed to be an architect," Mr. Linsky said. "I'm also glad you're thinking about more than one career. You're getting off to a good start in learning about careers."

To Discuss

→ 1. How is Mr. Linsky helping Keith learn about careers?

→ 2. How will the aptitude test help Keith decide whether he should become a lawyer or an architect?

→ 3. What might be some ways for Keith to find out more about being a lawyer or an architect?

Topic 12 Review

Topic Summary

You may plan to work in the future. There are many reasons you may decide to do this. You can earn an income and receive fringe benefits. Working can give you a sense of dignity and identity. Your family and community can also benefit when you work. You will need to decide if you want to hold a series of unrelated jobs or pursue a career. Your lifestyle will be affected by what you decide.

The job you choose will be affected by changes in society and technology. Being aware of trends in the world of work will help you follow these changes. You will be able to make better choices about a job or career.

To find the right career or job, you first need to identify your interests and skills. Then you need to learn about the different types of careers and jobs available. Once you take these two steps, you can match your interests and skills to a career or job. You need to set goals to help you find the job or career you want.

You may choose a career in family and consumer sciences. Careers in the family and consumer sciences job cluster help people improve their quality of life. This cluster includes jobs in foods and nutrition, housing, and clothing and textiles. It also includes jobs in child development, family relations, consumer education and management, and education and communication. Depending on your training and experience, you can seek an entry-level, skilled-level, or advanced-level job.

To Review

Write your answers on a separate sheet of paper.

1. List three reasons people work.
2. What are three examples of fringe benefits?
3. True or false. Most people change careers in their lifetimes.
4. How can jobs affect people's lifestyles?
5. Describe how trends will affect future jobs.
6. List three opportunities for being an entrepreneur.
7. List the steps you can take to learn about your job interests and skills.
8. An (interest inventory/aptitude test) will point out your natural skills.
9. Give examples of two sources of job information.
10. True or false. The *Occupational Outlook Handbook* describes over 35,000 different jobs.
11. List the seven main areas in the family and consumer sciences job cluster and give an example of a job in each area.
12. What is the difference between a skilled-level job and an advanced-level job?

347

Vocabulary Quiz

Match the definitions in Column A with the terms in Column B. Write your answers on a separate sheet of paper.

Column A

1. A job that requires a four-year college degree or an advanced degree.
2. A natural skill.
3. A position held by a worker.
4. A series of related jobs a person holds over time.
5. A test that shows areas in which a person seems to have the most interest.
6. Reward of a job other than income.
7. A person who starts and manages his or her own business.
8. A job that requires some training beyond high school.
9. A field that helps people improve their quality of life.
10. A job that requires the least amount of training.
11. A general pattern of events.
12. A group of jobs that requires some of the same skills and knowledge.
13. A sample of materials relating to a person's career plan.
14. A job or position held by a worker.

Column B

a. Career.
b. Family and consumer sciences.
c. Entry-level job.
d. Job cluster.
e. Advanced-level job.
f. Occupation.
g. Skilled-level job.
h. Trend.
i. Aptitude.
j. Fringe benefit.
k. Work.
l. Entrepreneur.
m. Job.
n. Interest inventory.
o. Career plan portfolio.

Topic 13 Preparing for Work

Lesson 13-1
Heading for a Career

Objectives

After studying this lesson, you will be able to

➡ *define job skills, apprentice, vocational program, and resume.*

➡ *list three ways to get job training.*

➡ *explain the benefits of working part-time.*

➡ *outline the steps in getting a job.*

New Words

job skills: *skills that are used in the world of work.*

apprentice: *someone who learns a job by working with a skilled worker.*

vocational program: *a training course that teaches specific job skills.*

resume: *a written description of a person's qualifications and work experience.*

New Ideas

➡ *You can prepare for a career in many ways.*

➡ *Part-time work can help you learn about jobs.*

➡ *You can develop skills that can help you find your first job.*

Being well prepared for the job market can help you get the job you want. It can also help you advance faster and earn a bigger income.

Find out what you need to do to prepare for careers that interest you. Preparing for a career involves getting job training. It may involve getting some work experience through a part-time job, too.

Getting Job Training

The purpose of job training is to learn **job skills**. These are skills that are used in the world of work. Having job skills can help you get and keep a job. Some skills, such as basic learning and relationship skills, are required for all jobs. See 13-1. Some jobs also require specific job skills. For instance, if you want to work as an artist, you need art skills.

13-1 Being able to communicate clearly is a skill needed for all jobs.

You can get job training in several ways. You may choose to take special courses in high school. You might decide to attend a training school or college after high school. You could choose to get military training. You could also choose to become an apprentice. An **apprentice** is someone who learns a job by working with a skilled worker. Depending on your goals, job training may last a few months or many years.

Your career plan portfolio can help you decide what courses to take in high school. For instance, suppose you want to be a teacher. Your research tells you teachers need a college degree. Therefore, you decide to take high school courses that will prepare you for college. See 13-2.

Your career plan portfolio may not require a college degree. In this case, a high school vocational program may provide the training you need. **Vocational programs** are training courses that teach specific job skills. Business education, child care services, and auto repair are vocational programs offered in many high schools. See 13-3.

Other vocational programs are taught at special *vocational schools*. Some programs involve on-the-job work experiences. Students attend school part of the day and go to work part of the day.

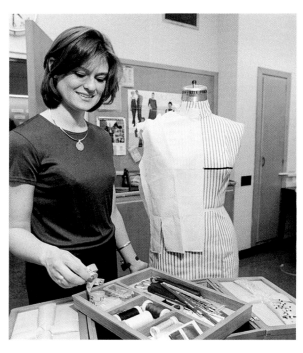

13-2 This college student is studying to be a fashion designer. In high school, she took clothing and art courses.

13-3 Many high schools offer vocational programs in child care services.

✓ **Check What You Have Learned**

1. Why do you think it might be important to get job training before you begin looking for a job?
2. Why might you want to enroll in a high school vocational program?

Working Part-Time

Another way to begin preparing for a career is to get a part-time job. Part-time work means less than 40 hours a week. Many teens have part-time jobs. They work during evenings and on weekends when they are not in school.

Part-time jobs have many advantages. You learn how to be a responsible employee. You learn job skills you can use in a future career. You learn how to handle an income. A part-time job can even lead to other jobs.

There also are disadvantages to working part-time while in school. You will have less time to do your schoolwork. You may not be able to participate in after-school activities such as sports and clubs. When you work, you will not have as much time with your friends. Deciding whether to work part-time requires an examination of the advantages and disadvantages.

Try to find a part-time job related to a career that appeals to you. See 13-4. This will give you a chance to see if you like that field. You may choose another career if you don't like the job.

You may decide to do volunteer work instead of getting a part-time job. You won't receive an income. However, you will learn many of the same skills you would learn at a job. See 13-5. For instance, you might volunteer in a clinic. This work would teach you skills you could use in a medical career. The skills you learn may be more helpful to your future than the income you'll be missing.

13-4 A part-time job in a clothing store could help you explore your interest in a fashion career.

13-5 Volunteer work at a hospital snack bar helps this girl explore food service, sales, and medical careers.

✓ **Check What You Have Learned**

1. What does working part-time mean? Why do you think part-time jobs are often held by students?
2. What are two advantages and two disadvantages of having a part-time job or doing volunteer work?

Getting Your First Job

There are skills you can use to get the job you want. These skills involve finding available jobs, placing an application, and interviewing for a job. These important skills will help you find your first job as well as future employment. See 13-6.

Where can you look for jobs? The newspaper runs employment ads each day. Your friends and family may know of jobs that are available. Your school counselor frequently gets calls from businesses looking for qualified people. Some communities have youth employment agencies to help teens find part-time work.

You also can use your initiative to find a job. You can place a "Position Wanted" ad in the newspaper. You can call businesses and ask if there are available jobs. You can look for "Help Wanted" signs in the windows of area stores and then apply for jobs.

13-6 Learning interviewing skills will help you get the job you want.

Before you apply for your first job, you must have a Social Security card. You can get this card by going to a Social Security office. Child labor laws affect the work you can do when you are under age 18. The types of jobs, hours, and work settings may be restricted. You may be required to get a worker's permit. Your guidance counselor can tell you about the laws in your state.

You can apply for a job in person, by telephone, or by mail. You should find out which is preferable. A prospective employer may ask you to submit a resume and give references. A **resume** is a written description of a person's qualifications and work experience. A *reference* is a name of a person who can be contacted about you and your work habits. Most employers require references on job applications. Always ask people if they will give you a recommendation before you list their name. References should be people who know about you and your work. Do not use relatives. Former employers are an excellent choice. Teachers, counselors, ministers, priests, and rabbis also are good references.

You probably will be asked to fill out a job application. Be neat and accurate when completing an application. Type or use a pen. Avoid making mistakes such as spelling errors. Provide all the requested information.

Most employers interview potential workers in person before they hire them. First impressions are important. Dress appropriately. Make sure you look clean and well groomed. Have a positive attitude. Smile and shake the interviewer's hand when you arrive. Use good posture. Be on time and use good manners. Thank the person for his or her time. Be prepared. Know as much as possible about the company. Ask a family member or friend to practice asking you interview questions.

Try not to get discouraged if you do not get a job for which you have interviewed. Most people have more job rejections than job offers. It takes a lot of trying to get the job you want.

✔ Check What You Have Learned

1. What skills are involved in getting a job?
2. List three sources where you can find jobs.
3. What are three hints for interviewing successfully?

The Main Ideas

Entering the career world requires preparation. One way to prepare is to get job training. High school vocational programs offer job training for some careers. A part-time job or volunteer work can also help you prepare for a career. Both job training and part-time work teach you job skills you will need in the future. There also are job skills you can learn to help you earn your first job. These skills include finding available jobs, applying, and interviewing.

Apply What You Have Learned

1. Find out what vocational courses are offered at a local high school. Interview a student from one of the programs that interests you. Ask the student what courses he or she must take. Ask what job skills he or she is learning. Find out how well the student feels the program is preparing him or her for a future career. Share your findings with the class.
2. Look at the want ads in a local newspaper. Clip any ads for part-time jobs that teens might be able to fill. Make a collage or bulletin board display with the clippings.

Topic 13 Preparing for Work

Lesson 13-2
Getting Ready for Job Success

Objectives

After studying this lesson, you will be able to

- *define basic learning skills, thinking skills, and criticism.*
- *give examples of how basic learning skills are used on the job.*
- *describe the importance of getting along with others on the job.*
- *list traits of a successful worker.*
- *explain why thinking skills are needed on the job.*
- *explain why workers must continue to learn.*

New Words

basic learning skills: skills in reading, writing, and math.
thinking skills: the ability to think creatively and critically, to make decisions, and to solve problems.
criticism: a judgment.

New Ideas

- *Basic reading, writing, and math skills are needed in almost every job.*
- *Your ability to get along with others can affect your career success.*
- *You can develop certain traits that will help you be a successful worker.*
- *Thinking skills will help you succeed on the job.*
- *Continuing to learn on the job will help you advance in your career.*

Some people are successful on the job. They receive more responsibility and more pay. They may receive other job offers, too. Basic learning, relationship, and thinking skills are the keys to this type of job success. You can develop and improve these skills now. They will be useful throughout your life. See 13-7.

Basic Learning Skills

Skills in reading, writing, and math are called **basic learning skills**. They are needed to get and keep a job. They are also needed to keep up with changes on the job.

13-7 Developing basic learning and thinking skills will help you succeed in the world of work.

Few jobs are open to workers who do not have basic learning skills. Checking a work schedule and reading directions require reading skills. Applying for a job and completing report forms require writing skills. Making change and taking measurements require math skills. See 13-8. (Math skills are also needed to manage your income.) These are just a few examples of common work tasks that require basic skills.

Basic learning skills are often taught in job training programs for adults. Learning these skills while you are in school will help you compete in the future job market.

13-8 Basic math skills are needed to use a cash register and count change.

✓ Check What You Have Learned

1. Why do you think skills in reading, writing, and math are called *basic skills?*
2. What is one example of how each of the basic learning skills might be needed on the job?

Getting Along with Others

Being able to get along with others is required in all jobs. If you cannot get along with others, employers will not want to hire you. Other people will not want to work with you. See 13-9.

13-9 Getting along with your fellow workers is a requirement of all jobs.

You need to get along with your boss. Obeying company rules will help you get along. Following your boss's orders will also help. If you disagree with your boss, you may be able to state your feelings. However, you will have to respect his or her decisions. Otherwise, you may lose your job.

You will need to get along with your coworkers, too. Working together requires patience and kindness. Other workers may be different from you. You cannot allow these differences to keep you from getting along with others. Some pointers for getting along with your coworkers are listed below.

- Listen to what your coworkers have to say. This will help you understand them.
- Get to know your coworkers. Take an interest in what they do.
- Take part in group discussions. This involves listening as well as offering ideas.

- Take part in group decision making. Do your part after the decision is made, even if the decision is not what you wanted.
- Avoid blaming coworkers for your problems. Talk over your conflicts. Review conflict resolution skills in Lesson 3-4. Try to reach agreements that will let you get along in the future.

Your job may also require you to get along with customers. You need to be friendly, helpful, and polite when dealing with customers. You are representing your company. How you treat these people will affect whether they do business with your company again. See 13-10.

13-10 Successful workers are cheerful and courteous when helping customers.

✓ Check What You Have Learned

1. How can getting along with others affect your job success?
2. Why is it important to be friendly, helpful, and polite when dealing with customers?

Being a Successful Worker

Successful workers have a number of traits that help them do their jobs well. They have good attitudes. They manage their time well. They are also loyal, honest, and hardworking.

One of the biggest factors affecting your job success is your attitude. You need to have a good attitude about yourself. This means you believe in your skills as a worker. This type of attitude gives you confidence and helps you do a good job. You also need to have a good attitude about your work. This means you enjoy what you do. If you like your job, you are likely to do better work.

Your attitude is seen in what you say and how you act. If you have a good work attitude, you will make nice comments about your job. You will act cheerful and confident. Having a good attitude makes you pleasant to be around.

To be a successful worker, you need to use your time wisely. Arrive for work on time. See 13-11. Avoid leaving work early. Use your time at work for company business, not private business.

13-11 Employers respect workers who report to work on time.

Don't take more than the allowed amount of time for breaks. Avoid wasting time on the telephone.

Successful workers are loyal. As a loyal worker, you should not gossip or make unkind remarks about your coworkers. Do not complain about your boss either. Above all, you should never discuss company secrets away from work.

You must be honest to be successful on the job. You may handle money or work with costly products. You may have an expense account if you travel for business. Employers need to be able to trust you. If you are suspected of stealing or cheating, you may lose your job.

To be a successful worker, you need to do your best. You need to work hard to complete your assigned tasks. When you make a mistake, be willing to admit it. Learn from it, so you will not make the same mistake again. See 13-12.

Guidelines for Success

★ Arrive on time.
★ Use work time for work, not for personal matters.
★ Take only the amount of time that is allowed for breaks or lunch.
★ Do not leave work early.
★ Ask for vacation only after it is earned.
★ Use sick time for illness only.
★ Use the telephone for business only.
★ Be cheerful.
★ Show interest in the job and the company.
★ Ask intelligent questions.
★ Get along with other workers.
★ Accept suggestions from others willingly.
★ Be willing to learn new skills as the job demands.
★ Do your share without complaining.

13-12 Following these guidelines will help you be a successful worker.

✓ Check What You Have Learned

1. How do workers with good attitudes feel about themselves and their jobs?
2. Why shouldn't you gossip about coworkers and complain about your boss?
3. What are three jobs in which a worker's honesty might be extra important?

Thinking Skills

Thinking is an important skill. Through it, you gain knowledge. **Thinking skills** are the ability to think creatively and critically, to make decisions, and to solve problems. Decision making and problem solving are considered to be thinking skills.

When you are creative, you can come up with new solutions to a problem. You have lots of ideas. Employers need creative people.

Critical thinking means you can look at different sides of a problem. You can understand different points of view. You are able to reason and analyze situations.

Decision making is an important skill, both in life and on the job. Review Lesson 3-4. Good decision making involves analyzing alternatives and picking the best one. It involves thinking through consequences. Good workers can help group members make good decisions.

Employers need workers who can solve problems. You are able to think through problems and resolve difficulties. You gather facts and suggest solutions. People advance on the job when they are able to solve problems. For example, parents like to hire Rashad as a baby-sitter. In his neighborhood, he is known for being able to handle emergencies using good problem-solving skills.

✔ Check What You Have Learned

1. What are thinking skills?
2. Which thinking skills do you have? Give reasons for your answer.

Continuing to Learn

In order to advance in your career, you will need to keep growing and learning. Tools, materials, and methods change. As you advance, your responsibilities will change, too. You must be willing and able to keep up with these changes. This means learning new skills.

How can you continue to learn? Reading can help you stay informed. You can also take adult education classes. Many businesses offer classes to help workers stay informed, too.

Another way to learn is through criticism. **Criticism** is a judgment. Some people use criticism to find fault with others. However, when used in a kind way, criticism can be helpful. Your boss or coworkers may use criticism to make you aware of errors. You can use their criticism to help you improve your work in the future.

You can also learn by asking questions. When you are given new tasks, ask for help when you need it. Be willing to learn from other workers and your employer.

Learning is a lifelong process. You cannot learn everything you need to know in school. By continuing to learn, you will help ensure your job success. See 13-13.

13-13 Taking classes can help workers keep up with changes on the job.

✔ Check What You Have Learned

1. Why is it important to continue learning even after you get a job?
2. What are three ways you can continue to learn after you finish school?

The Main Ideas

Certain skills and traits are needed for success in all types of jobs. You need to be able to use basic reading, writing, and math skills. You need to be able to get along with others. You should have a good attitude and be able to manage your time well. Being honest, loyal, and hardworking will help you be successful, too. Your success will also be affected by your thinking skills and willingness to keep growing and learning as a worker.

Apply What You Have Learned

1. Help your class prepare a survey. Each student should interview five people who are currently employed. Ask each worker the following questions:
   - How are basic skills in reading, writing, and math used in your job?
   - What people do you have to deal with in your job? Why is it important that you get along with these people?
   - What traits do employees need to succeed in your line of work?
   - Does your place of employment offer special classes or workshops for you to attend?

   When you finish your survey, compile your results into an article for your school newspaper.
2. Pretend you are working as a clerk in a local store. Role-play a situation showing poor skills in getting along with others on the job. Then repeat the role play showing good skills in getting along with others.
3. Invite a person who is a job supervisor to speak to your class. Ask the speaker to describe traits of a successful worker. Ask him or her to discuss the most common reasons workers are fired.
4. Find out what types of adult education classes are offered in your area. Report your findings to the class.

Case Study

Read the story below and look at Lesson 13-1 again.
Then answer the questions below.

Deciding Where to Work

The school year is about to end. Erika wants to earn some money during the summer to pay for her trip to camp. However, she is only 14 years old. She decides to talk to her mother about ways she can earn money.

"Well, Erika, you can baby-sit, deliver newspapers, or work at my bookstore," said Mrs. Weigner.

"If I work for you, what would I do?" Erika asked.

"You can do odd jobs around the store, such as stock books and dust. If we get really busy, I may even teach you how to run the cash register," said Mrs. Weigner. "If you work for me, you can see how a business is run and learn about different writers. This may help you later in school."

"Working there sounds kind of fun," said Erika. "How often would I have to work? I still want to be able to spend time with my friends, Lori and Lisa."

"You would only work for me part-time," said Mrs. Weigner. "I'd schedule you to work either mornings or afternoons. If we start to get really busy, I may schedule you more."

"Will I be able to make enough money to pay for camp by working part-time?" asked Erika.

Mrs. Weigner said, "I'll pay you minimum wage, which is more than you can earn baby-sitting or delivering newspapers. If you manage the money you earn carefully, you should be able to save enough to pay for camp."

To Discuss

1. How can Erika's need for a summer job be met by working part-time at her mother's bookstore?
2. What future career skills can Erika learn by working at the bookstore?
3. How can working at the bookstore help Erika learn to manage and handle money?

Topic 13 Review

Topic Summary

Once you choose a career, you need to start preparing for it. One way is to get job training. You can get job training by being an apprentice, taking special courses, or participating in vocational programs at school. Job training will teach you the skills you need to be successful at your job. They may be specific skills or skills related to learning and getting along with others.

Working part-time is another way to prepare for a career. You can learn how to behave in a work setting. Part-time jobs also give you the chance to explore careers in fields that interest you.

Having basic learning, relationship, and thinking skills will help you be successful in your chosen job. Basic learning skills are needed to get and keep a job. Relationship skills help you get along well with your coworkers and customers. Other important traits include having a good attitude; managing time well; and being loyal, honest, and hardworking. You need thinking skills to help you think creatively and critically, make decisions, and solve problems. You must also be willing to learn new skills.

To Review

Write your answers on a separate sheet of paper.

1. What are two types of skills that are required for all jobs?
2. Give two examples of vocational programs that are available in many high schools.
3. True or false. When you work part-time, you work more than 40 hours a week.
4. List three benefits of working part-time.
5. What are the basic learning skills?
6. Why are basic learning skills important for getting and keeping a job?
7. Why is it important to get along with others on the job?
8. List four hints for getting along with others at work.
9. True or false. Your attitude affects your success on the job.
10. How can you learn from criticism?
11. Why is learning a lifelong process?

Vocabulary Quiz

Match the definitions in Column A with the terms in Column B.
Write your answers on a separate sheet of paper.

Column A

1. A judgment.
2. Someone who learns a job by working with a skilled worker.
3. A training course that teaches specific job skills.
4. Skills in reading, writing, and math.
5. Skills that are used in the world of work.
6. The ability to think creatively and critically, to make decisions, and to solve problems.
7. A written description of a person's qualifications and work experience.

Column B

a. Job skills.
b. Basic learning skills.
c. Apprentice.
d. Vocational program.
e. Criticism.
f. Resume.
g. Thinking skills.
h. Reference.

Learning job skills and exploring careers will help you prepare for your future in the workplace.

Appendix

When You're on Your Own — A Lesson in Self-Care

Now that you're older, your family may decide you can be left by yourself for a short time each day. This may be because all the adults in your family need to be away from home at the same time. They may have jobs and cannot be home with you. You may have to take care of yourself while they are away. This may be in the morning before you leave for school or after you get home. You may also need to stay by yourself for a few hours during the evening. Do you know how to behave and what to do when you're alone? Do you know how to handle situations that might come up?

Some of the situations you might want to be prepared for are described below. Tips for handling these situations are also given. You may want to think about these ideas and talk about them with your family before you stay by yourself. Your parents may have their own ideas about what they want you to do.

Coming and Going

When you're the first one home, check to see that everything looks normal before you enter the house or apartment. Signs that an intruder might be present are

- lights are on when they should be off
- a car you don't recognize in the driveway
- a broken or open window
- an open or unlocked door

If you see any of these signs, take the following steps:
- DO NOT GO INSIDE!
- Go to a neighbor's house and call home. Maybe another family member came home early.
- If no one answers the telephone, call a parent. Ask what you should do. Perhaps a family member came home during the day and then left.
- If you can't reach a parent, call the police. Give the police your complete name and address. They will come and check your house for you.

If you arrive home and everything looks normal, enter your house or apartment. Be sure to lock the door after you enter. If you have lost your key, go to a neighbor's home. Your parents may want to leave a spare key with the neighbor. If they don't have a key, call a parent for instructions.

You may be the last one to leave your home in the morning. If so, there are some tasks you must remember to do.

- Make sure the windows are closed and locked.
- Turn off all the lights.
- Check the weather. Decide whether you need a coat, raincoat, hat, or gloves.
- Make sure you have your key.
- Lock all doors.

Using the Phone

When you are home alone, the telephone can keep you from getting lonely. You can call someone and talk. If you have an answering machine, your parents can leave messages for you. If you have a problem, you can call for help.

You should make a list of important telephone numbers. Keep this list by the telephone at all times. The list should include the following telephone numbers:

- parents' work numbers
- neighbor or relative who is home most of the time
- police and fire (if 911 is not available in your community)
- family doctor
- ambulance
- poison control

The telephone can also create problems. If you are talking on the phone too long, a parent may not be able to call and give you messages. Also, strangers may call. You need to discuss with your parents what you should do when strangers call. Keep the following points in mind:

- Always answer the phone. If you don't, intruders may think there's no one home.
- If the caller asks for your parents, don't say you are home alone. Instead, tell the caller that your parents cannot come to the phone right now. Keep the conversation brief. Hang up if you need to.
- Ask the caller if you can take a message. Be sure to write down the caller's name and telephone number.
- Do not give the caller your name, telephone number, or address!

Answering the Door

If you are by yourself, you should be cautious when someone comes to the door. Do not open the door until you know who is there. Look through a window or peephole. If you can't see who it is, ask. It may be a friend or neighbor.

If the person at the door is a stranger, keep the following rules in mind:

- Keep the door locked.
- Talk only briefly and then go away from the door.
- If the person wants to use the telephone, offer to make the call yourself.
- Do not let the person know you are alone.
- Do not let anyone inside your home unless you have a parent's permission. Your

family may have rules about when you can have friends over when you are alone. Know what these rules are. Let your friends know, too.

- If someone is delivering a package, ask them to leave it outside.

What to Do If...

There are many situations that may occur while you're on your own. Many of these have already been discussed. However, there are others. Some situations may be serious. You and your parents should talk about what to do if

- you get very sick
- you get hurt
- you smell smoke or a smoke alarm goes off
- the electricity goes out
- there is a severe weather warning
- a stranger offers you a ride home

You should also talk about what to do when

- you get hungry
- you get bored
- you feel lonely
- you feel afraid
- you have to take care of younger brothers or sisters
- you have homework

Being on your own is a big responsibility. If you and your parents think you can handle the situations discussed above, then you are ready. Good luck!

Having a pet may make you feel less lonely when you are home alone.

Glossary

abbreviation. Shortened form of a word.

accept. View as normal or proper.

accessories. Items worn to accent clothing.

accident. An unexpected event causing loss or injury.

addiction. A physical dependency on a substance.

adolescence. The stage of development between childhood and adulthood.

advanced-level job. A job that requires a four-year college degree or an advanced degree.

advertising. The process of calling attention to a product or business through the mass media.

affection. A fondness.

a la carte. A menu term meaning each food or course is listed and priced separately.

alterations. Changes made in the size, length, or style of a garment so it will fit properly.

alternatives. Options available to choose from when making a decision.

anorexia nervosa. An eating disorder in which people starve themselves.

antiperspirant. A product that helps control wetness and covers unpleasant body odors.

appearance. How you look.

appetite. The desire to eat.

appetizer. Small, light food served before a meal.

appliance. A tool run by gas or electricity.

appliqué. To sew one or more pieces of fabric to a large piece of fabric or a garment.

apprentice. Someone who learns a job by working with a skilled worker.

aptitude. A natural skill.

baby-sitting. Caring for children, usually during a short absence of the parents.

bakeware. Items used to cook food in the oven.

balanced diet. A diet that provides all the nutrients your body needs for good health.

basic learning skills. Skills in reading, writing, and math.

basting. Sewing fabric pieces together with long, loose, temporary stitches.

blend. A combination of two or more different fibers.

budget. A plan for spending.

buffet service. A style of meal service where people help themselves to food set out on a serving table.

bulimia. An eating disorder in which people eat large amounts of food and then purge themselves of the food.

C

calories. Units of energy provided by proteins, carbohydrates, and fats.

career. A series of related jobs a person holds over time.

caregiver. A person who takes care of children.

centerpiece. A decorative object placed in the middle of a table.

cholesterol. A fatty substance found in foods from animal sources.

classic. A style that stays in fashion for a long time.

communication. Giving or receiving information, signals, or messages.

computer. An electronic machine capable of storing, processing, and controlling large amounts of data.

computer network. A system where resources are shared among computer users.

confident. Being sure of yourself.

conflict. A disagreement among two or more people.

conflict resolution. When a disagreement among two or more people is settled.

conserve. To save.

consumer. A person who buys or uses goods and services.

consumer decisions. Decisions made about how to spend money.

cook. To prepare food for eating using heat.

cookware. Pots and pans used on the range.

cooperate. To act or work together with others.

course. All the foods served as one part of a meal.

cover. The table space in front of a person's seat.

credit. A way to pay that lets you buy now and pay later.

crisis. An emergency situation.

criticism. A judgment.

culture. The beliefs and customs of a certain racial, religious, or social group.

curdling. Lumping of milk proteins caused by cooking with high temperatures.

cut. To divide foods into small pieces.

D

Daily Value. Reference figures on food labels that help consumers see how food products fit into a total diet.

data. Information.

decision. A choice made about what to do or say in a given situation.

decision-making process. Steps followed to help make a decision, solve a problem, or reach a goal.

deodorant. A product that helps destroy or cover unpleasant body odors.

dependent. Relying on another for support.

dermatologist. A doctor who specializes in treating the skin.

development. Gradual changes that take place as the result of growth.

developmental tasks. Skills or behavior patterns people should achieve at certain stages of their lives.

diet. The food and beverages consumed each day.

Dietary Guidelines for Americans. Guidelines for a healthful diet.

dovetail. To do more than one task at a time.

dry-clean. To clean with chemicals instead of detergent and water.

dry heat cooking methods. Water and other liquids are not added when cooking protein foods.

E

ecology. The study of all living objects in relation to each other and the environment.

emotions. Feelings about people and events.

energy. The capacity for doing work.

enriched. To have nutrients added to a product to replace those removed during processing.

entrepreneur. A person who starts and manages his or her own business.

entry-level job. A job that requires the least amount of training.

environment. The conditions, objects, places, and people that are all around a person.

etiquette. Proper behavior in social settings.

evaluate. To judge an entire plan of action.

F

fabric. Cloth made by weaving or knitting yarns or by pressing fibers together.

fad. A style that is popular for only a short time.

family. A group of people who are related to one another by blood, marriage, or adoption.

family and consumer sciences. A field that helps people improve their quality of life.

family council. An informal meeting called to talk over issues concerning family members.

family counseling agencies. Groups that work with family members.

family service. A style of meal service where people serve themselves as dishes are passed around the table.

family structure. The makeup of a family.

fashion. A style that is popular at the current time.

fatal. Deadly.

feedback. Repeating what a speaker says to be sure you understand it correctly.

fibers. Hairlike strands that can be twisted together to form yarn.

finish. A treatment given to fibers, yarns, or fabric to improve the look, feel, or performance of a fabric.

fixed expenses. Regular expenses that cannot be avoided.

flatware. Forks, knives, and spoons used for serving and eating.

flexible expenses. Costs of goods and services that are not purchased on a regular basis.

food-borne illnesses. Illnesses caused by bacteria or toxins produced by bacteria in food.

Food Guide Pyramid. An outline of what to eat each day.

friend. Someone you care about, trust, and respect.

fringe benefit. Reward of a job other than income, such as paid vacations and health insurance.

G

generation. All people who are born and live in about the same time span.

goals. What you want to achieve.

grain. The direction yarns run in a fabric.

grooming. Cleaning and caring for the body.

group dating. When several people of both sexes meet for an activity.

growth. An increase in size, strength, or ability that occurs over time.

guide sheet. A sheet that gives directions for cutting and sewing a project.

H

habit. A repeated pattern of behavior.

hangtag. A large tag attached to a garment that is removed before the garment is worn.

heredity. The result of receiving traits from parents or ancestors.

home. Any place people live.

homemaker. Anyone who manages or cares for a home.

homogenization. A process where milkfat is broken into tiny pieces and spread throughout the milk.

hot line. A telephone service that offers immediate information to people who need help.

house. A freestanding, single-family dwelling.

human resource. What people have within themselves to get what they need or want.

I

image. The mental picture of a person.

implement. To carry out a plan of action.

impulse buying. Making an unplanned or spur-of-the-moment purchase.

income. The money you earn.

independence. The freedom to decide, act, and care for yourself.

infant. A child under one year of age.

ingredient. A food item needed to prepare a food product.

insulation. Material used to prevent the transfer of heat or cold.

integrity. A commitment to do what is right.

interest inventory. A test that shows areas in which a person seems to have the most interest.

inventory. A list of items on hand.

iron. To move an iron back and forth over fabric to remove wrinkles

J

job. A position held by a worker.

job cluster. A group of jobs that requires some of the same skills and knowledge.

job skills. Skills that are used in the world of work.

L

label. A small piece of paper, fabric, or plastic attached to a product that gives information about the product.

layaway plan. Placing a small deposit on an item so that the store will hold it for you.

leadership. The ability to inspire others to meet goals.

learning. Gaining information or skills through instruction or practice.

leavening agent. An ingredient that causes foods to rise during baking.

lifestyle. The continuing way in which a person lives.

limit. A boundary or restriction.

love. A strong feeling of affection for someone or something.

M

management. Using resources to reach goals.

management process. A series of steps for reaching a goal. The steps are setting goals, planning, implementing, and evaluating.

manicure. A method of caring for hands and fingernails.

manners. Guidelines for behavior.

mass media. A means of communicating to large groups of people.

meal patterns. Guides for planning menus.

measure. To determine the amount of an item.

mental disability. A condition that limits a person's ability to use his or her mind.

menu. A list of foods to be prepared and served.

microwaves. High-frequency energy waves often used to cook food.

mix. To combine ingredients.

modem. A device that allows computers to directly communicate with each other over telephone lines.

moist heat cooking methods. Water or other liquids are added when cooking protein foods.

money management. The process of planning and controlling the use of money.

N

natural resources. Conditions and substances that are supplied by nature and needed for survival.

needs. The basic items you must have to live.

nonhuman resource. Objects and conditions available to people to help them meet needs and fulfill wants.

nonverbal communication. Sending and receiving messages without using words.

notions. Items other than fabric that become part of a garment or project.

nutrients. Chemical substances from foods needed for the body to function.

nutrition. The study of how the body uses food.

nutrition label. A panel on a food product package with information about the nutrients the food contains.

O

occupation. A job or position held by a worker.

P

parallel play. When toddlers play near but not with one another.

pasteurization. A process where milk and milk products are heated to destroy harmful bacteria.

pattern. A set of guidelines for making a garment or project.

pedicure. A method of caring for feet and toenails.

peer pressure. The influence people's peers have on them.

peers. People in the same age group.

personality. The group of traits that makes each person a unique individual.

physical disability. A condition that limits a person's ability to use part of his or her body.

physical traits. Distinguishing characteristics of each human body.

plate service. A style of meal service where plates are filled in the kitchen. Then they are carried to the table and served to each person.

pollution. The state of being unclean.

pores. Tiny openings in the skin.

posture. How you hold your body when standing, walking, or sitting.

precycling. Buying products that reduce waste.

preschooler. A child between the ages of three and five or six years.

press. To lift and lower an iron onto an area of fabric.

priorities. Important goals that must be met before less important goals.

private resource. A resource owned and controlled by a person or a family group.

problem. Source of difficulty or distress.

procrastinate. To put off difficult or unpleasant tasks until later.

produce. Fresh fruits and vegetables.

public resource. A resource shared by everyone and paid for through taxes.

Q

quality. How well a product is made.

R

ravel. When threads pull out of the cut edges of a fabric.

recipe. A set of directions used to prepare a food product.

recycling. Taking a used product and turning it into a product that can be reused.

redesign. To change the appearance or function of a garment.

redress. To correct a wrong.

reflex. A natural, unlearned behavior.

relationship. A link with another person.

reputation. How others think of a person.

resource. Assets that can be used to meet needs and fulfill wants.

respect. A high or special regard for someone or something.

responsibility. Something a person is expected or trusted to do.

resume. A written description of a person's qualifications and work experience.

ripe. Fully grown and developed.

role. A person's place in a group.

S

sanitation. The process of making conditions clean and healthy.

saturated fat. Fat that is solid at room temperature.

scale floor plan. A drawing that shows the size and shape of a room.

scarce. A resource that is limited in supply.

schedule. A written plan for reaching goals within a certain time.

scum. A film that forms on the surface of heated milk.

seam. A row of permanent stitches used to hold two pieces of fabric together.

self-concept. The way a person thinks and feels about himself or herself.

self-confident. To be sure of yourself.

self-esteem. How you feel about your self-concept.

selvage. The smooth, tightly-woven edge of a fabric.

separation anxiety. A fear that if parents leave, they will not return.

serger. A type of sewing machine that uses an overlock stitch to prevent seams from raveling.

shank. A short stem that holds a button away from fabric.

share. To experience or enjoy with others.

shelter. Place that offers housing and food to people who have nowhere else to go.

shortage. A condition in which there's not enough to go around.

skilled-level job. A job that requires some training beyond high school.

software. A set of instructions that tells a computer what to do.

solar energy. Energy from the sun's rays.

solutions. Answers.

sort. To group clothes according to the way you will wash them.

standard measuring tools. Specially marked cups and spoons used to measure ingredients.

standards. A means of measuring how well goals are achieved.

stress. Emotional, mental, or physical tension felt when faced with change.

stutter. To repeat a word or parts of a word several times.

style. The design of a garment.

T

tableware. Dishes, flatware, and glassware.

technology. Use of knowledge, tools, and systems to make life easier and better.

thinking skills. The ability to think creatively and critically, to make decisions, and to solve problems.

time management. The skill that involves organizing your time so you can accomplish what you need to.

time-out. A technique used to improve a child's behavior by moving the child to a place where he or she must sit quietly.

time schedule. A written plan for a person that lists when tasks should be started and completed.

toddler. A child between the ages of one and three years.

toxic. Poisonous.

trade-off. The giving up of one thing for another.

traditions. Customs passed from one generation to another.

traffic pattern. A path people follow as they move within a room.

trend. A general pattern of events.

trust. To believe a person is honest and reliable.

U

unit price. Cost for each unit of measure or weight.

unity. A state of being in agreement; not being divided.

universal product code. A group of bars and numbers found on packages. This code provides pricing and other product information to a computer scanner.

use and care manual. Booklet of instructions for a tool.

utensil. Handheld, hand-powered tool used to prepare food.

V

values. Strong beliefs or ideas about what is important.

verbal communication. Using words to give or receive information.

vocational program. A training course that teaches specific job skills.

W

wants. The extra items you would like but must not have to live.

wardrobe. All the clothes and accessories you have to wear.

warranty. A written guarantee on a product from the manufacturer.

wellness. A state of physical, emotional, and mental well-being.

work. What a person does to earn money.

work center. An area of a kitchen that has been designed around a specific activity or activities.

work plan. A list of tasks to be done, who is to perform them, and the tools and ingredients needed.

Y

yarn. A continuous strand of fibers.

Index

N

Natural fibers, 283, 284
Natural resources, 157-160
    definition, 157
    protecting, 158-160
    use and misuse, 157, 158
Needs, 85-88
    emotional needs, 86, 87
    physical needs, 85, 86
    wants, 87
Nonhuman resource, 89
Nonverbal communication, 39
Notions, 306
Nutrients, 181
Nutrition, 181
Nutrition label, 205

O

Occupation, 335

P

Parallel play, 56
Part-time jobs, 351
Pasteurization, 210
Pattern, 303
Payment methods, 275, 276
Pedicure, 121
Peer pressure, 35
Peers, 35, 36
Personal development, 11-46
    communication, 39-43
    family, 23-28
    friends, 33-38
    growth, 16-22
    self-image, 11-15
Personality, 12, 13
Personal resources, 89
Personal responsibility, 98
Physical disability, 77
Physical needs, 85, 86
Physical traits, 12
Picnics, 234
Plate service, 216
Poisonings, 146, 147

Pollution, 158
Pores, 118
Posture, 114, 115
Precycling, 159
Preschoolers, 58-62
    definition, 58
    emotional development, 60
    intellectual development, 60
    physical development, 59
    social development, 61
Press, 291
Priorities, 95
Private resource, 89
Problems, family, 29-32
    seeking help, 31
Problem solving, 30
Procrastinate, 110
Produce, 208
Public resource, 90

Q

Quality, 126

R

Ravel, 298
Recipes, 235-238
    definition, 235
    following, 237
    reading, 235, 236
Recycling, 159
Redesign, 316
Reflex, 48
Relationship, 23
Reputation, 36
Resources, 89-92
    definition, 89
    developing, 91
    types, 89, 90
    using, 90
Respect, 26
Responsibility, 19
Rest, 115
Resume, 352
Ripe, 208
Role, 25

Acknowledgments

The authors gratefully acknowledge the interest of those people directly and indirectly involved in the preparation of this book. They especially recognize the important contributions of the late M. Yvonne Peeler, coauthor of the original *Living, Learning, and Caring*.

Appreciation is also expressed to Margaret B. Liggett, a highly respected family and consumer sciences editor and educator; Ann Satterwhite Tunstall, who proofread the manuscript; Leslie VanHoy Matthews, state consultant with the North Carolina Department of Public Instruction, who reviewed the content; the students at Carrington Middle School, Durham, North Carolina, who field-tested the lessons and provided insight and suggestions about the type of textbook they wanted to read; the students and faculty of Meredith College in Raleigh, North Carolina, for their creative contributions of photographs; Marie Hammer, Professor of the Cooperative Extension Service at the University of Florida at Gainesville for her suggestions on the hazardous waste disposal section; Ruth Ann Balla, Manager of Technology Services at Meredith College for her contributions to the lessons on technology; and families and friends for their encouragement.

A special thank you is extended to the following teachers who allowed their classes to be photographed:

- Gayle Cooke
  Apex Middle School, Wake County Schools, NC

- Ruth Ann Griggs
  Carrington Middle School, Durham Public Schools, NC

- Sister Jon Julie Sullivan, S.N.D.
  Teacher and counselor, Boston, MA

- Harriet Lasher
  Raleigh Preschool, Raleigh, NC

- Libby Moore
  Marblehead Middle School, Marblehead, MA

- Kathy Reider
  Governor Mifflin High School, Shillington, PA

- Connie Woody
  East Millbrook and Carnage Middle Schools, Wake County Schools, NC

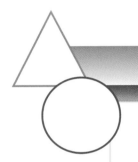

Photo Credits

American Egg Board 9-26
ARA Services 12-3, 12-17
Bernina of America, Inc. 11-1
Binney & Smith 1-15
Birkin, Joanne 1-5
Chef Boyardee p. 265
Chocolate Manufacturer's Association 7-11
Clawson, Barbara 10-1C
Currin, Virginia 12-23A
Debnam, Dianne 3-4, 3-10, 3-15, 4-11, 4-12,
    4-15, 4-16, 7-13, 8-9, 8-12, 8-16, 9-22, 9-24,
    10-4, 10-5, 10-6, 10-7, 10-10, p. 324, 12-4,
    12-5, 12-10, 12-11, 12-16, 13-10, 13-11, p. 366
DeLaRosa, Julia 1-2
Drucilla Handy Co. 9-29
Everett, Eugene 6-3, 7-15
FHA/HERO 3-17
Fleishmann's Yeast, 9-23
Gallen, Joseph 1-24, 6-6, 7-3, 9-7, 9-12, 9-21
Godwin, Lia 2-25
Gomez, Fran 1-27, 2-14
Gordon, Clyde 10-1B
Green, Kim 1-9
Hastings, Lynn 2-16, 3-6, 4-9, 5-9, 6-1, 8-18,
    10-18, 11-19
Images © 1996 PhotoDisc, Inc. 1-11
Kellogg U.S.A. 8-2
Kendzierski, Richard 8-14, 9-23
Konopasek, Nancy 2-3
McKenzie, Georgie 12-23B
Meredith College Publications, Chip Henderson
    3-12, 4-1, 4-4, 4-13, 4-19, 6-7, 6-10,
    13-9, 13-13
Meredith College Publications, Doug Van de
    Zande p. 82, 7-4, 8-17, 12-14, 13-1, 13-6, 13-7

Meredith College Publications, Steve Wilson
    6-9, 12-15
Mollica, Richard p. 8
National Cattlemen's Beef Association 9-13,
    9-25
National Cotton Council 10-11
National 4-H Council 7-2
National Pork Producers Council 7-1, 8-3
Nelson, Myrna 4-6, 5-12, 6-3, 10-2
New Zealand Kiwifruit 8-4
Pineapple Growers Assoc. p. 172C
Quinn, Patti 12-8
Sath, Savuth 2-27
Simplicity Pattern Co., Inc. 10-12, 11-7, 11-8
Smith, Kim 3-3
Spar and Spindle Girl Scout Council, Inc.
    4-17
Spragens, Lynn 1-7
Stouffer Foods Corp. 4-20, p. 174B
Strohecker, Ben 1-1, 1-8, 1-17, 1-25, p. 172A,
    8-5, 8-7, 8-8, 8-10
Stuber 2-9, 2-11
Sullivan S.N.D., Sr. Jon Julie p. 10, 1-3, 1-9,
    1-12, 1-13, 1-14, 1-19, 2-1, 2-5, 2-6, 2-7,
    2-12, 2-15, 2-18, 2-20, 2-23, 9-31
Thomas J. Lipton, Inc. 9-27
Visiting Nurses Asssociation/Salem 1-16,
    2-19, 2-22
Whitman, Lillian 2-10
Wilson, Steve A. 3-1, 3-14, 3-16, 4-26, 5-8,
    5-10, p. 172B, p. 174A, 9-9, p. 266, 10-14,
    13-2, 13-3
Young, Leslie/Barrier Free Environments
    2-28, 5-6